THE STORIES
THAT CHANGED
AUSTRALIA

THE STORIES THAT CHANGED AUSTRALIA

50 YEARS OF FOUR CORNERS

EDITED BY SALLY NEIGHBOUR

ABC Books

The ABC 'Wave' device is a trademark of the Australian Broadcasting Corporation and is used under licence by HarperCollins*Publishers* Australia.

First published in Australia in 2012
by HarperCollins*Publishers* Australia Pty Limited
ABN 36 009 913 517
harpercollins.com.au

© Copyright in the individual essays remains the property of their authors.

The rights of Kerry O'Brien, John Penlington, Peter Reid, Caroline Jones, Allan Hogan, Jonathan Holmes, Mary Delahunty, Chris Masters, Peter Manning, Jenny Brockie, David Marr, Liz Jackson, Sally Neighbour, Debbie Whitmont and Sarah Ferguson to be identified as the authors of this work has been asserted by them under the *Copyright Amendment (Moral Rights) Act 2000*.

This work is copyright. Apart from any use as permitted under the *Copyright Act 1968*, no part may be reproduced, copied, scanned, stored in a retrieval system, recorded, or transmitted, in any form or by any means, without the prior written permission of the publisher.

HarperCollins*Publishers*
Level 13, 201 Elizabeth Street, Sydney NSW 2000, Australia
31 View Road, Glenfield, Auckland 0627, New Zealand
A 53, Sector 57, Noida, UP, India
77–85 Fulham Palace Road, London W6 8JB, United Kingdom
2 Bloor Street East, 20th floor, Toronto, Ontario M4W 1A8, Canada
10 East 53rd Street, New York NY 10022, USA

National Library of Australia Cataloguing-in-Publication data:

The stories that changed Australia / edited by
Sally Neighbour ; introduction by Kerry O'Brien.
 ISBN: 978 0 7333 3105 3 (pbk.)
 Four corners (Television program)
 Television feature stories – Australia – Social aspects.
 Television broadcasting of news – Australia.
 Documentary television programs – Australia – Social aspects.
 Other Authors/Contributors:
 Neighbour, Sally.
 O'Brien, Kerry.
070.1950994

Cover design by Jane Waterhouse, HarperCollins Design Studio
Cover image by Lodi Kramer, ABC TV
Photograph of Jenny Brockie courtesy SBS; photograph of Caroline Jones © Peter Solness; photograph of Mary Delahunty © Mark Chew; photograph of David Marr courtesy Fairfax; photograph of Peter Manning from his private collection; all other photographs courtesy ABC.
Typeset in 11/16.5pt Adobe Caslon Pro by Kirby Jones

'Give me liberty to know, to utter, and to argue freely according to conscience, above all liberties.'

John Milton, *Areopagitica*, 1644

CONTENTS

	INTRODUCTION by Kerry O'Brien	1
1	'THIS PROGRAM WILL GO TO AIR OVER MY DEAD BODY' by John Penlington	7
2	TIMES THEY WERE A-CHANGING by Peter Reid	25
3	'GIRL TAKES OVER' by Caroline Jones	43
4	THE COOK WITH ALL THE FIREWOOD by Allan Hogan	59
5	RECOLLECTIONS OF A CUTTING-ROOM TECHNICIAN by Jonathan Holmes	79
6	AIDING OR ABETTING? by Mary Delahunty	97
7	THE BIG DIG by Chris Masters	111
8	THE ADRENALIN YEARS by Peter Manning	129
9	HANDLE WITH CARE by Jenny Brockie	151

10	REPORTING BLACK AUSTRALIA: THESE STORIES AREN'T OVER by David Marr	165
11	COMFORTABLE AND RELAXED: ENCOUNTERS WITH JOHN HOWARD, 1994–2007 by Liz Jackson	179
12	'THAT AWFUL BLOODY PROGRAM' by Sally Neighbour	203
13	REPORTING FROM ANOTHER COUNTRY: STORIES ABOUT ASYLUM SEEKERS by Debbie Whitmont	223
14	THE WAITRESS, THE REFUGEE AND THE KILLING BOX by Sarah Ferguson	245
	AUTHOR BIOGRAPHIES	267

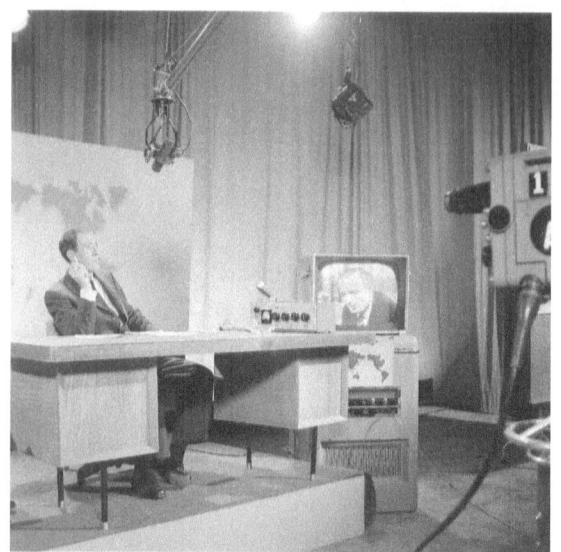

Clockwise from top: Michael Charlton conducts a studio interview via a remote link on screen, 1960s; Michael Charlton on the cover of *TV Times*, 18 August 1962; early advertising for the new program, 1967.

INTRODUCTION

by Kerry O'Brien

Put simply, *Four Corners* is a television miracle. It began life on a trial basis on 19 August 1961 in a medium that was just five years old in Australia; a medium whose managers have since routinely killed off programs because the audience was too small or the expectation too big, often not even bothering to ensure they were properly archived for history. Some programs have literally disappeared without trace. Many others has died a natural, even dignified death after a long run, but none has outlived this great television current affairs trailblazer.

There was certainly no great expectation when *Four Corners* was launched. Its start was as tentative as the first steps of a child. Stories vary about its beginnings, but what is not contested is that one day in 1960 a newsreader and sometime cricket commentator, Michael Charlton, managed to squirrel himself and a journalist colleague named Bob Raymond past the normal hierarchical and heavily public service-oriented processes of a resistant management into the almost deified presence of the ABC's General Manager, Charles Moses. This was a last-ditch appeal for a new program idea.

Charlton had some cachet in the place. His father, Conrad, was the first voice on ABC Radio, introducing Prime Minister Joseph Lyons to launch the national network in 1932. Charlton the son was the first face on ABC Television, introducing Prime Minister Robert Menzies to launch the network 28 years later.

In those days, television news was indeed radio with pictures; journalists struggled to understand and fully exploit the potential of the new medium, and TV current affairs didn't exist. By that time ABC Radio was a settled and indispensible institution for many Australians — from the most humble to the most elite. It had already helped keep the nation informed through the Great Depression and World War II, and had brought Test cricket alive on the airwaves. I can remember as a small child in the early '50s that whenever I travelled from the Queensland bush to stay with my grandparents in Brisbane, I had no choice but to sit with them each weekday at lunchtime, listening first to the ABC news and then to the classic radio serial *Blue Hills*, written by Gwen Meredith. I can still hum the theme.

But for Bob Raymond in 1960, public broadcast television was a pale shadow of its relatives abroad. In his memoir, *Out of the Box*, Raymond recalled: 'There was straight news — read with BBC-like solemnity by former radio announcers in dinner jackets — plenty of sport, a weekly "news magazine" of non-topical items, and an occasional brief illustrated lecture by a university political scientist on some "faraway place of which we know little" ... But beyond that — nothing. Topical background, contemporaneous comment, helpful interpretation was not just in short supply; there simply wasn't any.'

Raymond and Charlton managed to persuade Moses to embrace an idea for a topical weekly program that represented virgin territory for Australian television. They thought if they were lucky, it might last a few months, maybe even a year.

Moses must have occasionally wondered what he had done as the new program found its feet, seriously ruffling political and other institutional feathers along the way. Amazingly, one year has become 50, and feathers are still being ruffled.

But it wasn't just its own rich lode of groundbreaking investigative and social documentary stories that *Four Corners* was to produce. It also spawned a whole stable of troublesome offspring, from the first nightly national current affairs program, *This Day Tonight*, in 1967, to the current crop: *7.30, Lateline, Foreign Correspondent, Australian Story, Insiders, Landline, Lateline Business* and *Business Insiders*. Through all this, *Four Corners* has remained the Mother Ship; leaky at times, occasionally in need of serious work in the dry dock, but still the Mother Ship.

The philosophy of *Four Corners* today is simple enough, and hasn't changed much over the years: to invest time and resources identifying and investigating issues of significance to Australians and fashioning the end results into a coherent, informative 45-minute television narrative.

In 50 years, for all its imperfections, it has nurtured and showcased many of the finest journalists, editors, cinematographers and sound recordists this country has produced, of a standard that is in the global front line. Some, like Michael Charlton, Mike Willesee, Caroline Jones, Andrew Olle, Paul Lyneham and Chris Masters, became household names (the two Michaels for their pioneering interviews; Caroline as the trailblazer for so many other outstanding women in modern journalism; Andrew for his elegant writing and filmmaking; Paul for a clever, probing intellect that would not be denied; and Chris for his tireless and courageous pursuit of institutionalised corruption).

But from the earliest days there have been countless others who have also had an enormous impact, not only on their own craft and the television industry, but also on the broad national debate. They also at times have been catalysts for significant change. It's not hard to find examples year by year, decade by decade, and some are in this book; a book that offers real insight into the nature of the program and the people who made it.

Looking back, I realise I was still a babe in the woods at 30 when I first went to *Four Corners* in 1975, and something of a journeyman when I returned in 1985. It's been a rare privilege for me to come back again at this stage of my career to share a cautious pride in 50 years of accumulated achievement.

So what of *Four Corners* into the future? Journalism in all its forms is not so much at a crossroads as on a roundabout with a confusion of exits. Newspapers are fracturing, disappearing or morphing into something else; converging with television and radio. Television journalism is spreading itself across a number of platforms.

Despite the exciting potential that technological advances offer, the quality and depth of content in both print and television is being diluted before our eyes. The opportunities for distortion and manipulation by those who hold the reins of power across society are growing. Yet the reliance on cheap, emotive sensationalism, the hypocritical exploitation of tragedy, the pursuit of mindless celebrity and the ranting of would-be demagogues to sell publications or draw audiences is becoming pervasive, sucking the oxygen out of real journalism. And yet, I believe the public need and hunger for real information, for real debate, for real, thoughtful inquiry and revelation, have never been stronger.

At the same time, the evolution in the delivery of news is coinciding with a worrying decline in resources. The pursuit of quality journalism, of proper investigation, inquiry, and finally, the production of stories on any significant scale and consistency, will always require strong resources. In public broadcasting, too, those resources are being chipped away. As you will gather from some of the personal accounts in this book, it takes a great deal of time and digging and travel and expertise — plus blood, sweat and tears while up against remorseless deadlines — to produce the goods in long-form television current affairs.

In this era of massive change there are no guarantees for any print publication or electronic program into the longer term, and even as the dust is still settling on its 50th anniversary celebrations, and incidentally on a year of vintage investigative journalism, we have to acknowledge that *Four Corners* is not immune from the pressures of these times.

What *Four Corners* has proved in what can so often be a fickle and superficial medium, is that it is possible to pursue excellence and endure; fall at the hurdles from time to time, occasionally get weak at the knees and even stray off course, but endure. I don't even want to try to imagine life without it.

John Penlington (far right) with the *Four Corners* crew outside the Hiroshima Peace Memorial, 1964. Until he started at the program, Penlington had never been out of Australia and had no passport.

1

'THIS PROGRAM WILL GO TO AIR OVER MY DEAD BODY'

by John Penlington

As an eager young reporter who'd switched from newspapers to broadcast journalism in 1961, I found the weekly staff meetings of the ABC Talks department rather dull affairs; but this one was to prove a monumental exception. Michael Charlton and Robert Raymond had been invited along to outline their new project — a weekly magazine program on topical issues, to be called *Four Corners*. Had anyone suggested that morning it might still be running half a century later, everyone in the room, including Charlton and Raymond, would have fallen off their chairs laughing.

As I sat listening to their impressive plans, I had not the faintest idea that I would be one of three reporters parachuted in when Charlton and Raymond left the ABC two years later in frustration.

Television was approaching its fifth birthday in Australia. It was about to have its first current affairs show, for which Raymond and Charlton proved ideal pioneers. Raymond was an affable Australian journalist who had freelanced in Fleet Street, made films in Africa and returned home to work as an ABC documentary producer known for being willing to experiment. Charlton was a popular ABC Radio announcer, newsreader and television presenter with a warm cultured accent and a gift for live commentary, especially on cricket. He was also a keen student of international affairs.

The two had become close friends after working together on a live interview series called *Horizons*. They nourished their friendship with regular lunches at La Veneziana, a cheap Italian restaurant in Darlinghurst, where over many a bottle of house red they would lament Australia's lack of stimulating topical programs such as the BBC's *Panorama* and early American current affairs journalists like Ed Murrow on CBS.

Why couldn't Australia have the television equivalent of a quality Sunday newspaper, they kept asking. No one else seemed interested, so they designed one themselves, only to discover that finding a home for it looked hopeless. The ABC's Director of Talks told them 'leave it with me' — and there it stayed — while the Controller of News, a fierce protector of his fiefdom, made it clear that any such program would be done by the News department and not by Charlton and Raymond. Weeks passed and in desperation Charlton suggested they seek an audience with the General Manager, Charles Moses, who they knew to be a fan of Charlton's cricket commentaries.

Moses granted them a hearing, which Raymond recalled in his memoir, published in 1994: 'When we finished he rose heavily from behind his broad desk and went to a cupboard in the corner of his office. He took out a full-sized tree-felling axe, swung it once or twice with satisfaction, and carried it back to his chair.' Moses, later Sir Charles, had been an army officer in both Britain and Australia. His favourite hobby was competition wood-chopping, for which he was famous.

'And what makes you two think you can get this program off the ground, when all the advice I get is that it won't work?' asked Moses, before proceeding to grill them about whether they were up to the job while delicately running his thumb along the gleaming edge of the axe.

Finally, the General Manager put his axe away and slowly crushed his cigar butt in an ashtray. 'This program of yours sounds like something the ABC needs, but you'll never be able to do it through the normal channels. The only way it can be done is if you two just go ahead and do it. So I'm going to give you my personal permission to do it outside the departmental structure. I'll see that you get a small budget and the freedom to do it the way you want to. If it's a success the ABC will take the credit. And if it's a failure I, personally, will kick you both all the way up William Street.'

Still determined to preserve its domain, the News department developed an alternative proposal, but Moses knocked it back. A day or so later in a corridor at the ABC's Gore Hill TV studios on Sydney's North Shore, Charlton and Raymond came face to face with the Controller of News. As they passed, Raymond heard him snarl, 'This program will go to air over my dead body.'

The inspiration for the title, *Four Corners*, apparently came from the closing speech in Shakespeare's *King John*, though who came up with it has been contested over the years. Both Charlton and Clement Semmler, the Assistant General Manager for Programs (AGM), claimed it had been their idea. Raymond recalled first hearing it from Charlton when the presenter declaimed one day, with a wave of his arms, in their office, 'Come the four corners of the world in arms, and we shall shock them.' By Raymond's account, Charlton continued, 'People always make that mistake with the quotation from *King John*. It's not four corners, it's three. But four will do for us.'

Four Corners hit the airwaves for the first time on 19 August 1961. In the eight-item program, a visiting American astronaut, Scott Carpenter, talked about plans for America's first orbital space flight; the world record-breaking Olympic swimmer Jon Konrads discussed his race strategy; and Charlton quizzed an economist about that week's federal budget. Two anniversaries were commemorated — the end of World War II in the Pacific and Indonesia's Declaration of Independence. Viewers were also treated to a filmed rehearsal and interview with the popular harmonica player Larry Adler, who was in Australia for an ABC tour. Finally came the 'Voice of the People' segment, which featured street interviews on the topic 'What are you worried about?' Its aim was to show ordinary Australians to themselves and it proved both entertaining and popular. Raymond, the show's producer, saw it as 'a little light relief to finish the program'. In its own small way, it was a precursor of talk-back radio.

After the closing credits, Raymond took a call from an anxious ABC bureaucrat. His verdict: 'That was an excellent program. I don't think we could have offended anybody.'

That would soon change. A few weeks later Charlton and Raymond presented a 25-minute report on shocking living conditions at the Box Ridge Aboriginal settlement near Casino, where 110 people were crammed into 12 houses or shacks, with one communal water point and no electricity. All Charlton and Raymond had done was follow up a comment by the Bishop of Newcastle that the settlement at Box Ridge was 'a living cemetery'. Viewers saw a clergyman who tried to help the Aborigines at Box Ridge tell Charlton some people in Casino thought he was a Communist because he was concerned about Aboriginal welfare.

The report was a trailblazer in opening Australians' eyes to the plight of their Aborigines, and put Indigenous issues firmly on both national and state political agendas. Until *Four Corners* came along, no home-grown television program had bothered probing beneath the headlines in that way. The audience was outraged and protests poured into the New South Wales government. It would be six more years before Aborigines became citizens of Australia and were given the right to vote.

Working on a limited budget, Charlton and Raymond filmed reports in many parts of Australia, but ventured overseas with *Four*

Corners when Air India gave the team free seats on inaugural flights to its newest destinations. Whole programs devoted to the Soviet Union, India and Hong Kong enthralled viewers, thanks to these freebies.

Within two years of its launch *Four Corners* had become a spectacular success, well beyond the traditional ABC audience, and Charlton had won a Gold Logie for 'outstanding personality of the year', an award usually reserved for entertainers like Graham Kennedy and *Pick-a-Box* quiz show king, Bob Dyer. The significance of Charlton and Raymond's achievement was summed up by a later compere and Executive Producer of the program, Robert Moore:

> They legitimised the Australian accent on TV ... they allowed real Australians to be seen and heard and changed our consciousness of ourselves and our country. *Four Corners* made *A Big Country* and *This Day Tonight* possible, but it also made *Homicide* possible. It created an atmosphere in which producers and viewers could see themselves in a new confident light.

Four Corners' success aroused discomfort among some in the ABC hierarchy and the conservative Menzies government, then in its fourteenth consecutive year in power. ABC management enforced a policy of political balance which required program-makers to seek permission from the General Manager for any politician to appear. Raymond later recounted how they could only use an interview with an opposition politician if the relevant government minister also appeared. Thus, by avoiding an appearance, ministers knew they could kill a damaging report. Censorship by default was how Charlton described it.

The issue came to a head in May 1963 when *Four Corners* broadcasted a story on housing without including the Federal Housing Minister, Sir William Spooner, who had been unable to find time for an interview despite a persistent and flexible invitation. When the story went to air without him, he copped criticism from his colleagues for not putting the government's case. Sir William then demanded the right of reply, and ABC Chairman, Dr James Darling, directed Raymond to put him on air. Raymond sent reporter Bob Sanders to Canberra to ask the minister what he saw wrong with the story — and let him drone on and on and on. Charlton introduced the interview by informing viewers they had been 'instructed' to give Spooner his say, 'and here he is'. The interview went to air unedited, lasting nearly half an hour. 'It destroyed any credibility he had,' Raymond said afterwards, apparently satisfied with the result.

The Spooner incident confirmed a change that Charlton and Raymond were detecting in the immunity they had enjoyed from direction and control. With their patron Charles Moses nearing the end of his term as ABC General Manager, their protection from interference was no longer guaranteed. This made it easier for each of them to accept the attractive offers that followed their success. As Raymond said later, 'If we couldn't do it the way we wanted to do it, we weren't interested.' Charlton headed off to the BBC's *Panorama* while Raymond went to Channel 9 to create a special projects unit. As Moses had predicted, the ABC would take the credit for *Four Corners* and pour in more resources to keep it running.

My own career on the show had begun in Sydney as a production assistant for a fortnight, with the job of putting together the 'Voice of the People' segment for the final show of 1961, quizzing celebrities about how they were going to spend Christmas. After this I was promoted to the role of Talks Officer in Perth, where I eagerly awaited each week's *Four Corners* program and contributed a couple of items to it myself. I also started a half-hour weekly state current affairs show based in Perth called *West Coast '63*, unashamedly modelled on *Four Corners*.

Allan Ashbolt, who held the position of Federal Talks Supervisor (Topical), was put in charge of *Four Corners*, with Frank Bennett, Robert Moore and myself as reporters and John Power as producer.

[In his 1986 book *Four Corners: Twenty-Five Years*, Robert Pullan described Penlington as 'a young reporter who brought to his on-camera interviews the formidable combination of fresh-faced, boyish enthusiasm and relentless tenacity'. Ed]

Under Ashbolt's leadership, the program would sharpen its investigative skills — and earn some scars to prove it. Ashbolt was tall, confident and energetic. His career had included acting, book reviewing and filmmaking before he joined ABC Talks. He had recently spent three years in New York as an ABC correspondent and came home deeply affected by the inequalities in American society. He was seen by some in ABC management as a radical left-wing intellectual.

One month after the changeover, Ashbolt put to air his own film report, which analysed the political power of one of Australia's most sacred cows, the RSL. Today that report seems unexceptional, but in 1963 it was a bombshell. Looking back, it's so easy to see why. In the 1960s, two fears lingered in the minds of many Australians following World War II — fear of invasion by the so-called 'hordes of Asians' to our north, and alarm about the advance of Communism. On both issues, the RSL was the Menzies government's most insistent pressure group. As the Repatriation Minister admitted to Ashbolt, the RSL was 'the only public organisation in Australia that has direct and regular access to the federal cabinet'. The League's original role had been to lobby for welfare benefits; its critics in 1963 thought it enjoyed too much influence on national policies such as defence, Communism and immigration.

Ashbolt's questioning of the RSL Federal President, Sir Raymond Huish, confirmed that the League would strongly oppose any revision of immigration policy allowing Asians and Africans into Australia and would support another referendum to ban the Communist Party. Menzies had tried to abolish the Communist Party in 1951, but the High Court ruled the legislation invalid. Menzies then tried a referendum, but it was lost and the Communist Party remained legal.

One of the critics interviewed by Ashbolt was the editor of the Communist Party newspaper, *Tribune*, Alec Robertson, an officer in the army and the air force in World War II and an RSL member until the League expelled Communists. This must have been the first time a Communist had been interviewed on the ABC and it caused an uproar. It was like throwing a can of petrol onto a bonfire.

Menzies called for transcripts of the past ten *Four Corners* programs and the General Manager decided to intervene. Ashbolt would 'no longer be active' on *Four Corners* but would now concentrate on 'his other duties', it was announced. Gerald Lyons, host of the Melbourne *People* program, would replace him. This proved an unpopular move — both with the audience and with the Talks department staff in Sydney, most of whom signed a petition protesting Ashbolt's removal. Moses met the signatories and assured them that political pressure had not influenced the change. Many were not convinced.

Menzies' own view of the program was spelled out in a remark he made when introduced by the ABC Chairman, Dr James Darling, to Clement Semmler, then the senior executive responsible for *Four Corners*. 'Young man, I know you and your *Four Corners*,' Menzies told Semmler, 'and I want you to know that I know, and my ministers know, that the sole reason for that wretched program is to discredit me and my government.'

According to Semmler, Menzies then turned his back on him.

I missed most of this trouble. After three months on the program, as planned I had returned to Perth to get married, only to be told to stay there for the time being. By the end of the year, with the audience dwindling, Ashbolt was reinstated to run the program and Lyons returned to Melbourne.

The RSL affair heralded a continuing battle over the program's, and indeed the ABC's, role and commitment to investigative journalism. Despite having championed the program, Moses held the view that *Four Corners* should inform without taking sides and must not set out to 'expose' anything. This of course challenged the essential role of journalists in a democracy — exposing problems, mistakes and issues — and that tension sat uneasily for years in the public service ethos of the ABC.

My first assignment when I returned to Sydney was a report on the right of Aboriginals to drink alcohol in the Northern Territory. But a far greater challenge lay a few months ahead. An ABC camera crew was finishing a documentary in Japan and Ashbolt assigned me to join them to report on the deepening conflict in Vietnam and Laos. I'd never been out of Australia and needed a passport. Time was pressing so, as the ABC was a government commission, it was decided I should travel on a diplomatic passport, a dangerous practice that fortunately didn't last. *Four Corners* reporters should be seen as independent journalists, not representatives of the Australian government.

Saigon, known then as 'the Pearl of the Orient' and now as Ho Chi Minh City, was in bad shape, with sandbagged bunkers outside main buildings, sentries with bayonets fixed on their rifles and wire-mesh screens on cafes and nightclubs. The Viet Cong were infiltrating the city with plastic bombs in the terror phase of the war in the South Vietnamese capital. The previous month had seen 18 bomb attacks in the city. We interviewed an American lieutenant who'd been in a cinema when a bomb went off, killing three people and injuring fifty.

The scene for this war had been set in 1954 at peace talks after the French were defeated by Vietnamese Communist forces at Dien Bien Phu. Vietnam was split into two temporary states — the Communist-controlled North and the anti-Communist South — and elections were promised two years later to reunify the country. But the South's dictatorial president, Ngo Dinh Diem, was tardy about holding elections, so the North Vietnamese regime and its supporters in the South, known then as the Viet Cong, turned to 'revolutionary warfare' to achieve their goals.

We met an Australian missionary doctor, Alan Walker, who had come face to face with the Viet Cong on a trip in the Vietnamese countryside before Australia became so committed to the war. 'We were coming up from the river bank,' he told us, 'and all of a sudden we found ourselves surrounded by guns pointed at us, men shouting and blowing whistles.' At first the missionary party was treated roughly, but when no weapons were found in their baggage they were marched into the jungle for a two-hour lecture and told the Viet Cong had no objection to their working as missionaries so long as they didn't interfere in politics.

Dr Walker, who worked at the Saigon Adventist Hospital, also corroborated stories of Viet Cong terror tactics. 'Right here in the city we see men and women without ears, with tongues cut out. These are some of the things the Viet Cong do when they want to victimise a person. The worst cases don't survive to come here.'

Reports of such cruelty sickened me as I began to grasp the impact of this ideological battle for the loyalty of hapless Vietnamese peasants. We filmed the Strategic Hamlet Program, whereby peasants were forced to live in villages surrounded by barbed wire and sharpened bamboo stakes and were trained in civil defence against Viet Cong attack. The insurgents were targeting village chiefs and officials sympathetic to the Saigon regime. As the war intensified, the United States used napalm, carpet bombing and defoliant sprays on the Viet Cong's jungle sanctuaries and supply routes.

Even in that July of 1964, it was clear that Saigon and Washington had a near impossible task ahead of them. They could capture and hold a stretch of country, but could they rely on the loyalty of the peasants who lived there?

It was also a battle fought with foreign aid — channelled into a civic action program that helped villagers build houses, schools and hospitals. An American adviser on psychological warfare told us, rather naively, I thought, 'If, for example, we could get all the Viet Cong in a large football stadium and let the Premier explain his policies to them and say, "Just go back to your home town and wait three months and if you don't see results, go on back to the woods", I'm convinced we could defect about a half of them.'

Our Vietnam report went to air just after the first Australian soldier was killed in the conflict. *Four Corners* devoted many programs to that war as it unfolded into a tragedy of epic proportions. It took the lives of 500 Australians, 50,000 Americans and at least two million Vietnamese in a frantic but flawed attempt to stem the advance of Communism in Asia.

* * *

Reporting on a war can prove harrowing but, as I was to find out a few months later, so could dealing with ABC management as a *Four Corners* reporter.

In October 1964, Ashbolt assigned me to do a story on capital punishment in Perth, where a notorious serial killer, Eric Edgar Cooke, was about to be hanged. He wanted the story for the following week's program. I filmed some street interviews about the hanging, but was having great trouble getting anyone in authority who supported capital punishment to appear on the program.

When news of our forthcoming report was revealed in the Perth press, an incensed local politician stood up in Parliament and urged the WA Premier to get the ABC to stop the story.

On the Wednesday afternoon four days before the hanging was scheduled, I went to the ABC's Perth office to contact Ashbolt about the lack of progress. Before I could phone him, I was handed a press release issued by Clement Semmler, now AGM for Programs, saying it was a 'mere coincidence' that I was in Perth ahead of the Cooke hanging and the ABC had no intention of running a story on capital punishment: 'Not only would it be in poor taste to do so and indeed smacking of sensationalism, but it would obviously be impossible to expect to get a balanced and objective viewpoint at this particularly unfortunate time when feelings were bound to be high among sections of opinions concerned.' Dr Semmler claimed the statement had 'no relationship whatsoever' to the political objection raised in the WA Parliament. I was ordered not to talk to the press.

I accepted management's right to control what went to air but deeply resented its distortion of the truth. I remember telling Ashbolt on the phone, 'We've been sold down the river.' I had had no trouble filming comments in the street both for and against the hanging of Cooke, without resorting to sensationalism. People expressed their views calmly and intelligently. Had Dr Semmler checked on the progress of the story before issuing his statement, the embarrassing explosion that followed could have been avoided.

That night, when contacted by a reporter from the *West Australian*, Ashbolt gave a truthful account of the matter and said he was worried that the statement reflected on my integrity by implying that I was not up to the basic task of a journalist — providing a balanced report on such a controversy. When the same reporter told me what Ashbolt had said I felt I could not let him stand alone, so I broke my promise to stay silent and confirmed that I had been assigned to a capital punishment story for that week's program; it was no 'mere coincidence' that I was in Perth.

I returned to Sydney to receive a verbal walloping in Dr Semmler's office, with the closing words, 'Just keep your trap shut!' Ashbolt and I were removed from *Four Corners* as punishment for speaking to the press, but the widely reported controversy refused to die. Viewers and concerned citizens bombarded the ABC with complaints that questioned both its programming policy and the probity of Semmler's statement. Some of the replies went out over the signature of the Chairman, Dr James Darling. One of those replies was brought to the office by a viewer, who handed it to me saying, 'I think you should read this.' The Chairman had accused Ashbolt and myself of having 'against standing instructions and against all decent practice, contradicted their senior officer in the public press', and said we had been returned to our previous positions 'because they have shown a lack of the responsibility necessary to conduct a program of the type of *Four Corners*'.

I found the letter deeply offensive and sought the opinion of a lawyer at the firm where my wife was working, who told me the letter was defamatory. After much agonising, I decided to approach the Chairman directly and sent a telegram saying, 'I can hold my peace no longer. I must talk with you.' Again I was carpeted by Semmler for going over his head, but this time I did most of the talking, telling him I had legal advice that the letter was defamatory and wanted to give the Chairman the opportunity to withdraw it.

I had a half-hour meeting with Dr Darling, who appeared not to be aware of the whole story. He said he could not condone what I had done, but was prepared to withdraw some of his criticisms of me. He later gave me a letter to that effect which I was free to show to anyone who had received one of his replies. After the summer holidays I was sent back to *Four Corners* and worked with the ABC for another 12 years.

* * *

In 1967 *Four Corners* faced its biggest challenge to date — the arrival of nightly current affairs in the form of the ABC's *This Day Tonight*. It drew the spotlight away from *Four Corners* with a cheeky style of reporting that became extremely popular. It encroached on our territory by covering stories we might have done and had the advantage of being able to follow up its stories night after night. To survive in the new climate, *Four Corners* had to evolve. Single-issue programs became more regular, and overseas assignments helped in the quest for exclusive stories. Among my most memorable assignments were a Middle East series on Israel, Egypt and the Palestinian refugees in Jordan, and reports from South Africa and what was then Rhodesia — when Ian Smith's government made its unilateral declaration of independence.

Documenting the social and political changes taking place in Australia also proved fertile ground for *Four Corners*. I recall filming a story in Brisbane where two women chained themselves to a public bar to protest against the law that forbade women to drink there. Those were the days when women were obliged to drink in the 'ladies lounge'. The story exposed the absurdity of laws that allowed women to work as barmaids in public bars while forbidding them to be there as customers.

Australia's controversial White Australia Policy was still in place, although it would gradually fade away under the more liberal approach of Menzies' successor, Prime Minister Harold Holt. In 1966 a university-educated Philippines banker's application to migrate was refused by the Australian government. I went to Manila to canvas the reaction. Viewers saw what many educated Asians thought of Australia at that time: a racially discriminating country that subsidised white immigrants while making it extremely difficult for non-white immigrants to enter. 'We'll never be appeased or stop criticising the White Australia Policy until all the inequities have been erased,' a top Manila newspaper columnist told the *Four Corners* audience.

The task of finding fresh topics was aided by the coming of age of the post-war baby-boomer generation. Unencumbered with the fears and social rules ingrained in their parents, they sought freedom and a more open society. Inevitably, sex became more widely discussed.

Oddly enough, one particularly confronting exclusive story proved the easiest of my time on *Four Corners*. In 1968 a Sydney judge who had sentenced six teenagers convicted of rape spoke out about the prevalence of that crime in the outer suburbs. At executive producer Sam Lipski's Monday planning meeting we discussed how *Four Corners* should cover it. It was agreed that I would go out to Bankstown in Sydney's outer southwest that night with a producer, David Stiven, and see what we could find.

Within the first half hour we spent chatting with young men, the story emerged. It wasn't rape that was prevalent, they kept insisting, it was 'gangbangs' — consenting sex between one girl and a group of young men. But would they talk about it on television? Yes, they would — and they did the next evening, after the 24 hours I gave them to think it over.

Their ease and candour in discussing such a touchy subject shocked many in the audience, but proved a fascinating insight for lawyers and social researchers.

> PENLINGTON: **How many gangbangs do you think you've been along to?**
> INTERVIEWEE: **Oh about six. Just did it for kicks, I suppose, to be part of the group, you know. They're all mates, we all went to school together, grown up together, just out for kicks, something to do. There's about nine of us altogether.**
> PENLINGTON: **How do you prevent a gangbang becoming a pack rape?**
> INTERVIEWEE: **Well, you can't really unless only the guys that are selected turn up. If it's any more, you know, like crashers come, that's when it starts to be pack rape. When the girl says she's had enough, but these guys, they haven't had theirs yet so they start to get a bit cranky about it, start bashing the girl around a bit forcing her into it. That's rape then.**

* * *

In Canberra, the Catholic Women's League of Decency tried to have the regular Sunday repeat of the program cancelled, but Dr Semmler withstood the pressure this time and let it go ahead.

I left *Four Corners* at the end of 1971 to become an overseas correspondent, but returned as acting Executive Producer for a few months in 1981 when Paul Lyneham suddenly left for Channel 7. Soon afterwards I also decided to move to commercial current affairs, partly because I was convinced the program needed fresh blood. It got it the following year with Jonathan Holmes, recruited from the BBC's *Panorama*, who turned out to be one of the best acquisitions the ABC ever made.

'Where Have All the Poisons Gone?' (1972). 'One of the most disquieting environmental reports screened on the ABC': Peter Reid's investigation into the hazardous waste being dumped each week in Australia, to which governments turned a blind eye.

2

TIMES THEY WERE A-CHANGING

by Peter Reid

Australia was in the throes of far-reaching social and political transition in the late swinging '60s when I joined the *Four Corners* team making its mark as Australia's first national TV current affairs program. I was a young producer back from a stint overseas honing skills in advanced electronic news-gathering with Visnews and ITN (International Television News) in London.

I returned to a nation still embroiled in the divisive Vietnam War, with anti-war protests escalating coast to coast. Women, too, were demonstrating in the streets, demanding greater equality in society, with the advent of the contraceptive pill rekindling moral debate about premarital sex.

With the demise of the White Australia Policy, new immigration patterns were reshaping us into one of the world's most ethnically and culturally diverse countries, while a national referendum eventually gave Aboriginal Australians citizenship rights.

The Rolling Stones, the Beatles and Bob Dylan toured Australia as the hippie movement embraced rock'n'roll, drugs and free love.

Alternative lifestyles challenged outmoded values, typified by beach inspectors fining a bikini-clad young woman for being 'unsuitably dressed' on Bondi Beach, and supermodel Jean Shrimpton shocking staid matrons at the Melbourne Cup by posing in an audacious miniskirt — that became an iconic image of the decade's supposedly permissive society.

Around the globe, the mega-news events of the 1960s could hardly have given rise to a more journalistically fortuitous period for *Four Corners* to debut. The Cold War was at a peak. So, too, was rivalry for supremacy in space, with the United States and the Soviet Union locked in an historic race to put a man on the moon. Global leadership was in flux with the passing of two Western leaders of prodigious stature: John F. Kennedy, the first Catholic and youngest man to become US president, assassinated in the prime of life; and the death at 90 of Britain's World War II leader, Sir Winston Churchill, acclaimed in a BBC poll as the greatest ever Briton, his state funeral attended by the biggest gathering of dignitaries yet seen. In Australia, our longest serving prime minister, Sir Robert Menzies, quit after a record 16 years.

Pivotal changes, too, were under way at *Four Corners* when I joined in 1967. The program was expanding its largely observational style of coverage, by not only holding a mirror up to Australian society but also shining a spotlight into dark places, with a new emphasis on investigative reporting.

A significant step in this direction was the formation of 'Focus Report', an editorial unit within the program devoted chiefly to penetrating investigative coverage. It added another dimension to *Four Corners* — a hard-edged documentary approach with less personalised reporter involvement and more top-grade producer input and in-depth story research. The series was conceived and co-produced by myself and Gordon Bick, a senior journalist recruited from ABC TV's *This Day Tonight*. The format was akin to the British Granada TV's current affairs series *World in Action*, then regarded in the UK as TV investigative journalism at its best.

One of the first major issues we set our sights on was Australia's involvement in the Vietnam War, destined to become the longest and most controversial military conflict in our history. Public support for the war had waned in both Australia and the United States, particularly after the infamous My Lai massacre in the late 1960s, when 514 noncombatant Vietnamese villagers, ranging from a year-old baby to an elder of 81, were killed by a US infantry patrol. Most of the victims were women, raped and tortured before being slain. The atrocity provoked outrage in many countries, including Australia, and was credited with advancing the end of the war by eroding public support.

Only one person, US army lieutenant William Calley, was convicted — of premeditated murder for ordering the My Lai killings. Calley claimed in his defence that he was justifiably obeying his senior officer's orders while leading a 'search-and-destroy' troop patrol against a suspected Viet Cong presence near My Lai. He was sentenced to life in prison but, following intervention by President Nixon, served only a few years under house arrest. Calley's case evoked calls by military analysts to review the standards of officer selection and training after it was revealed that Calley had been a jobless college dropout who was rushed through basic training; as the war dragged on America's recruitment intake had started dwindling.

In Australia, the issue of training standards became a topic of debate among instructors and cadets at the elite Royal Military College, Duntroon, which prided itself on the quality of its graduate officers being equal to, if not better than, the world's best. Duntroon also had another distinction: it was probably the most conservative institution of its kind in Australia, with deep-rooted British army traditions that didn't readily yield to change. To its harsher critics, the college had become a military anachronism, a cosy haven for time-serving Colonel Blimps turning out tin soldiers in the same mould.

But to its top brass Duntroon symbolised the acme of military leadership and the ideals of duty, honour and loyalty, on a par with Britain's Sandhurst and America's West Point.

Duntroon's reputation had been tarnished the previous year — in 1969 — with the exposure of bastardisation, a debasing form of cadet punishment that caused the worst scandal in the college's history up until then and prompted a federal government inquiry. New cadets had been forced to do 200 push-ups at a time, stand naked in the mess hall and perform sexual acts with frozen chickens. In the aftermath, it seemed timely for *Four Corners* to chronicle the ethos and mood at the nation's premier military training establishment, and the sort of moral challenges that officer graduates would encounter when deployed in Vietnam, commanding conscripts in combat zones in an increasingly unpopular war.

Gaining media access to an institution of Duntroon's venerable status was easier than we'd thought. But tensions soon surfaced when I began asking what were deemed 'difficult' questions about college training methods, particularly during on-camera interviews with cadets, which their supervisors insisted on monitoring closely. The answers hinted at a regimented environment that fostered conformity and subordination of self to group.

Most cadets I spoke to hoped to serve in Vietnam after graduation that year and ultimately to lead others into action. I asked them how much thought had they given to how they'd perform under fire, having to kill and face the hazard of being killed.

'Very little,' replied one cadet. 'You don't join the army ... to be a professional killer. You join the army to become an officer.'

REID: **Hypothetically, if you were ordered to shoot innocent women and children, would you do so?**

Typical responses included:

> I hope I'd react in the right way, if there is a right way.

> I don't know what I'd do if I was in that situation whereby my superior officer told me to shoot people I knew were innocent. He would obviously have some superior reason for them to be shot. But I really couldn't say what I'd do.

> When it's merely your opinion against a superior officer, you must realise a superior isn't a superior for nothing, and that he's giving an order because he's qualified to do so and is probably in possession of facts you don't have.

> It's up to the individual. If he considers he shouldn't carry out an order he should make his appropriate protest.

The custodian of the college's moral compass was Duntroon's padre, Lester Thompson. I asked him what sort of ethical and moral problems cadets brought to him for advice. He replied that a common question was whether Christians in the armed services were permitted to kill.

'We would go straight to the Scriptures for the answer,' he said, 'and point out that soldiering has always been a profession within the Scriptures when Our Lord makes contact with soldiers.'

So how did Padre Lester personally reconcile war with Christian principles? Did he find conflict within himself in that regard?

He replied, 'I do find conflict. We all do. And I'm sure every soldier who goes to Vietnam and comes under fire questions himself. This is a good thing, and I'd like to assure everybody outside that we do question ourselves because we hate death. But then, of course, we believe that we're there as a protecting force as well, and we've seen a lot of death caused by other people.'

Relationships between Duntroon's academic staff and military instructors had soured after a college lecturer, Gerald Walsh, had publicly exposed bastardisation the previous year. 'I don't regret it at all,' Walsh told me. 'Actually, I think all the publicity is the best thing that's happened to Duntroon in 60 years because it's now cleared the air. A lot of Duntroon people agree with me on this. They can see that now the stage is set for even greater developments at the college, and that it was extremely necessary to have this public exposure.'

I asked if he believed bastardisation at Duntroon was finished for good or was there a risk it could recur in the future.

'It's certainly finished for the time being,' Walsh said. 'But I'm not sure about it being finished for good. We should draw the lesson from America's West Point Academy, where it came back again.'

When the *Four Corners* program was broadcast, audience reaction was mixed. The Duntroon administration resented what it saw as an attack on its traditions, particularly as the Queen was in Australia on a royal tour and had visited the college that very week. There was also pointed criticism of the visual reconstruction sequences, a technique used to illustrate how bastardisation occurred. The then Army Minister, Andrew Peacock, called the program 'unbalanced' and 'partly fake'.

The *Four Corners* report had featured the academy's new commandant, Major General Sandy Pearson, who had been tasked with moulding a new-look Duntroon in the era of push-button warfare. 'It's important we keep the good traditions and throw out the bad,' he said. 'Let's face it, we've had some bad traditions not only here but in the army. We should all be challenging these traditions from time to time.'

Yet one of Duntroon's oldest traditions — its unswerving refusal to admit woman students — still remained deeply entrenched. It wasn't until the mid-1970s that the Whitlam Labor government legislated to absorb Duntroon into the newly integrated Australian Defence Force Academy, which accepted women students for officer training.

Fast forward to 2011 when the ADFA found itself mired in scandal after students allegedly filmed and broadcast over the internet a female cadet having consensual sex.

An independent inquiry found that while for most women students, most of the time, ADFA was a safe and rewarding place, more than 70 per cent of female students at ADFA had reported gender-related or sexual harassment. But within just weeks of the inquiry's report came allegations of another sex incident that could further sully ADFA's reputation: a male officer cadet was charged at the ACT's Magistrates' Court in April 2012 with two counts of sexual intercourse without consent. He pleaded not guilty. The alleged victim was reportedly a young woman civilian living at the college.

A great deal had changed since Duntroon's integration with ADFA, but it seemed some things stayed the same.

* * *

If the 1960s were the genesis of *Four Corners,* the '70s became its decade of consolidation, when it evolved into one of the nation's most watched programs, featuring a range of talented, TV-savvy journalists and presenters, some of whom became household names. The reporters included Paul Barry, Gordon Bick, Jenny Brockie, Peter Couchman, Mary Delahunty, Jim Downes, Bob Hill, Allan Hogan, Jonathan Holmes, Caroline Jones, Tony Jones, Brian King, Stuart Littlemore, Paul Lyneham, Peter Luck, Peter Manning, David Marr, Ray Martin, Chris Masters, Jeff McMullen, Robert Moore, Kerry O'Brien, Andrew Olle, Richard Oxenburgh, John Penlington, Clare Petre, Peter Ross, Maryanne Smith, Jeff Watson, Deb Whitmont, Marian Wilkinson, Michael Willesee and Charles Wooley, buttressed by peerless researchers like Patti Warn, Robyn Smith, Anne Parker and Wendy Borchers, with producers Gordon Bick and Brian Davies, and executive producers Allan Martin and Tony Ferguson.

Another pervasive issue that would become a focus for *Four Corners*—influenced by US biologist Rachel Carson's paradigm-shifting bestseller, *Silent Spring*—was the environment. The conservation movement, though still in its infancy, was gaining momentum. In 1967 I was assigned with a *Four Corners* camera crew to join a research team headed by Dr Robert Endean, one of Australia's most respected marine scientists, traversing the waters of the Great Barrier Reef to assess coral devastation caused by the crown-of-thorns starfish, named for the mass of deadly poisonous spines covering its body, which can inflict a wound of agonising pain. It is the world's biggest starfish, growing to the size of a car tyre, and ravages reefs by feeding off vulnerable coral polyps. Most Australians had never even heard of the crown-of-thorns, let alone seen one. When the *Four Corners* report went to air, viewers were taken aback by the program's opening sequence of the starfish in repellent close-up being plucked from the sea, accompanied by voice-over narration:

> If God created a satanic villain of the ocean, this surely is it: a grotesque specimen of starfish that is slowly but surely devastating one of the world's largest natural wonders. In the sea, the starfish is virtually indestructible. On the Barrier Reef, in vast labyrinths of coral that sprawl over thousands of kilometres, the chances of halting the starfish infestation are now considered remote. The crown-of-thorns now infests the reef in untold millions. To seek them out over such immense areas of reef and kill them by hand is virtually impossible. Is it only a matter of time before Australia loses its most precious natural heritage?

Our research revealed the probable causes of the starfish scourge included an ecological imbalance in the reef's delicate habitat, partly the result of over-fishing by trawlers, toxic chemical pesticide run-off from coastal farms, and coral bleaching due to climate change.

In an investigative follow-up titled 'Oil in Troubled Waters', I teamed up in 1970 with Michael Willesee, who'd joined the program as its presenter after an outstanding spell anchoring ABC TV's *This Day Tonight*.

The Great Barrier Reef was again making headlines. Now it was controversy over renewed attempts by sectors of the petroleum industry to drill for oil on the reef despite conservationists' fears about the risks of pollution from oil-rig blowouts or tankers going aground in waters designated to become the world's largest marine park.

The story's newsworthy peg was the upcoming national conference of the Australian Petroleum Producers' Association at Surfers Paradise. It came amid growing public concern after Queensland's worst oil spill which occurred when a Liberian-flagged tanker ran aground off the state's eastern seaboard. The conference was opened by its guest of honour, Sir Joh Bjelke-Petersen, Queensland's maverick premier, who had recently championed oil exploration on the Barrier Reef and who reportedly had a financial stake in an oil company, raising questions of potential conflict of interest. The terse on-camera exchange with Bjelke-Petersen was one of the most penetrating interviews Willesee did on *Four Corners*.

WILLESEE: **Premier, I'd like to look at your personal involvement in the oil search. Can I ask you if you still hold shares in oil exploration companies?**
BJELKE-PETERSEN: **Well, I've made my decision very clear in the past. There's no question on where I stand in this way. There's absolutely no conflict in the interests I have in oil exploration companies.**
WILLESEE: **Can we establish what your interests are?**
BJELKE-PETERSEN: **No. This has nothing to do [with] my private interests in what oil exploration companies I'm interested in.**

I don't think this has got any real interest for anyone other than I —
WILLESEE: **You are the Premier of Queensland —**
BJELKE-PETERSEN: Yes. But I want to say this — there is absolutely no conflict. The minister brings his recommendations to cabinet in the matter and cabinet as a whole makes the decision ... And these are interests that I held long before I ever became premier —
WILLESEE: **Are there applications for leases or leases granted but held in abeyance because of the current dispute over the reef?**
BJELKE-PETERSEN: Well, this is a matter for the Mines Department and has been canvassed and spoken for a long time.
WILLESEE: **I'm asking you, as premier, do you know —**
BJELKE-PETERSEN: And I'm telling you, as premier, this is something I'm not going to tell you —
WILLESEE: **Can we then presume that there are some applications for leases?**
BJELKE-PETERSEN: You can presume anything you like ...

While the Great Barrier Reef remained Australia's most precious natural heritage, other environmental concerns were unfolding during the 1970s, not only in the continent's coastal and inland waterways but also in our cities and industrial centres, in tandem with ballooning consumerism and population growth.

As technology produced more potent substances, problems associated with safe disposal of industrial toxic waste were becoming increasingly acute, and had given rise to an entire industry in itself, proliferating in every state. The oversight of hazardous waste material, often dumped out of sight on land and sea, had been neglected for years by lax government agencies.

Compounding the problem, in most states there were dwindling numbers of outlets where toxic waste could be disposed of with relative safety. Warnings from environmentalist groups, highlighting fears that seepage could contaminate precious underground water resources, had induced some local councils in most states to prohibit municipal refuse tips from accepting liquid or substance waste, especially if tainted with deadly cyanide, arsenic, mercury, pesticides or viral contaminants.

Many factories had to stockpile their toxic waste, but sooner or later they ran out of storage space. Some firms illicitly emptied hazardous liquids into bushland and creeks or down roadside drains, where it usually ended up in the sewerage system — and was eventually pumped into the ocean, posing health risks to recreational beaches and coastal fishing.

Other companies got hazardous waste accepted covertly in return for bribes at council effluent works. This practice had become recurrent among some, if not most, waste-disposal firms throughout Australia, according to a whistle-blower who contacted *Four Corners* during our initial research. He had recently worked for a Sydney waste disposal merchant and disclosed he had proof of illegally dumped toxic wastes, backed up by documentation, possibly incriminating, which he'd compiled over several months. And he was willing to spill the beans to *Four Corners*.

It was against this background that *Four Corners* in 1972 embarked on what was to become one of the most disquieting environmental reports screened on ABC TV, revealing evidence of corruption in the waste-disposal industry in New South Wales and other states, with significant implications for public health and safety. I was joined on the assignment by producer Gordon Bick. A first step was to interview our key informant, who divulged on camera detailed files on toxic waste consignments and locations where they were accepted for illegal dumping, mostly at municipal effluent works in exchange for kickbacks to council staff.

REID: **On each occasion these loads were dumped illicitly, did money pass hands?**

INFORMANT: **On each occasion, yes.**

REID: **In the form of a direct bribe?**

INFORMANT: **A direct bribe, yes.**

REID: **How often would this occur?**

INFORMANT: **Every second day, if not every day.**

The illicit dumpers often operated under cover of darkness and offenders usually had to be caught red-handed before they could be prosecuted. We filmed a park ranger inspecting a woodland reserve where a road-tanker driver had illicitly dumped hazardous liquid waste — a rare case in which the offender was eventually traced — only to be fined a mere $120, a penalty the ranger regarded as woefully inadequate. Asked what would happen to the site we'd filmed, the ranger pointed out several dying trees and shrubs. 'Nothing will grow again here,' he said. 'The whole area is dead.' He went on to say the liquid chemical residue would seep into a nearby creek and end up in Sydney Harbour, harming foreshore vegetation and fish life. 'It'll kill anything it touches.' Some chemicals, he added, could mix with others, forming a deadly toxic combination.

We decided to gauge for ourselves the effect that millions of litres of hazardous waste was having on the city's marine environment and iconic beaches. From a helicopter our film crew took aerials of the Bondi ocean outfall, one of several outlets continuously discharging vast volumes of sewage and diluted chemicals. Starkly visible from the air was a huge multi-hued stain, the size of several sports ovals, discolouring the ocean surface and exposed to changing winds and currents which could spread the effluence to nearby surfing beaches.

But to gain a more graphic impression we needed closer, on-ground visuals. There was only one way: get camera access and interiors of Bondi's sewerage system.

'Sure to be a once-in-a-lifetime experience,' our Executive Producer said dryly. 'Challenging and character-building. Don't forget nose pegs.'

Clad in oilskins, a cinematographer, sound recordist and myself as reporter–producer soon found ourselves drifting in a rickety punt among a murky labyrinth of dripping tunnels deep below central Sydney's busy streets. The sewer, Australia's oldest, originally built in 1889, showed its age. Our guide was cheerfully upbeat. 'Bit pongy down here, but you'll soon get used to it,' he said. 'And in case you're wondering, this *is* where that old saying "up shit creek without a paddle" originated.'

One of the more bizarre methods of effluent treatment we filmed was the disposal of human hair. Masses of accumulated hair strands from Sydney's countless bathrooms were sifted and drained in tanks before being compressed into massive chunks, wrapped in hessian, like outsized wool bales, and trucked to a suburban landfill.

Our main breakthrough came with a tip-off that enabled us to get our film crew aboard a barge crammed with a load of drums containing thousands of litres of chemical tar waste. The barge left Sydney Harbour quietly at dawn, towed by a tug out to sea where the drums — more than 160 of them, some rusty and leaking — were heaved overboard. Several of the drums failed to sink and were left floating while the barge wallowed in a slick of self-made pollution, filmed from aloft by a second camera crew in a helicopter.

The dumping operation was carried out on behalf of the former British corporation ICI (Imperial Chemical Industries), which had been disposing of substances off the coast for well over a year.

Later we learned that dumping of industrial wastes was occurring around the continent, mostly in coastal waters, involving some of Australia's biggest, most respected industrial corporations; not only ICI, but also the Ford Motor Company, Shell and General Motors Holden. Some of the more lethal substances dumped were cyanide, pesticides, hydrocarbons and lead sludge. But it wasn't only industrial wastes that were disposed of under the waves. A number of nations, Australia included, had for years used the ocean to get rid of military hardware and other munitions. Shortly before *Four Corners* began its investigation, the Federal Department of Supply had dumped 23,000 tons (about 21,000 tonnes) of explosives off the Queensland coast.

Australia was then considering ways to curb such dumping by means of an international convention. Some nations had endorsed the treaty, but not Australia, which environmentalists accused of procrastination. I asked the then Minister for Shipping, Peter Nixon, if the federal government was dragging its heels on the issue.

> NIXON: **We've been active. Don't let me mislead you on that, we've been active, but —**
> REID: **But it still goes on?**
> NIXON: **We've done our best … New forces have emerged [bringing] greater awareness of possible damage to the ecology of dumping at sea. These factors have brought a new consciousness on the part of government to study the problem.**

A few days later, Mr Nixon's department disclosed that the federal government had in fact recently sanctioned companies dumping substantial amounts of chemical wastes, including cyanide and pesticide poisons, into coastal waters.

The *Four Corners* program was the first in-depth report on a major Australian environmental issue screened on national television. Afterwards, in a jaw-dropping turnaround, the government promptly foreshadowed uniform federal and state measures to curb further ocean dumping, moves that were to bolster *Four Corners*' reputation in the making as a pioneer of environmental reporting on ABC TV.

Since then, the expanding use worldwide of chemicals for economical and social development has also posed human health as well as environmental hazards, according to a 2010 United Nations report citing Australia as one of the world's largest generators of municipal waste per head of population. Noting that the absence of major environmental disasters in Australia, similar in magnitude to those overseas, had been due more to good luck 'than good management', the report points out that the accumulation in many countries of waste substances laced with toxic chemicals were now capable of affecting human brain development and behaviour. 'Some chemicals build up in body tissues over years. Adult human beings today carry up to 500 measureable chemicals in their bodies.'

Be that as it may, the storage and movement of hazardous wastes in recent decades have spawned multi-billion dollar waste-disposal trade worldwide, giving rise to links with organised crime in various countries, including Australia, where bikie gangs have been reportedly involved in hazardous waste dumping and other environmental offences.

Human beings have been fouling their nests since civilisation began, to the detriment of their own and future generations. As one major Sydney waste merchant, who preferred to remain nameless, put it, 'Everyone, everywhere, every day generates waste in some form or other. It's our job to get rid of it — at a price. Sure, some shonky operators try to muscle in on the trade, but I don't reckon we'll ever go bust. After all, it's an unending biz.'

Whether hazardous waste disposal companies, like the mining industry, will evermore be laughing all the way to the banks is anyone's guess. But chances are the ravages of their legacy in terms of human and environmental harm could remain with us for generations to come. Can we afford to ignore it?

* * *

During a dynamic period of stand-out programs during the 1970s and '80s, *Four Corners* attained record audience ratings, and struck it rich with a swag of journalism and TV industry awards (as documented by Rob Pullan in his book *Four Corners: 25 Years*, ABC, Sydney, 1986).

As one of *Four Corners*' longest serving producers, often I've been asked what the program's more memorable stories have actually achieved in terms of positive outcomes. To me the question is somewhat akin to the personal dilemma faced by some aid workers in the aftermath of a disaster, as they and the caravan of media teams move on to another calamity. In the long run, what have they achieved? Ultimately, they — like us — have no control over the outcome, but can only do the job before them as best they can. What I felt counted most — before considering subsequent audience or critical reaction — was the initial gauging of what we considered each story's ABI — accuracy, balance and impartiality (or sense of fairness) — which underpins sound journalism. Another criterion, of course, was how well a story stood the test of time.

When this is applied to *Four Corners* itself — a program with the staying power to score half a century not out and become a worthy runner-up to BBC-TV's prestigious *Panorama* as the world's longest running investigative current affairs program — the outcome, I guess, is about as good as it gets.

'A lot of lady': the program's first female presenter, Caroline Jones, setting out on assignment from the ABC's Gore Hill studios.

3

'GIRL TAKES OVER'

by Caroline Jones

'GIRL WILL TAKE OVER 4 CORNERS' was the banner headline in the Melbourne *Listener In-TV* on Remembrance Day 1972: 'The ABC this week named a girl in her early 30s for one of its top on-camera jobs — new compere on ABV2's prestige program *Four Corners*.'

Allan Martin, the executive producer who had invited me to come to *Four Corners*, was quoted as saying: 'I agree that this is a very big post for a girl, but you must remember that Carolyn [sic] has not just suddenly "arrived". She is a competent and experienced TV professional who has served in Canberra for *TDT* [*This Day Tonight*] during her six years with the ABC.'

The *Melbourne Sun* announced: 'Carolyn [sic] Jones, the attractive ash blonde who has landed the compere's job on ABV2's *Four Corners*, would be one of the few women in the world to get such a position … In US television, current affairs top jobs are basically reserved for the men. It's something of a breakthrough for women's lib in Australia.'

A one-day publicity trip to Melbourne produced a full page in the *Listener In-TV*, revealing little more than my painful inexperience at being in the media spotlight. I allowed myself to be photographed perched on a high stool, in a mini-skirt, applying lipstick and answering questions from a reporter much smarter than me. The headline read (again, in blaring upper case): 'CAROLINE DOESN'T KNOW HER VITAL STATISTICS, "I'M JUST SKINNY"'. The reporter observed, 'She smells very feminine', and ended with the punchline, 'A lot of lady is *Four Corners*' new lady.'

My new colleagues were kind enough to offer no comment but must have wondered if this was the sort of attention the program needed, especially when a columnist at the *Daily Telegraph* in Sydney felt moved to confess, 'The Jones girl does not particularly appeal to me — as a sex symbol.'

The sexist language, unacceptable today, was not unusual then. But I felt embarrassed and miscast. My pride was in being a reporter. I was unprepared to become a public figure. It was not part of our ABC training and I had to learn the hard way, and with no professional advice, how to deal with media attention.

Feeling I had been gullible, next I took an unwise turn to over-vigilance. When the controversial new *Cleo* magazine did a lengthy article about my appointment, I rang the editor, Ita Buttrose, to take issue with one of the photographs, in which a smaller nose than mine appeared to have been superimposed on my face. Looking at it today, I don't know why I complained; it's a pleasant enough image. Perhaps they thought they were doing me a favour.

We had a mild altercation but I soon forgot about it and we have enjoyed a warm and respectful association over the years. In 1991, very graciously, she put a flattering photo of me on the cover of her own magazine, *ITA*. So I was astonished when, in 2011, the highly rating ABC television drama *Paper Giants* featured my insignificant phone call in 1972 as one of the trials Ita had had to endure as *Cleo*'s editor. Such is the hothouse atmosphere of the media, in which many a trivial storm rages in a teacup.

It was left to Matt White in the *Daily Mirror* eventually to elevate the tone of commentary about a woman presenting *Four Corners* for the first time, when he wrote: 'For some strange reason a current affairs program seems to take a good deal of its character from the personality of its anchor man. *Four Corners* is luckier than most in its anchor woman, Miss Caroline Jones, with her air of quiet distinction and dignity.' (He even spelt my name right.)

While I endorsed Mr White's scepticism about the undue influence attributed to current affairs presenters, it was a fact of television life. And we could hardly avoid it, *Four Corners* having made its first presenter, Michael Charlton, a household name. Now, overawed to be seated in 'his' chair, I tried to channel some of his authority, if not his voice. Fortunately the day had passed when presenters were expected to adopt an English Home Counties accent.

My transition from the nightly *TDT*, where I had worked as a reporter from 1968 to 1972, to the weekly *Four Corners* was challenging. In his book *Those Fabulous TV Years*, Brian Davies describes the *TDT* production unit as a cross between an undergraduate review, an anarchist camp and an Oxbridge 'High Table'. He wasn't wrong, and I had enjoyed every exciting minute of it.

I remember hectic drives through Sydney afternoon peak-hour traffic to get our film to the lab for processing; pelting in my miniskirt, well-suited to the purpose, along the corridors of Gore Hill to the announcers' booth to record commentary; the aroma of Bill Peach's cigar (smoking had not yet been banned on ABC premises) and the reassuring sound of his laughter as tension grew towards the 7.30pm deadline; playing hilarious, boisterous games of corridor cricket during the rare spaces in our 11-hour days; sharing a work cubicle with Iain Finlay and Bob Connolly (later to become a noted documentary-maker); and riding with Bill Peach on a *TDT* float through the city — with a regrettably laddered black stocking on public display — pinching myself to believe that I was really part of it all.

At high school, I had been a sprinter, not a distance runner, and while the frantic daily turnaround of *TDT* suited my temperament, I had to adapt to the greater depth and patience required to produce reports for *Four Corners*. But I was so ready to take that step.

Towards the end of my five years with *TDT*, I had gained a lesson in the real power of television after producing some revealing programs about several unscrupulous inner-city Sydney landlords and the suffering of their tenants. The reports, edited by Dusan Werner, created controversy, but my cameraman, Ray Byrnes, and I were disturbed that our reportage resulted in reprisals against those tenants who had been brave enough to speak to us on camera. Some were evicted. For several weeks we kept in touch with them to check on their welfare, but the demands of daily television soon directed us to new assignments, and we could not continue our concern in any effective way.

For these reports I was given a Logie Award for contribution to television journalism in 1972 but the prize was bittersweet. With it came the realisation that exposing problems did not necessarily solve them, and that media attention could hurt innocent people. Ever since, I have been uneasy about receiving awards. As I began work on *Four Corners*, I resolved to calculate more carefully any risk to vulnerable people against the news value of an exposé.

I was at *Four Corners* from November 1972 to the end of 1981. The new Whitlam government ushered in a decade of change and *Four Corners* was questioning the status quo in many areas. John Penlington, Peter Reid and Frank Bennett had led the way in exposing the squalid living conditions and deprivation in Aboriginal communities. For many Australians, this was their first insight into a shameful inequity which *Four Corners* would continue to reveal, up to the present day.

The program was also characterised by its determined challenge to vested interests, bringing it occasionally into conflict with an ABC hierarchy still getting used to finding itself out of step with the political establishment of the day. Peter Reid's investigations pioneered environmental reporting in Australia, demonstrating that some of the biggest, most respected industrial firms were serious polluters. Who could forget the dramatic sequence in his 1972 report, 'Where Have All the Poisons Gone?', filmed by David Brill and Richard Baillie-Mace, with sound by Bob Sloss, in which drum after drum of toxic waste was rolled into the ocean from a barge towed out to sea? In 1977, Paul Lyneham's report on Utah Development Company of America's mining bonanza in Queensland's Bowen Basin revealed that not only rich coking coal but also $3 million clear profit were going offshore each week. I introduced the report by saying, 'If Australia Proprietary Limited was a company listed on the stock exchange, we'd be considered as having been taken over.' It would appear that little has changed in 35 years.

In the 1970s Australia was turning its attention beyond our shores, with *Four Corners* leading the way on television. Allan Hogan was reporting from Vietnam in 1975 on the eve of the fall of Saigon and interviewing Idi Amin in Uganda in 1976. Jim Downes went to Sweden to detail the innovative industrial relations experiment at Volvo, where the company was turning its workers into shareholders. He also ranged around the Pacific, reporting on how 'big brother' Australia was facilitating — or hampering — the tiny, dependent economies of our island neighbours. And his personal account of giving up smoking, through a Seventh Day Adventist course, drew enormous interest from fellow smokers.

John Temple was producing essays on Australian society. One of his finest was a 1978 reflection on Manning Clark, in which Temple explored a current criticism of the prominent historian's scholarship with a memorable lead-in to the subject: 'Some people have complained that Manning Clark doesn't write objective history. He agrees with them.' It was typical of Temple's thoughtful, sardonic style.

Reporter Peter Ross developed a talent for the political profile. A notable example was in 1975 when Queensland Premier Joh Bjelke-Petersen appointed Brisbane French polisher Albert Field to the senate to replace an ALP senator who had died, defying political convention by ignoring the candidate nominated by the Australian Labor Party. The ploy resulted in Field's immediate expulsion from the ALP and placed him in a position to bring down the Whitlam government. Thrust into this pivotal role, Field was completely out of his depth and his replies to Ross's questions led him into a self-parody which was both excruciating and somehow touching to watch. Politicians were less sophisticated then. Spin doctors and minders had not yet come on the scene.

As my colleagues' stories came in, I found them endlessly fascinating. And I had perhaps the best job of all — writing a succinct introduction to reports on sometimes unfamiliar or difficult subjects to make them relevant to an Australian audience. Working with Peter Reid during his term as Executive Producer, I learned from his journalistic wisdom for seven years. For shorter periods I worked happily with EPs Tony Ferguson, Brian Davies and Paul Lyneham.

Evaluations of my presentation of *Four Corners* varied. In his book *This Is the ABC*, K.S. Inglis kindly wrote that I was 'as unflappable as Peach, as crisp as Charlton, and transmitted by face and voice a humane and liberal concern that was exactly right for the program'.

Others were far less impressed. In *Programmed Politics: A Study of Australian Television*, three academic authors, Bell, Boehringer and Crofts, referred to my 'style of hand-clasping concern' and seemed disturbed by my simultaneous presence on daily morning current affairs radio, which, according to them, provided 'a unique form for her particular brand of socially concerned liberal reformist journalism'.

'No other ABC journalist had such apparently uncontrolled editorial access to ten or more hours of radio per week,' they added.

Until I read their book, I had not realised that the construction of my every sentence revealed that I 'rejected the validity of analyses which assume society to be structurally conflict-based, preferring the assumption that the ad hoc rectification of social illnesses is appropriate to the interests of the social whole.' I had not consciously identified my own philosophical position, so these analyses made me reconsider the notion that one could report from a neutral standpoint.

On occasion, restraining, or concealing, personal bias was a challenge. In 1975 I was assigned to report on a prevailing perception that the pharmaceutical drug diazepam, marketed most commonly as Valium, was being over-prescribed, especially for women. A member of my family had committed suicide while taking another of the new mind-altering prescription drugs (not Valium), to treat depression, and I had a strong view on the subject.

Counselling and support groups were not yet readily available as alternative treatments to anti-depressant drugs.

I found and interviewed a well-respected psychologist and social commentator who expressed the view that astute drug company advertising was targeting general practitioners with a promise to alleviate *their* stress when confronted with an increasing cohort of unhappy women. The implication was that this advertising could be a factor in an increasing rate of prescription. Of course, neither the drug companies, nor their advertising agents, nor the medicos were doing anything illegal, but I considered it a feasible suggestion and I gave it some prominence.

Next my crew and I went to film a recently installed playground, established beside a high-rise housing block. Here we interviewed young women, including a number of single mothers, who were enjoying the new facility, and discovered that their prescription drug-taking had decreased.

The Housing Commission had the humane insight that women may need to escape the loneliness of their domestic confinement to enjoy companionship, to share mothering experiences and to benefit from cooperative child-minding arrangements. I thought that this was a desirable initiative and I am not sure that I avoided displaying my personal bias in that report.

As presenter, my opportunities to produce reports for the program were fewer than those of my colleagues, and when they came, I relished them. In 1973, with cameraman Ray Byrnes, sound recordist Peter Lipscomb and editor Ian Gonella, I produced a program on Jack Mundey, controversial secretary of the NSW branch of the Australian Building Construction Employees' & Builders' Labourers' Federation — until recently it had been known as the BLF — which was pioneering the use of so-called 'green bans' to stop development of heritage sites. Their actions led to the preservation of much of Sydney's history, including The Rocks district around Circular Quay. The inclusion of Dick Dusseldorp provided the balance of a prominent developer's view. We interviewed him at his Lend Lease Corporation headquarters high up in Australia Square, the first modern international-styled office tower in the country, a landmark at 50 storeys, designed by Harry Seidler.

Among my most memorable assignments was a trip to Papua New Guinea, one of the world's last colonies, which gained self-government in 1973 and independence from Australia in 1975. With the same camera crew, I reported on the prelude to that transition. One sequence featured film of the Mount Hagen Cultural Show in the Western Highlands, a gathering in which tribesmen from many districts danced and sang for hours on end in traditional dress designed to distinguish each unique group. Their adornments included full face and body paint, mud, grass, bone, beads, penis gourds, palm fronds and brilliant headdresses of bird of paradise feathers. The show was an almost overwhelming experience. The rhythmic stamping of hundreds of bare feet accompanied by hypnotic chanting made the earth tremble, while the coordinated movements of massed bodies with arms linked rippled in waves through the vast throng. Our footage brought the spectacle of the Stone Age tribesmen of our near neighbour into the living rooms of *Four Corners* viewers.

Reporting from overseas, I found it difficult to avoid judging an unfamiliar culture with Australian eyes. This problem is exacerbated if you are accommodated each night in Western-style four-star hotels. In Papua New Guinea there was none, and I got a better insight into the resilience needed to survive in a tribal society by sleeping with the local people on slats in a bamboo hut, and trying to evade the enthusiastic attentions of their many prized pigs when attending to the calls of nature in the open air. The experience allowed me to reflect on the particular discomforts for women, and to imagine myself into their lives.

By complete contrast, also in 1973, I presented *Four Corners* live from the opening of the Sydney Opera House. (The ABC bought me a dress for the occasion!) That really felt like being a part of history. As Queen Elizabeth walked past me up the many stone stairs I became nervous; even more so when my commentary was punctuated by an ebullient greeting from the organiser of this grand occasion, Sir Asher Joel, and I disappeared momentarily in the flurry of Lady Joel's feather boa.

One story I'm not proud of was a 1973 report I made with producer Gordon Bick on Jerilderie, New South Wales, as a 'typical' country town. I grew up in such a town. I could see that the satirical tone of our program, which canvassed parochial conflicts and hinted at social improprieties, would hurt local pride. And it did. A follow-up program the next week did not heal the wounds. Years later, stranded in Sydney with a flat battery in my car, I rang the NRMA for roadside assistance. The mechanic who came was Jerilderie-born and bred. He remembered the program very well, and he let me have it, before fixing the battery and driving off in triumph. I couldn't blame him.

Having a job on television bestowed a status that was not necessarily warranted. It was a constant surprise to me that my television role seemed to recommend me for a variety of public appointments. In 1971 Don Chipp, the Minister for Customs in the Coalition government, appointed me to the National Film Board of Review, a new authority constituted to hear appeals against decisions of the Commonwealth Film Censorship Board. Appropriately, our screenings were held underground in government offices beneath a shopping arcade, where we viewed an eye-popping parade of films featuring pornography, sado-masochism and the outer reaches of violence. The would-be distributors were often world-weary, middle-European gentlemen in felt hats and trenchcoats. One of the favourite arguments they put in support of their films' release onto the general public was delivered with a shrug and palms upturned: 'On the continent, this would be considered merely educational.' The ten years I spent on the board were certainly an education for me. The Whitlam government gave me a place on the new Australian Council for the Arts, chaired by H.C. 'Nugget' Coombs, whom I admired greatly, with a Who's Who of some of the most prominent people in the land. I was overawed but did my best to make a contribution.

I was also invited by the Governor-General, Sir Zelman Cowan, to dinner at Admiralty House in Sydney to meet Prince Charles, on a visit to Australia prior to his marriage to Lady Diana Spencer. (Thank goodness for that Opera House dress!)

I am sure that none of the above opportunities would have come my way had I not been presenting *Four Corners*.

Accepting the prized position at *Four Corners* — and all that came with it — meant putting the rest of my life on hold. Over the course of my working life I turned my back on several opportunities for marriage and family life. Forty years on, I admire all the women who juggle work and family with apparent dexterity but I could not see myself fulfilling the two roles without compromising both. Perhaps

I was lacking in imagination or courage but I saw it as a choice and my decision seemed straightforward. I had been brought up to place a high value on purposeful work as the way to a good life and the stimulating, privileged job I had been given was my priority. I loved the work and, in my 30s, I preferred it to the demands of negotiating a relationship. Although I worked well in a team, my personality was not well suited to partnership. I found the exclusivity of it put limitations on my participation in a wider world of friendships, work, interests and causes.

Later there was a period of sorrow that I did not have children of my own, but I accepted it as a consequence of my earlier decisions. I was born just before the baby boom and raised under a wartime sense of values that was more modest, less self-confident than that of the post-war generation. I think we were not imbued with such great expectations of personal fulfilment: I never believed that I was entitled to 'have it all'. I have been graced with a fortunate life, in many ways, and being single has allowed me the opportunity for a variety of rewarding relationships. For instance, there are plenty of younger people to whom one can be a mentor — and I find great satisfaction in that.

During my years on *Four Corners*, I became increasingly aware of the potential of my position and the pioneering opportunity it offered, not only for me but for other women journalists. I thought that if I could do this job well, preferably without aggravating my all-male peers, it would open the door for other women. This was my quiet contribution to the women's movement, although I took care to blur my motivation. I was aware that there were divisions between the more radical and conservative women's groups and that some women were feeling threatened or excluded by the stronger expressions of feminism. I preferred not to fuel disunity. A challenging idea has more hope of realisation if you can bring people with you, rather than backing them into a corner.

With this in mind, in December 1973 I produced a *Four Corners* report on Elizabeth Reid, the newly appointed special adviser to Prime Minister Whitlam on women's affairs. In the *Australian* on 4 December 1973, Michael Le Moignan described it as 'an unsensational, perceptive film report on the work and the woman … Ms Jones was able to show us both the mother and the academic with equal warmth … Her commitment is based on humanitarian rather than party lines.' Mr Le Moignan wrote that he was disappointed when the report came to an end halfway through the program and thought the subject warranted fuller treatment. His response was just as I had hoped: it left the door open for more of the same.

I was fortunate to have the professional support of some excellent women working on *Four Corners* behind the scenes. I remember with gratitude the researchers, librarians, film researchers, script assistants and secretaries. None received equal pay with men, yet their work was vital to the success of the program. We were all modestly paid. I was excited when elevated to the status of senior reporter in the early '70s, with an annual gross salary of $8000. It seems so little now, but everything was cheaper then. I bought my home unit in Sydney in 1971 for $19,000. I had to borrow several thousand dollars and, despite being a media identity, I had to ask my father to be my guarantor in order to satisfy the bank.

In my nine years at *Four Corners*, I encountered only fairness and encouragement, as I had from the early '60s when I joined the ABC in Canberra as a trainee broadcaster. I was given many opportunities, most of them by men because they held most of the senior positions. I found them generous in sharing their experience and in mentoring me. I have never had to apply for a position, except the very first one. Although conscientious, I did not see myself as being outstanding. Through good fortune, I was in the right place at a particular time in Australian broadcasting history.

During the '70s, much of our working social life centred on Sydney's 729 Club, a magnet for media workers because it remained open until late at night. Drinking was an element in our relaxation, as well as the occasional romance, and a lot of talk. We played snooker and I smoked slim cigars (sophisticated, I thought) with my Danish friend Kirsten, a film editor. (No smoking over the billiard table — we knew better than that.) We enjoyed being a few women among all the men, who were entertaining and good company. Because I was, for a while, the only woman in a prominent post in television current affairs, I was not seen as being a threat to anyone else's ambition. I was not very assertive. It was not necessary. I was happy being 'one of the boys'.

On assignment, we travelled as a team of three: reporter, cameraman and sound recordist; the latter two were always male. Together we worked out how to cover the story. They were my best teachers, especially when I was still a novice at filmmaking. In news and current affairs television, it is always the reporters who get most of the credit, yet it is in large measure the camera crews and editors who create the production values and the impact of a program.

When travelling overseas with a crew, I tried to judge when it was not appropriate for me to join in all their activities. Quite early on I got it wrong and earned the nickname 'Matron' because I thought it must be my duty to dispense the malaria tablets and wait up at the hotel until 'the boys' got back from their evenings at leisure. I soon got the message, but the nickname has stuck. To this day, Mike Carlton takes delight in loudly addressing me as Matron at any public gathering where our paths may cross.

From 1977 to the end of 1981, while I continued to present *Four Corners*, the demands of my daily morning current affairs radio program, *City Extra*, broadcast on the ABC in Sydney, virtually ruled out travelling or reporting for television. Although the dual roles made for a challenging week, they complemented and informed each other. Renowned radio current affairs Executive Producer Russell Warner offered me this challenge and, after the initial terror, I loved working on live radio. It's a high-wire act with only a seven-second delay as a safety net. With good producers and researchers, the program was richly varied in content and rated well, even against the then king of commercial radio, John Laws. Surprisingly, 30 years on, people still remember the whimsical exchanges I enjoyed each day at 7.25am with the iconoclastic breakfast announcer Clive Robertson. But as the program took a more investigative turn, exploring the reach of corruption into local and state government, we became part of the headlines, and I realised that there was a time limit on working at this level of intensity.

In 1979, I was on a tour sponsored by the US State Department in the United States with a group of international women broadcasters. I was sharing a room with the Indonesian delegate, Diati Ganis. We were startled awake by a phone call in the early hours. It was Gerald Stone, calling me from Sydney, inviting me to join his first team of reporters for the new Channel 9 program, *60 Minutes*. I had worked with Gerald when he was a producer on *TDT* and I was pleased that he had asked me, but I decided to stay with the ABC, which had given me all my opportunities.

No doubt I missed out on an adventure, a generous salary and the celebrity treatment. But I had been trained to keep myself out of the story. I'm not sure I would have succeeded in the role of reporter as 'star'. It's worth observing that my 'no' opened a door for Jana Wendt. I was happy to see how capably she walked through it, into an impressive career.

If, over the years, my lead did pave a way for other women, then I am glad. I rejoiced whenever I saw another female face appear on TV. And today women are among the best in news and current affairs reporting, especially at the ABC, with *Four Corners* women excelling, equalled by my colleagues on ABC TV's *Australian Story*.

I left *Four Corners* at the end of 1981 to work with social researcher Hugh Mackay at his Centre for Communication Studies in Bathurst,

New South Wales. I'm deeply grateful for my time with *Four Corners*, the ABC's flagship program. It gave me a worthwhile job, good people to work with and a marvellous education about Australia and its place in the world.

I began my life as a shy person from a small, weatherboard cottage on Mayne Street, Murrurundi, New South Wales, in wartime. *Four Corners* gave me a passport to find a welcome almost anywhere in the land, with the exception of Jerilderie! It gave me a privileged place in the national conversation of a country I love very deeply. It is a country with many wounds to heal, many inequities to correct. Yet it is the best place in the world, if only we remain vigilant to the welfare of the land and all our people.

Today, more than ever, Australia needs intelligent, sceptical, forensic reporting on every aspect of national life, with those in power at the top of the list, including those of us in the communications media. This is an essential element in a healthy society and it can best be done by a fearless, determined, independent, well-resourced public broadcaster.

Top: *Four Corners* was one of the few programs to cover 'that gigantic mystery — overseas'. Cameraman David Brill and reporter Michael Willesee filming the war in Vietnam, with the South Vietnamese army. Bottom: 'Vietnam: Triumph or Tragedy' (1971). John Penlington and Gordon Bick on the role Australia played in Vietnam.

4

THE COOK WITH ALL THE FIREWOOD

by Allan Hogan

In his account of *Four Corners*' first 25 years, author Robert Pullan referred to it as 'a time when Australia was turning to the gigantic mystery out there — overseas'. While ABC News and Current Affairs could never be accused of neglecting foreign stories, until *60 Minutes* began in 1979, *Four Corners* was the only Australian television program whose reporters travelled abroad to produce comprehensive reports on international issues, providing Australians with a window on the world outside their nation's borders.

Bob Raymond and Michael Charlton paved the way with their airline-sponsored travelogues in the early '60s, followed by reporters Frank Bennett, John Penlington and later Mike Willesee, who chronicled Australia's plunge into the Vietnam War. In 1971 there was controversy over a planned visit by reporter John Penlington to 'Red China'; Prime Minister William McMahon was outraged that the trip was to be 'facilitated' by Ted Hill, secretary of the Communist Party of Australia (Marxist–Leninist), and the assignment was cancelled.

As my own experience would later show, that was by no means the last time ABC management would try to censor programs dealing with events overseas.

In 1971, at the ripe old age of 28, and after two years as a reporter on *This Day Tonight*, I was encouraged by Tony Ferguson, *TDT*'s Executive Producer, to apply for an ABC correspondent's job in London. My main tasks were reporting for the radio programs *AM* and *PM*, but my TV experience opened the door to sending back reports for *TDT* and *Four Corners* and producing TV stories by other ABC journalists, including a *Four Corners* report by Ray Martin on the 1972 US presidential campaign; he was the ABC's New York correspondent. It was my first role as producer, a job description that was in those years virtually unknown in TV current affairs.

Given *Four Corners*' long-term coverage of environmental issues, I'm proud that the first time I fronted the camera for the program was to report on the 1972 Stockholm Conference, sponsored by the United Nations. The conference was attended by 113 countries and marked the beginning of international political awareness of global environmental problems. One of its declarations urged governments 'to be mindful of activities in which there is an appreciable risk of effects on climate'. Sadly, some 37 years later at another UN convention — in Copenhagen in 2009 — the good intentions of the 1972 conference did not transform into a binding agreement on how the problem might be addressed.

For a young man on his first stint overseas, it was a great privilege to be an ABC reporter based in Britain. Suddenly, I was in the midst of those stories that had seemed so distant when I read about them in Australia. I travelled to Egypt and to Libya, just four years after the coup that brought Colonel Muammar Gaddafi to power, and made a number of trips to Northern Ireland, where I met and interviewed a young Irish Republican Army leader named Martin McGuinness in the 'no go' area of Londonderry, controlled by the IRA. When I asked

McGuinness how many British soldiers he had killed, his steely blue eyes were a clear warning that this was a line of questioning not to be pursued.

In 1973 I was assigned to cover the fourth Arab–Israeli war, which had begun on Yom Kippur, the holiest day in the Jewish calendar, when a coalition of Arab states mounted a surprise attack on Israel's borders. I travelled to the Golan Heights, where Syrian forces had made major inroads to regain territory they had lost in the 1967 war waged by Israel. I had never been to a war zone before, and this was the biggest artillery battle since World War II; Israeli brigades confronted 28,000 Syrian soldiers with 800 tanks.

When we got there the Israelis had miraculously repulsed the Syrian attack and were within 40 kilometres of the Syrian capital, Damascus. The battleground was strewn with wrecked tanks and artillery, but amazingly there were no bodies. Both sides had already removed their dead. The Syrians had been brutally rebuffed by Israeli air raids and it was clear from the wreckage that many of their soldiers had died suddenly, caught in surprise attacks.

By a burnt-out Syrian tank, there was a trail of personal belongings where a soldier had been killed. A toothbrush lay on the ground alongside some toothpaste, a comb, a mirror, a razor, a Syrian newspaper and a pannikin, at the spot where the soldier had perhaps had his last breakfast. Nearby lay an open wallet. Inside it was a photo of a young man with what appeared to be his wife and children. Tears filled my eyes, and I had to walk away from the crew so they didn't see me weeping. Our Israeli minder saw that I was upset and came over to me. 'Our boys died, too,' he said. 'You shouldn't feel sympathy for these bastards.' Of course, my tears were about something far more complex. My father was killed in World War II, and somehow this scene had touched something deeply personal.

* * *

At the invitation of Executive Producer Peter Reid, I returned to Australia in 1974 as a Sydney-based, full-time reporter on *Four Corners*. The Australian political landscape had changed dramatically while I was based in London. A Labor government was in power after 23 years of conservative rule and long-running battles between ABC management and the producers and reporters of *TDT* and *Four Corners* had subsided. Gough Whitlam planned to replace the ABC Chairman and commissioners, all of whom had been appointed by conservative governments and had acted as their surrogates in battles with program-makers. But if Whitlam thought he now had a tame ABC on his side, there were still some tough interviewers who could and would ask difficult questions.

My assignments for *Four Corners* in 1974 were mainly domestic. One story I attempted never went to air. In October, the iconoclastic Sunday newspaper *Nation Review* published a report revealing the address of Vladimir Petrov, the Soviet diplomat who had defected to Australia in 1954 after confessing to his role in a Russian spy ring. He was living under an assumed name in Melbourne with his wife, Evdokia, who had also defected to Australia in spectacular fashion. She had been dragged on to a Moscow-bound aircraft by KGB agents at Mascot airport, then escorted back off the plane by ASIO officials when it reached Darwin.

The Petrovs' whereabouts was the subject of a 'D Notice' — a government list of matters that were off limits to the media on the grounds of national security. Breach of a D Notice carried no penalty since the system relied on voluntary agreement by media organisations. Peter Reid believed we would not breach the D Notice if we did not disclose the Petrovs' address and sent me to Melbourne to try to interview them. Early one morning I knocked at their door, but there was no answer. I waited with the crew outside the house for 30 minutes or so before Mrs Petrov emerged and drove off in her car. We followed, and soon I realised that she had been well trained in her previous career as a Russian spy. She quickly worked out that she was being tailed and her efforts to lose us would have done justice to a Formula One driver.

A wiser person than me might have given the game away at that point, but I doggedly pursued her until she turned into the driveway of a local police station. It wasn't long before a senior plod came out and told us to move on, saying we knew we shouldn't be following her. That certainly was the moment to cease and desist, but I made the serious mistake of returning to the Petrovs' residence, via a local florist. Along with the bunch of flowers I left on the doorstep was my handwritten note to Mrs Petrov, apologising for anything I might have done to offend her, but informing her I intended to keep pursuing her for an interview.

A few days later I suffered the humiliation of being the subject of an unflattering character analysis delivered on the floor of the senate by the Attorney General, Lionel Murphy. He read out my letter to Mrs Petrov, which he described as an outrage, accusing me of invading her privacy. A Liberal senator asked whether my conduct would be referred to the ethics committee of the Australian Journalists' Association, and the president of the AJA said the incident showed the need for a media council. The Minister for the Media, Senator McClelland, wrote a 'please explain' letter to the ABC Chairman.

Given that, years earlier, Labor's leader, Dr Evatt, had been badly damaged by Robert Menzies' exploitation of the Petrov affair, I had thought Senator Murphy might not be particularly concerned by Mrs Petrov's possible discomfort. But perhaps the senator saw some value in being the champion of a woman in distress, albeit one who had been a spy and a bureaucrat in the Soviet Union's notorious gulags. What I hadn't realised was that Mrs Petrov was employed by ASIO, so it was hardly surprising that my letter fell into Senator Murphy's hands so quickly. It was also not surprising that ABC management thought that the story should not be pursued, and made that clear to Peter Reid. In any event, in the absence of an interview with Mrs Petrov there was no story worth pursuing.

Soon there was a more pressing assignment. The end was in sight in the protracted war in Vietnam. South Vietnam's third largest city, Hué, had fallen to the Communist North Vietnamese forces, and now they had the capital, Saigon, in their sights. Peter Reid made it clear covering the story was for volunteers only, and so it was that cameraman Les Wasley, soundman David Norton-Smith and I boarded a plane for Saigon. I was nervous because, unlike a number of my more seasoned colleagues, I had no previous experience in Vietnam and there was no doubt it would be dangerous.

Something personal drove me to take on the assignment. As a student I had been passionately opposed to Australia's involvement in the war, taking part in demonstrations and writing strident editorials in the University of New South Wales student newspaper, *Tharunka*. The *Four Corners* assignment would give me the opportunity to see for myself what I had been so vociferous about, and to discover if I had the strength of character to handle a tough assignment. Today, occupational health and safety policies require journalists going into war zones to undergo extensive training by skilled professionals, and be counselled on their return. When I headed for Vietnam it was literally on a wing and a prayer, but fortunately Les Wasley had served in the Korean War and would provide me with a security blanket, for which my gratitude can never suffice.

After we arrived I managed to negotiate two precious seats on a South Vietnamese helicopter flight to the city of Xuan Loc, 64 kilometres east of Saigon. When the chopper dropped us in fields just outside the city, three North Vietnamese divisions had been pounding it for a week. They were meeting fierce resistance from the South Vietnamese, who were outnumbered six to one. At a staging post the South Vietnamese commander told Les and I, 'No matter how many they send, we will knock them down.' We found a helpful South

Vietnamese soldier with a jeep who drove us through the city streets, where buildings were on fire and bodies lay on the road. Occasionally, a shell would lob and explode nearby. If the South Vietnamese had hoped to show us they were winning the war, this scenario wasn't working.

It wasn't long before we noticed a stream of panicked civilians and soldiers heading out of town. After a few hours Les and I also decided it was time to go, but in our haste to get into Xuan Loc, we'd given little thought to getting out. And it turned out there were a lot of people who wanted to leave, all of whom had gathered where the choppers had brought us in, in the hope that they could get a lift out before it was overrun.

On the skyline some Chinook helicopters made their way towards us. The Chinook is the elephant of helicopters, a giant twin-rotor beast with a wide drop-down loading ramp at the rear. As each of them came in to land there was mayhem, everyone with one intention — to make it onto a chopper and get out, ASAP. A Chinook would come in, but rather than land it would hover just above the ground, loading ramp down, while the panicked crowd rushed towards it. The pilot would decide when he'd taken enough passengers on board and then simply head off, with people still trying to climb the ramp. The normal precaution of standing back from the huge wash of the chopper blades was something this crowd was not prepared to do as it could mean missing out on boarding.

Les Wasley and I had been bowled over by the wash of three departing choppers by the time we made our last attempt. Deserting soldiers pushed past wounded civilians in their determination to scramble up the slippery ramp, which was awash with leaking hydraulic fluid. Les turned on his Arriflex film camera, tucked it under his arm and followed me in our desperate dash to get on board. The loading ramp dangled at a steep incline that I climbed on all fours, carrying a heavy Nagra tape recorder. And even as the chopper lifted off there was still the fear we would attract the attention of North Vietnamese artillery. Over pictures Les shot from the chopper of the ruined city, the last line of voice-over in my report was, 'If this was victory at Xuan Loc, God knows what defeat would look like.'

I sent back two more stories from Vietnam for *TDT*: one about the grim future facing local journalists who had supported the South Vietnamese regime and the other about the plight of children who had been orphaned by the war, many of whom were destined to come to Australia. I was back in Sydney when Saigon fell two weeks later, and the veteran reporter Neil Davis recorded that iconic footage of North Vietnamese tanks arriving at the Presidential Palace. Whenever the footage of our escape from Xuan Loc is shown, I feel an imposter, knowing I never paid the dues incurred by other more experienced reporters in Vietnam. Tragically, Neil was killed in Bangkok ten years later covering a minor coup attempt in Thailand that lasted only a few hours. As he died, his camera fell to the ground, still running.

* * *

In October 1975, the Australian senate voted to defer debating the budget, beginning the process that would ultimately lead to the dismissal of the Whitlam government. When Malcolm Fraser had deposed Billy Snedden as Liberal Party leader in March, my report on the Liberal leadership battle hinted that Fraser was determined to use unconventional tactics to bring down the Whitlam government. I interviewed Malcolm Fraser for *Four Corners* on three occasions in the crucial period before November 1975, asking him whether he was prepared to defy the parliamentary convention that the budget of a popularly elected government should not be blocked by a hostile senate. Fraser reminded me that Gough Whitlam had said in opposition that he would defy this convention if he thought it necessary. The Governor General put an end to the standoff in

December, sacking the Whitlam government and installing Malcolm Fraser as caretaker Prime Minister.

The change of government boded ill for the ABC. In the lead-up to the dismissal, the ABC had come under increasing fire from the conservative opposition. Peter Nixon, the Shadow Minister for the Media, was critical of an ABC news report on Vietnam which had used the term 'forces opposing the Saigon government'; Nixon thought the description 'Viet Cong' or 'Communist' should have been used. Nixon was quoted as saying there were 'too many pinkoes or out-and-out socialists on the ABC's News and Current Affairs programs'.

There were no prizes for guessing that one of the first acts of the Fraser government would be to cut the ABC's budget. Across television and radio, costs were trimmed, programs axed and travel budgets reduced. Surprisingly, in this climate, Peter Reid encouraged me to plan a trip to Africa, where historic events were in play; but to make it cost-effective I had to come up with three stories. It wasn't hard. At the time apartheid was being cruelly enforced by the South African government, Rhodesia was a rogue state denying majority rule, and Idi Amin was the crazy and deadly dictator in control of Uganda. I proposed that *Four Corners* produce separate reports on the status of the black majorities in all three countries.

So in January 1976, with cameraman David Brill and soundman Chris Fileman, I boarded a British Airways flight in Perth bound for London. When the aircraft stopped to refuel at Entebbe Airport, 35 kilometres from Kampala, the Ugandan capital, the cabin crew were astonished and concerned that we planned to leave the flight. Didn't we realise this was Uganda, run by that madman Idi Amin? The airport was a shambles, deserted except for a few soldiers asleep by the baggage carousel. Amin had kicked out all Western media and we had no visas or any document suggesting we might be welcome, so the soldiers locked us up for the night, in the airport 'hotel'. At some previous time it might have provided shabby accommodation for those who wanted to stay at the airport, but in our case it was functioning as a detention centre.

Early next morning there was a knock on my door and a short, portly Englishman introduced himself as Bob Astles. He was dressed in a suit with a New Zealand Rugby tie and boasted of his close connection with President Amin. He told me the walkie-talkie he was carrying connected directly with 'H.E.' (His Excellency) and the prospects for our visit were not good. A French documentary crew had visited Uganda some nine months earlier, and the film they had made was screening widely across Europe, where audiences were laughing uncontrollably at the antics of Amin. 'If you try something like that,' Astles told me, 'you'll be in big trouble.' I babbled something about our story wanting to celebrate the fifth anniversary of Amin's regime, which I'm sure Astles didn't believe for a moment, but somehow we found ourselves in his black Mercedes on the way to a Kampala hotel.

Bob Astles had come to Uganda as a British soldier in 1949 and after independence had worked for Milton Obote, the leader who was deposed by Amin. Astles managed to survive the coup and transferred his allegiance to Amin. Amin called him 'Major Bob' and his role was mysterious — many considered he had a Svengali-like influence on Amin. He made it clear we would be travelling nowhere without him, and when we left or returned to our rooms at the hotel we were always being watched by Amin's not-so-secret police. Every morning Astles would arrive in the black Mercedes to take us to Amin's public appearances, and it wasn't long before the president was smiling and waving for our camera.

One morning Astles arrived to pick us up and I told him I had had difficulty in making an overnight phone call to Australia. 'I know,' said Astles. 'We don't like that kind of inefficiency. The hotel telephonist was executed this morning.'

It was an Alice in Wonderland moment. Sometimes it was hard to get a firm grip on reality in Amin's Uganda; Astles may not have been telling the truth. I wasn't sure whether I was horrified or incredulous.

Amin was a brutal dictator. He had expelled all Asian-born Ugandans, resulting in the collapse of the Ugandan economy, and had ordered the murder of at least 100,000 of his own countrymen. Stories of his macabre cruelty abounded, including one that he kept the severed head of one of his enemies in a refrigerator. No one was safe from his murderous rampage, including the Chief Justice, the Anglican Archbishop, the Governor of the Central Bank, and two of his own cabinet ministers, all of whom disappeared or were murdered on Amin's instructions.

Bob Astles made sure *Four Corners* was not given the chance to report those crimes. Instead, we attended endless formal functions where military bands played very badly out of tune, and His Excellency, The President for Life, The Father of All Twins, The Cook with All the Firewood (the list of these hilarious honorifics was endless), Field Marshal Dr Idi Amin Dada made speeches that were so inappropriate they were extremely amusing. Opening a factory backed by Japanese finance, Amin praised the Japanese for their kamikaze pilots during World War II.

Astles was not willing to arrange an interview with Amin for me. He said he had been jailed by Amin previously for his role in the Obote government, and wasn't keen to repeat the experience. But he did suggest I should ask H.E. myself for an interview. 'Just phone the State House, Entebbe,' he said. 'It's in the phone book.' This seemed preposterously simple, but amazingly, moments after making the phone call and asking the receptionist if I could speak to the President, Amin was on the line. When he asked me what questions I wanted to put to him, it didn't seem wise to suggest that his appalling human rights record would be a suitable starting point. Instead I rambled on about his role in the Organization of African Unity, and it wasn't long before His Excellency had agreed to an interview the next day.

When we arrived to set up for the interview, it turned out that a crew from Uganda TV was preparing to broadcast it 'live'. This added only slightly to my apprehension about what lay ahead — it was the sight of the president arriving with a large pistol in a holster on his hip that made me think things could go badly wrong. I have to admit that my reputation as a fearless inquisitor was not enhanced by my interview with Amin. Somewhere I injected an anodyne question about reports of his abuses, but he brushed it off by saying these allegations were the subject of an independent inquiry, and I cowardly failed to follow up his response. I regret that my report added to the international perception of Amin as a buffoon, rather than a murderous despot.

From Uganda we travelled to Rhodesia, where most blacks were denied the vote by the white minority government led by Prime Minister Ian Smith. My progressive views from my student days on black nationalism in Africa had been tempered by the horrors of Amin's regime, and now they were again challenged by the apparent prosperity and calm of Smith's Rhodesia. Blacks in Rhodesia enjoyed the highest standard of living in any African country; they had access to good schools and hospitals; and there were no apartheid laws, as in South Africa. But gathered on Rhodesia's borders were guerrilla armies, backed by the Soviet Union, determined to unseat Smith's government and install black majority rule. Two factions were vying for power, one (ZAPU) led by Joshua Nkomo, a former trade union leader, the other (ZANU) led by Robert Mugabe, who had been jailed in Rhodesia as a political prisoner from 1964 to 1974. It was a moot question whether the two men hated each other more than they hated the Smith regime.

Despite being engaged in a deadly war with these forces, the Rhodesian government made no attempt to prevent me interviewing Nkomo in his home town of Bulawayo, where he openly expressed his support for the armed rebellion. Nor was I prevented from recording the views of ordinary black Rhodesians who backed the struggle for their rights. One of the questions in my interview with Smith was, 'Surely black men must run black men's countries, even if they make a mess of it?' Smith replied, 'I don't think people should run countries for the worse, and make a mess of it.' In the end it was Robert Mugabe who won the battle for control of the new nation of Zimbabwe. Some 30 years later, in 2012, Mugabe was still in power, his regime universally condemned for its human rights abuses and economic incompetence.

* * *

In 1977 and 1978, the Fraser government's budget cuts continued to rob the ABC of the resources necessary to do its job. The national broadcaster could not afford the rights to major sporting events, local drama production had almost stopped, and the facilities for news-gathering were falling well behind those at the commercial stations. A retiring ABC commissioner, Richard Harding, said at a press conference that the Fraser government had reduced the ABC to a 'timid, dispirited, and punch-drunk organisation'. There were stop-work meetings, and strikes that put programs off air and caused blank screens.

In 1979, along with Ray Martin, George Negus, Gordon Bick and Jeff Watson, I joined an exodus of ABC staff accepting Gerald Stone's invitation to join Channel 9, where *60 Minutes* was taking shape. It wasn't the salary that attracted me; it was the program budget, which promised generous funding for overseas travel and the resources to make high-quality television reports. It was also comforting to know that so many former ABC staffers were involved, including Stone himself. We may have been working for Kerry Packer, but other than requiring us to make a popular program, that didn't seem to require any fundamental change in our journalism.

Gerald Stone delivered on his promise of the resources to travel widely. In three years at *60 Minutes*, I produced reports from Japan,

Korea, India, Thailand, Singapore, Malaysia, Uganda, Zimbabwe, Egypt, Germany, El Salvador, Israel and Spain. The assignments included an interview with Egyptian President Anwar Sadat, and a Walkley Award-winning story on three Australians jailed on drugs charges in Bangkok. I had no regrets at leaving *Four Corners*, despite my former colleagues' criticism that *60 Minutes* was shallow and superficial. When John Penlington defected to *60 Minutes*, the ABC lost one of its most widely admired journalists.

In 1981 I started the *Sunday* program for the Nine Network, poaching a neglected ABC journalist, Andrew Olle, to join Jennifer Byrne, a promising young reporter from the *Age*, as the program's two reporters. To cut a long story short, despite the program enjoying great critical acclaim, at the end of its first year, Channel 9 instructed me to cut *Sunday*'s budget and sack five of its staff. I could not sack people who had taken the risk of joining the program, and who had been responsible for its success. I said that if Nine insisted on the cuts, I would be one of the five who went. Nine tried to get me to change my mind but I refused, and so I sacked myself.

And that's how I ended up as a reporter back at *Four Corners*, with Jonathan Holmes as Executive Producer. I thought Holmes had acted admirably in refusing Nine's blandishments to take my highly paid job at *Sunday*, and he made me feel extremely welcome in the job I had left some five years earlier. Holmes was in the process of revitalising a tired program, and was determined to restore its reputation.

In May 1984 Holmes assigned me to Port Moresby for a story I never suspected would lead to controversy and confrontation. Thousands of West Irian refugees had crossed into Papua New Guinea, fleeing what they claimed was persecution by Indonesian authorities. It created a major diplomatic headache for Michael Somare's government. If he sent them back, many Papuans would be angry at the fate of their fellow Melanesians; if he let them stay in PNG, he risked the wrath of the Indonesian government. Somare wanted to show Jakarta he was not sympathetic to the cause of the OPM (Free Papua Movement), a ragged army of Melanesian guerrillas who were fighting the Indonesians for independence in West Irian.

On arrival in Port Moresby I met Sean Dorney, the ABC's PNG-based correspondent. He was welcoming and extremely helpful, even though he might have regarded me as an invader on his territory. With his advice, I made contact with the OPM and made secret plans to interview its leader, James Nyaro. The meeting was to take place in a remote part of the country, close to the West Irian border, and the *Four Corners* crew and I flew there covertly in a chartered aircraft. Shortly before we took off, Dorney phoned me to say the PNG government knew of our plans and was extremely angry. We were breaking the law, the government claimed, because we were enticing Nyaro to cross the border and enter PNG illegally. The truth was that Nyaro lived most of the time on the PNG side of the border, but the government wanted to maintain the fiction that it was able to prevent him doing so. I had interviewed Michael Somare earlier in our visit, so once the interview with Nyaro was recorded we headed for home.

On our return to Sydney the report was given the title 'Borderline', and I began writing the story and editing the footage. It wasn't long before Sean Dorney was on the phone, saying he had been told by the PNG government he would be deported if *Four Corners* ran the interview with Nyaro. Sean had also informed ABC management of this threat and the matter was referred up to the acting Managing Director, Stuart Revill, in the absence of Geoffrey Whitehead. The Australian Department of Foreign Affairs, following discussions with the PNG government, sent Revill a telex, saying that I had broken a promise not to interview Nyaro and that I had violated the immigration laws by doing so. The Department told Revill that the Foreign Minister, Bill Hayden, believed that if these allegations were true, the *Four Corners* interview would cause tensions with PNG.

Revill contacted Jonathan Holmes and asked him to consider the value of the interview if the consequence of broadcasting it was to be Dorney's deportation. At that stage the program was still being edited, and the interview with Nyaro remained uncut. I told Jonathan that Nyaro's halting English meant that I would use little of the interview anyway, and he in turn informed Revill that the interview was important to the story but not vital. Current Affairs management made the decision that the interview was not to be shown, and Revill contacted the PNG government to inform them of that decision. I was disappointed because the interview was a scoop, and even if it wasn't riveting television, it was important to an understanding of the issues.

The threat to expel Dorney remained unreported by the media until PNG's Foreign Minister told an AAP correspondent that he had complained to the Australian government about the *Four Corners* interview. Then it hit the front pages — and when the decision to ban the interview became known, it was even bigger news, covered extensively by the ABC's own programs. Tony Jones, then a young reporter for *PM*, followed the story closely. Battlelines were drawn: some argued the ABC was being censored by a foreign government; others believed that management had the right to manage. Jonathan Holmes defended my integrity, making it clear I had neither given nor broken undertakings to the PNG government.

Now the value of the Nyaro interview took second place to the principle of the ABC's independence. Holmes asked Revill to reconsider his decision, but Revill argued that the ABC's presence in PNG was his primary concern. This was understandable — the ABC was protective of its overseas bureaux: some had been established only after delicate diplomacy, and anything that might cause the expulsion of an ABC foreign correspondent was not to be taken lightly. Some years earlier the broadcast of the Italian director Michelangelo Antonioni's film about China on ABC TV had led to the Chinese government severely limiting the activities of Paul Raffaele, the ABC's first correspondent in Beijing. Revill would not change his mind about the ban on the interview, and he was supported by the Managing Director, Geoffrey Whitehead, when he returned from holidays.

The controversy deepened when ABC Chairman Ken Myer gave an interview in which he said that in Asian countries the media was totally controlled by government, and 'you have got to follow the rules set by those governments or you won't get in'. He was undeniably correct, but it was not a ringing endorsement of independent, truthful journalism, and in the context of the Nyaro interview it reflected badly on PNG. Myer was attacked on all sides and compounded his embarrassment by releasing a poorly worded statement which seemed to contradict his earlier view.

When the ABC board met a few days later, it was the founding father of *Four Corners*, Bob Raymond, now a board member, who declared that the issue went to the heart of the ABC's independence. He was joined by five other board members who voted to overturn the ban on the interview. That meant that Myer and Whitehead, who found themselves among a minority of four board members, had been overruled. Whitehead insisted that the decision was one for management, not the board. The meeting was adjourned until the next day, when Myer told the board he had received letters of resignation from Whitehead and Revill. This was not an outcome those who had voted to overturn the ban wanted, so a statement was prepared supporting the earlier management decision, but saying the board believed the issue had been elevated into a matter of principle by the PNG government's threat to expel Dorney. At the same time it was announced the Nyaro interview would go to air as part of the *Four Corners* story the next day.

The 'Borderline' report was half an hour in length, and the Nyaro interview took up about one minute of that time. The fallout from the ABC's prevarication was much greater than the issues raised by the story itself. Newspaper editorials questioned the competency of the board, and the *Australian* declared that 'at no time has there been so much public dissatisfaction with its performance'. I felt like an innocent bystander throughout the controversy. I was angered by the false allegations that I had broken the law or breached agreements with the PNG government, but I acknowledged that management had the right to make a decision about whether the interview should be broadcast.

Some months later, the PNG government carried out the threat to expel Dorney, but made it clear he was not held personally responsible for what had happened. I felt great sympathy for Sean, who is an excellent journalist, and greater sympathy for his wife, Pauline, who was a PNG citizen with extensive family connections in her homeland. Sean returned to PNG in 1987, and in 1991 was awarded an MBE 'for services to broadcasting and sport'.

Soon after 'Borderline' was broadcast, Ian Carroll, the Executive Producer of the nightly ABC TV program *Nationwide*, spoke to me about plans he had to shake up the evening TV news bulletin. He wanted to shift the starting time to 6.30 and soften the sharp demarcation between news and current affairs. The program would be called *The National*, and Carroll asked me to be his Deputy Editor. In what was perhaps one of my poorer career decisions, I agreed, and left *Four Corners* to help set up the new program. But that's a story for another time.

'*Four Corners* needed big stories. It always has.' Two of the big stories from the Holmes era: Jeff McMullen (above) reporting on Nicaragua's secret wars, and (below) Mary Delahunty's investigation into the misuse of Australian aid to the Philippines which won a Gold Walkley.

5

RECOLLECTIONS OF A CUTTING-ROOM TECHNICIAN

by Jonathan Holmes

By the end of 1981, *Four Corners* was in a bad way. Its budget had been cut until its crews could barely travel beyond the Blue Mountains. With a handful of veteran reporters it was struggling to fill 50 minutes each week. It had had three executive producers in a single year, all of them reporters who would much rather have been in the field. I've heard it said that at the end of that year, management came close to dropping the program altogether.

Instead, they took some drastic decisions to salvage it. *Four Corners'* duration was cut from 50 to 30 minutes; the budget for travel and expenses was almost doubled; and since no one in Australia wanted to take on what was seen as a somewhat thankless task, management decided to go to Britain to find a new executive producer.

The first two of those decisions, as much as the third, were the ones that helped to save the program. Suddenly it became possible to travel again all over Australia, and indeed to at least some of the four corners of the earth. And the program's weekly efforts were now concentrated on a single story, instead of two or three. All that had already happened before I arrived in Australia in April 1982.

My first instinct was that if *Four Corners* was still in trouble, it was because it lacked up-to-the-minute topicality. I soon discovered that the program's limited technical resources were a barrier to the 'fast turnaround' story.

I left a Britain that was in a fever of jingoistic excitement as its fleet sailed south through the Atlantic Ocean towards the Falkland Islands. I travelled the long way around the world to take up my new job in Sydney; *Four Corners* reporter Jeff McMullen was based in Washington DC, so I went via the United States to meet him. In total the journey took about five days. Thus, I arrived in Australia with the worst case of jet lag I have ever experienced, before or since. I was met by the ABC's Head of TV Current Affairs, Peter Reid — my new boss, who for seven years in the 1970s had himself been the Executive Producer of *Four Corners*. I think he was probably alarmed by my youth. I had been hired at long distance, interviewed not by him but by the ABC's London manager. I was 34 years old and looked about five years younger.

As we drove north through Sydney's central business district and over the Harbour Bridge towards the ABC's television studio at Gore Hill (no harbour tunnel in those days), I asked Peter what the program had done about the coming Falklands War. Nothing so far, he said.

I could hardly believe it. In London the story had been all-encompassing for months. It seemed extraordinary that a weekly current affairs program, even on the other side of the world, could have ignored it. I determined that the very next program would deal with the question of why Argentina had taken the colossal gamble of invading the Falklands (or recovering the Malvinas, as the Argentines saw it).

We had neither the time nor the money to even think about travelling to Argentina. But the idea for the story had occurred to me because four years earlier, I had myself produced a 50-minute report for the BBC's *Panorama* about Argentina's military junta and its 'dirty war' against left-wing guerrillas and anyone who might conceivably support them. We persuaded the BBC to send bits of that program to Australia by satellite. But that meant that it ended up on videotape, whereas *Four Corners* was shot and edited on film. Videotape editing in the early 1980s was crude and cumbersome; we had to go to the ABC in Canberra to get the facilities, and after that to a production house in North Sydney.

Writing and improvising as we went, veteran reporter John Temple and I put together a half-hour program, an amalgam of the old BBC report, more recent news footage and new material shot by our own people with Argentine exiles in Sydney.

Four Corners went to air on a Saturday night at 7.30, as it had done for 21 years. At 7.20 there were still a few embarrassing holes in the soundtrack where the pictures were absolutely mute. But we had run out of time. With a one-inch video reel clutched in my hand I leaped in a cab and tore through the back streets from Crows Nest to Gore Hill. We got it onto the ABC videotape machine at 7.29pm. One minute later, and my first week would have ended in complete disaster.

As it was, the program was a mess, technically and journalistically. That was nobody's fault but mine. *Four Corners'* staff wondered what had hit them.

I learned my lesson, and from then on we did very few fast-turnaround programs. The strength of *Four Corners*, everyone agreed, lay in stories that took weeks to research, film and edit.

But it turned out there was a gulf of understanding between the senior reporters and their brash new English Executive Producer. *Panorama*, where I had spent the past seven years as a producer, was *Four Corners'* closest equivalent in the English-speaking world; yet it was a wholly different beast. For a start, the BBC program was far better resourced. It had more money for travel; it had access to, and was beginning to learn how to use, new-fangled computer-assisted video post-production techniques, which only advertisers used in Australia; and above all, it had a lot more staff. When I left the UK, *Panorama* had six full-time reporters and 12 producers, giving it an emphasis on production quality that *Four Corners* lacked.

Four Corners had the same number of reporters but just one associate producer — my deputy, Mike Berry — and one producer, the formidable Peter Manning. We had three researchers, who helped the reporters get their stories under way. But once they left the office with their two-man film crews, the reporters were mostly on their own. They were used to that autonomy. They liked it. They were at the peak of the profession. Elsewhere in the ABC, *Four Corners* was known as the 'House of Lords'. As I began to recruit more producers, the reporters struggled to see the point of them.

Naturally enough, I regarded the job I'd been doing myself for years as indispensible. I wasn't used to having its value questioned. The philosophy at *Panorama* was that doing long-form television journalism was hard; there was too much to think about for one person alone. Since in those days most experienced journalists had their grounding in print, it was felt that they needed the help of people who, though they might be and usually were much younger, were television-makers first and foremost.

The producers had a lot of power at *Panorama*. Because we had often spent weeks on a story before a reporter was even assigned, we usually knew more about it than they did. What the reporters brought to the job was on-air gravitas and authority. But our job was to make sure that our combined efforts worked as television. In crude terms, they worried about the words — the narration and interviews — and we worried about the pictures and the sounds. We obsessed about 'sequences' and 'actuality' and 'pace' and 'structure' — technical terms that were barely recognised at *Four Corners*. We spent hours in the cutting rooms with the editors, shaping scenes, long before a formal script arrived. At times, we rather grandiloquently called ourselves 'filmmakers'.

To my eye, *Four Corners*' television style was at least ten years out of date. It seemed to me that its programs were too often illustrated lectures rather than living television. Mellifluous scripts were written without much regard to what pictures had been shot to accompany them. Interview grabs would run on interminably. It was a style of television that had long since gone out of fashion in Britain.

I set about changing things with plenty of vigour and precious little tact. No one who had survived for 12 years at the BBC ended up humble. We were confident that we simply knew better than everyone else in the world how to do what we did. And if the BBC had too little humility, the ABC had too much: why else would it hire a foreigner, younger than anyone else on the program's staff, who barely knew the names of the Australian states, let alone anything about the social, political or economic history of the country, to run Australia's premier current affairs program?

It is unthinkable that such a decision would be made today (though far more important jobs are regularly dished out to well-remunerated CEOs from overseas). But that was a time of cultural cringe. It puzzled me that while all around me I heard Australian accents — not just in the streets and in my kids' school playground, but among the off-air staff at the ABC, and on-air on every commercial radio and TV channel — many of the voices that you heard on ABC Radio and TV, including those of most *Four Corners* reporters, could have come straight from the Home Counties of England.

And so, with the blithe arrogance of (comparative) youth, I set about trying to turn *Four Corners* into a cheaper version (for there was nothing I could do about its comparatively meagre budget) of *Panorama*, albeit with an Australian voice. Somehow Peter Reid procured funding for two or three more producer positions.

Finding suitable people was another matter. In Britain there were numerous training grounds, in commercial television and at the BBC, for young television journalists who wanted a career behind the camera, in features and documentaries and in daily current affairs programs. In Australia there were virtually none — and the few who had the right combination of journalistic and television experience were snapped up at twice the salary we could afford to pay by the newly arrived big kid on the current affairs block, Nine's hugely successful *60 Minutes*.

The producers we did recruit — often people who came more from the documentary world than from journalism — discovered that collaborating with reporters accustomed to near-total autonomy was tough. Often a producer or reporter would come to me and ask, 'When the crunch comes, who's the boss?' At *Panorama* it was a question that was seldom asked. If the argument was about words, the reporter usually won; if about pictures, the producer — but most of the time there wasn't a conflict. At *Four Corners*, I found there wasn't sufficient common culture for that to work.

Within a year or two *Four Corners* had its own answer: the reporter was the boss — and still is. It's simpler. It resolves the creative tension — but at the cost, I've occasionally felt, of the creativity.

The producer we had when I began, Peter Manning, wasn't subservient to anyone. His qualifications were overwhelmingly journalistic, not televisual. He had wanted my job as Executive Producer, and in a journalistic sense was far better equipped than me to do it, as he proved when he took over from me in 1985. Meanwhile he provided much of the journalistic grunt at *Four Corners*.

Both Peter and I agreed that as well as a slicker television style, *Four Corners* needed big stories. It always has. Not necessarily many of them: if once or twice a year, weekly programs like *Four Corners* produce a story which makes headlines and becomes a talking point around the nation's water-coolers, they more than justify their place in the schedule. But if every week they do no more than a competent, thorough treatment of a worthy topic, they will be vulnerable when the razor gang starts looking for cuts. It had been too long since *Four Corners* had had a truly groundbreaking story. The lack of budget was no longer an excuse.

We first made headlines in 1982 when Peter and reporter Jim Downes went to Fiji to investigate the role of Clive Speed, an Australian adviser in the Prime Minister's office whose salary was paid by Australian aid, and his connections to a group of business consultants, also mostly Australian, who had been commissioned by a Fijian businessman to write a report for the ruling Alliance Party. The report included some ethically dubious advice about how to win the forthcoming election.

The PM, Sir Kamisese Mara, did us a favour by stalking imperiously out of his interview with Jim Downes. Tapes of the program, acquired by the Fijian opposition, played a major part in the 1982 election — although arguably they had the effect of uniting Indigenous Fijians behind Sir Kamisese Mara. His party won, and afterwards his government set up a Royal Commission, with a New Zealand judge as commissioner, to look into Australian interference in the political process — not only by Sir Kamisese's 'consultants', but by *Four Corners*. The Commissioner exonerated the program of collaborating with the opposition or interfering in Fijian politics.

But 'The Fijian Project' was dwarfed, in terms of impact, by 'The Big League', which went to air on 30 April 1983. At the start of the year, I'd invited Chris Masters to join *Four Corners* from the ABC's Rural department, where he'd been making films for *Countrywide* and *A Big Country*. I liked his air of Aussie honesty; I had no inkling, and nor did he, that he would turn into the country's most formidable investigative journalist.

I paired Chris with Peter Manning to make his first report — about the state of rugby league, something that Chris knew a bit about since his brother Roy was one of the best-known coaches in the game. But within a couple of weeks, Peter and Chris sniffed out a story that was far bigger than football. They uncovered suspicions in the New South Wales magistracy that seven years earlier a fraud case involving the Executive Director of the NSW Rugby League had been dismissed by a compliant magistrate on the instructions of the Chief Magistrate, who claimed to be passing on the wishes of the Premier, Neville Wran.

Hearing a rumour was one thing. Getting the report into a state where it could be put to air was another. Chris and Peter interviewed hundreds of people and tirelessly worked on their sources in the magistracy. It turned into what we came to call 'a big dig' — a story that instead of taking six or seven weeks took months to research and shoot. Everyone else on the program had to work harder and faster while Peter and Chris ground on remorselessly.

When it finally went to air, 'The Big League' caused Australia's most powerful premier to stand aside while the Chief Justice of New South Wales, Sir Laurence Street, took on the role of Royal Commissioner. Neville Wran was exonerated, but the Chief Magistrate, Murray Farquhar, went to jail.

There were epic battles fought in getting that program to air. Some in Australia — especially in the Australian Labor Party — still believe it never should have been aired, because it sullied the Premier's name with allegations that in the end we could not prove. Our view was that the allegations had been swirling around the magistracy for years, deeply damaging morale and trust in the judicial system. It was essential they be made public, and the issues resolved.

Still, if Dame Leonie Kramer, a Fraser appointee, had not been chairman of the Commission (it did not become a Corporation until later that year), 'The Big League' might never have got to air. It's the only program I know of, before or since, that was referred up beyond the Managing Director (or the General Manager as he was then) to the board, before it aired. In the end, a committee of the three commissioners who were based in Sydney — Kramer herself; Ken Tribe, a solicitor and prominent classical music administrator; and Laurie Short, the veteran secretary of the Federated Ironworkers' Association and a hard-boiled member of the ALP Right — decided two to one that it should air. Laurie Short, unsurprisingly, was the dissenting voice.

Even before that decision was taken, other battles had gone on behind the scenes — far less important in the political history of New South Wales, but significant in the evolution of *Four Corners*. Once again, they stemmed from my determination to make investigative journalism into television.

I believed that the story we had to tell, and the evidence upon which it was based, would not be understood by first-time viewers unless we dramatised the events we were describing. So we used actors to re-create some crucial scenes: the Chief Magistrate, Murray Farquhar, casting about for a suitably pliant magistrate to hear the case; his secretary announcing to Farquhar, in front of other magistrates, 'The Premier is on the phone'; Farquhar telling his deputy, 'The Premier wants the case dismissed.'

The ABC's lawyers were horrified. We were going to put words in the mouths of actors representing the Chief Magistrate, other magistrates and the Clerk of the Court. Not many words, it is true — indeed only a couple of sentences, based on notes that Chris and Peter had made after conversations with our three most vital sources. We'd shown the notes to the sources and they had signed or at least initialled them, but had refused to make out statutory declarations. They had promised that if it came to an official inquiry or a defamation proceeding they would give evidence — but the lawyers could not be sure that our sources would repeat on the witness stand the precise words we had put into the mouths of our actors. At the subsequent Royal Commission, I should add, they did. However, that came to nought as the Commission found that Wran could not have made the call.

And in any case, actors act, and sometimes overact. Meaning is conveyed not by words alone, but by tone and body language. How could we be sure we'd got that right in a dramatic reconstruction? 'Can't you read out the statements instead?' the lawyers asked.

I was adamant. This was long before iview and digital recorders; for most people there would be no second look at the program. We needed to create visual and aural impact if viewers were to understand the significance of what we were reporting. So the reconstructions remained — though we went to great lengths to make it plain that reconstruction is what they were. They were shot in a studio, in front of black drapes, not a simulated magistrates' common room; Chris Masters strode through the set before and afterwards, explaining that we'd based these scenes on the evidence of witnesses whom we could not name but who, we believed, were telling the truth.

It was a device the program used frequently for at least a decade thereafter, with ever-increasing subtlety and sophistication. Chris Masters' Walkley Award-winning films about a failed rescue in Bass Strait and the French Secret Service's bombing of the Greenpeace ship *Rainbow Warrior* in New Zealand both included extensive reconstructions. Re-created scenes of an empty dinghy tossing in the Bass Strait waves or a wet-suited diver sliding into the black waters of Auckland Harbour at midnight brought alive the events we were describing. Reconstructions have slipped in and out of fashion in the 30 years since 'The Big League', but I don't think we have ever again included dialogue. The circumstances were unique: the dialogue was essential, and based on the recollections of first-hand witnesses; anything more speculative than that would not have been journalistically, or legally, acceptable.

'The Fiji Project' was the first really memorable story to go to air on my watch; 'The Big League', without a doubt, was the biggest. But of course there were other significant programs. In 1983, reporter Mary Delahunty and producer Alan Hall won Australia's highest journalistic award, the Gold Walkley, for 'Aiding or Abetting?', a program about the use and misuse of Australian aid in the southern Philippines. Though I was delighted, Chris Masters probably had mixed feelings about that — with a defamation suit from Neville Wran hanging over it, 'The Big League' could not be submitted for awards that year.

Chris's turn came the year after, when the multi-millionaire electronics entrepreneur and helicopter enthusiast Dick Smith approached me with a proposition: he would part-fund a *Four Corners* investigation into how an aeroplane had crashed and its pilot drowned in Bass Strait because of what Smith saw as the inadequacies of the search-and-rescue system. In an arrangement which would never be contemplated today by ABC News management, Dick Smith provided the producer, and cash to pay for chartered helicopters and other expensive essentials, while we provided the reporter — Chris Masters — the crew, the editor and facilities. The program, 'Search Without Rescue', won Chris Masters a Walkley Award (the first of many) in 1984.

Then there was the battle over reporter Allan Hogan's brief interview with an armed militant from the OPM, the movement for the independence from Indonesia of Irian Jaya, or West Papua. The PNG government insisted that Hogan had 'lured' Nyaro across the border from Irian Jaya to do the interview, in defiance of promises he had made when he was given a journalist's visa. We never said publicly where the interview was conducted, but Allan Hogan always maintained that Nyaro lived most of the time in PNG, a fact that the government did not want to admit.

Under huge pressure from the PNG government and the Department of Foreign Affairs and Trade, and with the ABC's correspondent in Port Moresby, Sean Dorney, threatened with banishment, ABC management ordered that the interview be pulled. I always accepted their right to do that — the decision was well above my pay-grade. But I was incensed that they did not defend our reporter against the PNG government's allegations of breach of faith. In the end, ABC management's decision became a national scandal, the board overruled it, and the program went to air complete with the contentious (though, in all honesty, unremarkable) little interview.

The 'big digs' and the headline stories are the ones people still remember decades later. Nevertheless, week by week, *Four Corners* goes to air with the best program it can manage. For reporters and producers there's a rhythm to working on the program, increasing in intensity as they progress through research and shooting, to writing and editing, reaching a climax in 'program week'. For the executive producer, every week is program week. The intensity is draining.

I did not make myself popular, that first year or so. Indeed, for some of the veteran reporters at *Four Corners*, most of them 15 or 20 years my senior, I made myself insufferable. I would tear the initial rough-cut versions of their programs into 20 different parts and put them back together in a different order; we called it 'restructuring'. I would take their scripts and ruthlessly edit and change them, shortening sentences, dropping adjectives, simplifying syntax; we called it 'polishing'. I would push reporters and producers to think, and think again, about how they could bring glimpses of real life into their reports, with real sound, of people talking not to an interviewer but to each other in real situations; we called it 'actuality', and it was a hard thing to achieve. I urged cameramen to take their cameras off the tripod, sound recordists to trade off sound quality for genuine spontaneity.

Looking back on it, I feel I did more good than harm, but there were plenty who didn't think so then. One veteran reporter, no longer with us, dismissed me as a mere 'cutting-room technician'. Another remarked bitterly within my hearing, after a particularly tough rough-cut viewing: 'And for years I've been kidding myself that I understood television!' Three times, our best film editor, Alec Cullen (who amazingly would keep working at *Four Corners* until the end of 2011), announced that he had had enough and began packing cardboard boxes. It required a prescribed degree of executive grovelling to persuade him to stay.

Some reporters gave up making much effort to shape their stories the way they wanted them. 'What's the point?' I heard one ask a colleague. 'Jonathan will only change it all anyway.'

So the effort was not without cost, on both sides. It was not a happy experience for me either, at least in the early days. I was a newcomer to the country, and to the job. I had to make my friends and allies where I could and try not to worry about the nay-sayers. Hardest of all, at the end of my first year, I had to tell a couple of people who had served the program faithfully and well that I thought the program would be better off without them.

But gradually we forged a team — camera crews, editors, producers, a whole new reporting line-up — that understood what we were about.

Some of the new recruits during the 1980s — Andrew Olle, Kerry O'Brien, Chris Masters, Mark Colvin — had been working in television for most of their careers. Tony Jones came from radio, but became adept in the medium in no time. Others came direct from newspapers, and for them the transition was hard. As a medium, television has three or four times more heft and impact than the written word. But it takes time to learn how to use it.

For a journalist from a non-television background, the fact that everything you write has to be read to a series of pictures, and must have relevance to them, can seem an infuriating limitation on your ability to say what you want. You have to learn to use the pictures to help you rather than hinder you. A convoy of trucks can illustrate the slow progress of peace talks or the remorseless approach of war; a man gazing through a window at a bank of televisions can stand in for an entire population deciding how to vote. The viewer hardly notices these verbal sleights of hand; and after a while, like a driver instinctively changing gear, the reporter barely notices them either. But they make the difference between a program that a viewer struggles to understand, as image fights with words, and one that slides into the brain like a sword into its sheath.

For all that, it never gets easy. It wasn't until the early 1990s that I made the full switch from producing and supervising to reporting in my own write (to pinch John Lennon's pun). I have done many jobs in television, and a few outside it, since I graduated 40-odd years ago. Writing a *Four Corners* script is still, intellectually, the hardest thing I've done. Decide what the story is. Decide how to tell it, in what order. Decide which short grabs from lengthy interviews work best on screen, and how to link them together. Decide what your best visual sequences are, and how to use them to say what needs to be said, and where to place them so that the program has light and shade, moments where viewers can rest their brains, where words take a back seat. Then write your narration so that it doesn't conflict with what viewers are feeling as they watch the screen, so that information slips effortlessly into their ears without distracting their eyes.

But all that was in the future. Of those crowded three and a half years in the early 1980s, far more than individual programs, what comes back to me most vividly is the atmosphere in that cramped suite of offices on the fifth floor at Gore Hill. The battered wooden table around which we sat for our weekly meetings or to scour through the script after a rough cut. The old Remington typewriters on which we bashed out memos and scripts and research notes. The scissors and sticky tape with which we literally cut and pasted scripts, to save having to type them all over again between one version and the next: no word processors then.

No fax machines either. Jeff McMullen sent his scripts from Washington by telex, and I sent back my revisions the same way —

unimaginably cumbersome in this age of the instant email. I remember the Bakelite telephones with the silvery dials — push button phones didn't come in until the mid 1980s. And everywhere — in offices, in cutting rooms, in studio control suites — a haze of cigarette smoke, and ashtrays overflowing.

It was a life apart. For an EP, nothing much exists outside that little world: a small group of fiercely intelligent, competitive, ambitious men and women, striving to do better. There were rages and tears and tantrums. There was laughter too, and lunches, every fortnight or so, at which prodigious amounts of alcohol were consumed. Every Saturday night, another program to put to air, and every Tuesday afternoon, another rough cut to worry over.

I was due to go back to Britain after two years. But just before Christmas 1983, after I'd said my goodbyes (and been given a leaving present, an Aboriginal bark painting, which I still have), Peter Manning and reporter Jenny Brockie came to visit me and persuaded me to stay. A year later, for the 1985 season, the program was expanded back to 50 minutes — a vindication, I suppose, of three years' effort. In its half-hour incarnation it had needed no presenter, but now I managed to poach Andrew Olle from Channel 9 to be the program's weekly face. That was one of my better decisions. Another was the move to create new theme music and graphics to introduce the program; Rick Turk's distinctive tune and the *Four Corners* spinning cube — my very own graphic idea — have both stood the test of time, albeit much changed and updated, and are now 30 years old.

When eventually I handed over, with relief, to Peter Manning, my wife and I weren't convinced that we wanted to return to the grey skies of England. We went instead to Boston, Massachusetts, where I helped to make a documentary series about nuclear weapons. Two years later we were back in the searing light of Sydney. That, too, is a decision I've never regretted.

Since then I've put in three stints at *Four Corners* as a reporter, most recently for five years from 2003. In its spacious offices at the ABC's new headquarters in Ultimo, it's lost some of its scruffy intimacy. No executive producer I've worked for has been anything like as interventionist as I was. If they had been, I probably wouldn't have stood for it.

Wherever I've been working since 1985, every Monday night at 8.30, with very few exceptions, I've had the TV tuned to Channel 2. Sometimes the program is average, sometimes it's exceptional. But let no one doubt that over every one of those programs, sweat has been sweated, and metaphorically at least, blood has been shed.

I've met reporters from television news who've remarked that putting 45 minutes together in seven weeks must be a breeze. You will not hear anyone say that who has ever actually done it.

'A chance to enter the House of Lords': Delahunty reports on the disastrous Ash Wednesday bushfires, Mount Macedon, 1983.

6

AIDING OR ABETTING?

by Mary Delahunty

It began with a call. An English voice with a laconic air. 'I'd like to talk to you — in private.'

Private ended up a wide, empty and echoing lounge of the Ryde RSL, burnt orange and mission brown tiles hovered over by alarmingly green plastic potted palms. Funny what you remember.

Jonathan Holmes's beanpole legs were wrapped in jeans and he appeared supremely relaxed in the Executive Producer's skin, even though he'd seemingly been in the job five minutes. But the man did come with a reputation; I observed he carried it lightly. He was a gun producer from the BBC's *Panorama* program, creating waves of energy in Australian current affairs circles, and here I was a young journo from the Wimmera wheatlands, sitting opposite him on a plastic two-seater, with the distant afternoon jangle of the pokies in the next room, trying to take in a brilliant offer.

With the insouciance of youth, I didn't really know my own luck. A chance to enter the ABC's 'House of Lords', as *Four Corners* had become known by the early '80s, to be part of its transformation and to absorb by osmosis the finest skills in the business from the talents around me was the opportunity of a lifetime. *Four Corners* picked at the carapace of life and politics, and like the cat that got the cream I was both surprised and elated. Sitting there on the ugly couch, in my mind I was already straining to be the journalist I hoped to become.

I had been trained in the chrysalis of the ABC — social-affairs documentaries and *Nationwide* current affairs in Melbourne. I'd wandered a counterculture festival with a stripped-to-the waist Deputy PM Dr Jim Cairns and trembled in a grubby Williamstown pub waiting for a crim from the Painters' and Dockers' Union to find me and spill the beans on the 'Bottom of the Harbour' tax rorts. I'd almost been sacked when an April Fools' Day spoof on doctors exploiting the tax benefits of this scheme went to air with seemingly more truth than spoof. My next move had been to Sydney, to *The Reporters*, the program plaything of one media mogul, Rupert Murdoch, trying to best another media mogul, Kerry Packer at 9. It didn't. So I happily exited the glossy world of commercial current affairs, where editorial conversation too often had ranged around slogans rather than sentences.

It's been pointed out since, but I don't remember an obvious sense of being the only female reporter at *4Cs* when I arrived. What sticks in my mind was that under Jonathan's leadership the place was a hive of research and rigour.

Vigorous debate was the lingua franca of *Four Corners*, but I recall an exchange between Jonathan and me that carried the frisson of a deeper cultural mismatch. It was over Northern Ireland and the civil war between the Catholic Nationalists and Protestant Unionists. A researcher and I were deep in the story looking for an angle when I was asked into his office.

'You're too close to the story.'

Me, fifth-generation Aussie, being told by an English immigrant, just arrived, that I was too close to 'the Troubles' half a world away!

Red hair and pale skin mark me as part of the Irish diaspora but I had never even been to Ireland. Anyway I lost the argument and was taken off the story. It still rankles. I eventually got to the Emerald Isle well after the peace settlement, as a government minister on an education delegation in 2000 — invited by the English!

If 1983 was a seminal year for this young reporter, it turned out, for totally unrelated reasons, to be a hell of a year for the country — savage wildfires, the Franklin dam stopped by brave protests, and a sudden early federal election.

On the morning of 3 February 1983, daring a double dissolution to exploit Labor leadership instability and hoping to snatch control of both houses of the parliament, Prime Minister Malcolm Fraser called a snap election. But Fraser had made a monumental miscalculation. As he was doing the necessary constitutional business at Government House, the Labor caucus was efficiently changing leaders from the bland Bill Hayden to the charismatic former trade union leader Bob Hawke. That day at Yarralumla Fraser was on the wrong side of history. It was a day that reverse-mirrored the drama and political unpredictability of an earlier clandestine visit to the Governor General, in the spring of '75, when Gough Whitlam was sacked while Fraser waited in an anteroom to become the interim PM. What goes around comes around, and in 1983 the political tectonic plates were realigning. Though we didn't know it then, Labor would govern the country for 13 years, even, almost impudently, seeking 16.

That leadership change in '83, as dramatic and telling about the state of the Australian Labor Party as the Rudd–Gillard switch in 2010 (with the same salve for the vanquished — foreign minister), was a thrilling event for a young reporter like me. Political executions, with the blood always seeping out into the wider body politic, are a heart starter for journalists. Like a new engine in an old car, it revs up the show and you are never sure what direction it will go or how fast it will run. It cemented a fascination with politics that started before university and would later propel me into my own political career.

Of course *Four Corners* doesn't bother itself with the daily reporting grind. We had our eyes on the long game, the social and political effects of daily decisions, the ramifications of good and bad policy.

While Bob Hawke, the new opposition leader, was bristling during the 'blood on your hands' interview with Richard Carleton on the ABC's *Nationwide*, and Malcolm Fraser was exhorting Australians to 'put your money under the bed' to save it from Labor, I had my L-plates on at *Four Corners* dissecting the tragedy of the Ash Wednesday bushfires. This investigation was personal as well as professional. Friends' places had been scorched, though our hobby farm in Victoria had survived. I was disturbed by the failure of the state disaster plan and emergency services' communications. Many of these failures would be repeated nearly 30 years later in Victoria's Black Saturday inferno.

As the '83 election approached, 'the Silver Bodgie' — as Hawke was nicknamed by some wag in the party — ran on the mateship anthem 'Bringing Australia Together', while the tactically gazumped and wooden PM, Fraser, struggled to look like the national leader we needed, even in the townships of Victoria and South Australia, where wildfire had taken lives and certainty.

The election of 5 March 1983 brought Bob Hawke's Labor to government after seven and a half years of the Liberal–Country Party Coalition. Malcolm Fraser's lip quivered as brash Bob whooped into the tally room to claim victory. Labor gained 23 seats, on only a swing of 4 per cent, and its greatest election win in 40 years. As the surrendering opposition leader, Bill Hayden, had famously predicted, 'Even a drover's dog could lead the Labor party to victory.'

Hayden's consolation prize was the post of Foreign Minister. The man and the job would loom large in my life six months later, when

Four Corners was pursuing an explosive foreign aid story right in the middle of his portfolio patch.

It was about an Australian aid policy indolently executed on Mindanao Island, in the southern Philippines, which in the '80s — as now, though for different reasons — was the centre of a festering civil war over land ownership and self-determination. Through the nine-year-old Philippines Australia Development Assistance Project (PADAP), Australia was spending $80 million, a big chunk of its foreign aid budget, building roads on this primitive island. The aim was to provide a network of passable roads so subsistence farmers could get their produce and stock to markets. It seemed on the surface — and was presented to Australian government and taxpayers — like a straightforward infrastructure spend with demonstrable community benefit. But was it?

Four Corners' research, led by Robyn Smith, had discovered breathtaking Marcos diplomatic duplicity. A 1981 Community Aid Abroad survey had exposed as a sham the project's supposed benefits to the local community. Our assignment in the Philippines was to ascertain whether Australia was aiding the farmers or innocently abetting the Marcos dictatorship by paying for the asphalt and expertise that carried trained soldiers and military hardware to an undeclared and unequal civil war.

The Philippines is a beautiful country blessed with rich and productive soil and bountiful crops. Back then, 30 years ago, its natural assets were being plundered by Ferdinand Marcos, his plump wife, Imelda, their family and cronies. Ten years into martial law, they dominated this largely illiterate Catholic nation like demigods. They enjoyed a lot of earthly support.

Bloated landowning oligarchs poured money into Marcos coffers to protect their patch, as did the United States to shore up their bigger patch. A compliant nation in Southeast Asia, the Philippines was strategically critical after the fall of Vietnam in 1975. Under Marcos, the Philippines was a US-supported anti-communist rampart and commercially lucrative for American sugar interests. With the giant US naval base at Sepik Bay and regular cash-flow from Washington, Marcos and his mates were comfortable in Uncle Sam's embrace.

The new Labor government in Canberra felt some ambivalence over the pull of an American puppet and cosying up to a despot. It announced a review of foreign aid, keen to demonstrate judicious use of Australia's largesse. However, like probably all Australians back then, Hayden was a supporter of foreign aid. 'There are major benefits for Australia in investing in a poorer country in the region … Turning it on or off like a tap, no I'm not in that business at all,' he told us.

This was sensitive terrain for the government and for journalists. The Philippines, despite its dictatorship, was an ally.

Finally our *Four Corners* team was granted a visa — conditional on the approved itinerary and the company of a military minder. The ABC film crew — the wily, decorated and hilarious producer Allan Hall, who became a lifelong friend, cameraman Chris Doig and young sound recordist Scott Hartford-Davis — and I sensed the delicacy of the assignment. Did Jonathan counsel us? I don't remember that specifically but I do know we carried the stringent *Four Corners* ethics — be fair, tough, balanced and always question the official line — almost by osmosis. I think we knew, though Allan and I had not directly discussed it, that we would somehow have to ditch the government minder if we were to have any chance of testing the truth of this massive aid project. To record the reality on the ground of where the roads were being built and who was using them, we would have to become, to turn today's foreign correspondents' patois on its head, 'unembedded'.

In the Philippines there were hot days of glowing testimony and buoyant government-sponsored interviews and pictures, then the weather changed. As tropical sheets of rain whipped and lashed the island, we eluded the military meant to monitor us and were driven deep into the jungle by political activists wearing the priest's collar.

This was my first encounter with Liberation theology, a potent form of political activism practised particularly by Jesuits in the Third World; Catholic priests and nuns worked in the dirt-poor hamlets while their bishops mollified Marcos from gilt-edged pulpits in Manila.

The vehicles bogged on the crude tracks but before frustration or the soldiers could engulf us, silent villagers working with these men of the cloth rescued the convoy. One woman offered me tea. Her weather-beaten face creased into deep tired lines as she smiled; strong black tea and a gentle touch on the arm, a gesture of encouragement to a stranger. A stranger she and her family were trusting to understand. Simple grace. These brave people were farmers and rebels taking huge personal risks, like the priests, in non-violent protest — a lopsided struggle against a murderous regime.

What the tea lady knew of international diplomacy and Manila politics I cannot say. But as I sat across from her and other determined locals in a Jesuit safe house, through many discussions by candlelight with the priests and leaders, I learned she could not feed her family, though the land they worked was fertile. No rebel uniforms, guns or swagger, instead a powerful intellectual and moral consistency. To survive they needed some of the land and profits enjoyed by their feudal landlords — fruits of their labour, almost biblical — and the Jesuits saw the justice in their cause.

They all took risks to hide us, show us the actual destination of the disputed roads and trusted us to tell the real story on national television in Australia. What they helped us uncover was that while our embassy officials and Filipino functionaries lauded PADAP, Marcos's men — particularly the egregious local governor of Mindanao — were conniving in a dirty political harvest. Yes, the roads were shiny and storm-proof, but they were empty of farmers' produce moving merrily to market; indeed many didn't even go towards a commercial centre. Instead they snaked deep into rebel territory carrying armed platoons to harass civilians.

In fact peasants were being forced off their land in a brutal strategy known as 'hamleting' — a straight steal from Vietnam. To supposedly cut off the rebels' supply lines and effectively surrender plots for the oligarchs to plant with lucrative export crops, whole families were herded into confined hamlets far from their source of food. It was a grim picture.

Yet the governor could grin and chirrup for our camera, 'The people are happy about everything. Me and all my other candidates win the elections hands down.'

Not surprisingly, he told us, 'We want the Australians to stay forever.'

'And what of the "hamleting", the killing?' I asked him.

'The army are not here to kill, they are here to help.'

Governor Corrilles is probably long gone but the civil war in this place festers on 30 years later.

The evidence of Australian aid unwittingly abetting Marcos was compelling. And I was never the sort of journalist who sat on the fence when the facts, honestly researched and tested, held a truth that needed clear telling, regardless of the risks. And the risks, freely confronted, were magnified for the men and women who ferried us from safe house to safe house, staying ahead of embarrassed minders sent out to find us.

In a war zone you never really know where danger lurks, and we were careful. I certainly never felt the white-knuckle fear of witnessing the colour drain from the face of our interpreter as fast-talking militia held us at gunpoint during an assignment covering the civil war in El Salvador. Death squads were executing Western journalists there to intimidate the media just as the Indonesians had murdered the Balibo Five and another Australian journalist in a calculated attempt to hide the facts of their 1975 invasion of East Timor. Of course these deaths cast a shadow over our work, but though 'going underground' was risky and losing contact with minders and the Australian Embassy worried some at home, I never felt in the Philippines the deep anxiety I would later feel on occasions in politics. In the Philippines I was confident of the people closest to me during those weeks in the jungle. Confident that their networks were secure, that Jesuits aren't foolhardy and that they wanted our footage to prove the abuse of Australian aid on Mindanao. Indeed they would organise a trusted courier to spirit the critical canisters out of the country.

Back in Australia Bill Hayden was grumpy. We had been out of contact with the embassy and Australia for weeks and it was diplomatically awkward to lose an ABC journalist and crew in the middle of an ally's jungle. Perhaps he wondered if *Four Corners* was intent on embarrassing the new government. Remember, this was the same year that 'The Big League' went to air, the Chris Masters exposé that had caused Hayden's Labor colleague, Premier Neville Wran, to step down until he was exonerated by an investigation that led the chief magistrate and others in New South Wales to be jailed. Or maybe Hayden, the ex-Queensland copper, was as dubious of Marcos and his corrupt cronies as we were.

Dirty, hungry and exhilarated, we returned to Manila. We had a ripper story 'in the can', with the most telling footage, we hoped, already on its clandestine way to Sydney. Australian Embassy officials turned up the next morning at our hotel, anxious to know where we had been and why we were out of contact for so long. There was mutual suspicion. Had they got some grief from Canberra? The armed forces of the Philippines, they implied, were negligent in losing us. There was a lot of double talk. Government flunkies from both nations were particularly curious about the film of our travels. The Filipino officials who also arrived were direct in asking to see it. Under no specific obligation but not wishing to prolong our stay on these lovely islands, we agreed to show them our footage — some of it, at least. Crammed into a hotel meeting room solid with the fug of cigarette smoke, Alan Hall rolled the travelogue version: shiny military men hosting shiny road construction, optimistic departmental plans of what we would now call 'infrastructure fostering development', local town mayors on

Mindanao Island buoyant with supportive script. It was all resolutely 'on message'. None of this ever went to air!

The showing tickled the men from Manila. Soothed by picture postcards of terraced plantations, beaming workers and exquisite sunsets, no one asked about the jungle footage of the Australian-funded roads. The Australian diplomats crammed into that room appeared sceptical — *Four Corners* doesn't have a reputation for cant — but fortunately they remained diplomatic enough to encourage our hosts to stamp our exit visas.

I remember that first drink on the Qantas plane swooping away from the archipelago towards home, a toast to the Jesuits and a job well done. Relief. We were meticulous about protecting the identity of those brave souls who harboured us so no film was taken of them. No images remain but I'll never forget their faces.

A good story grips you until you get it on air. We landed and practically headed straight into the editing suite, Jonathan cracking the whip. Around the time of the final edit, perhaps after the first 'promo' for the show, the Foreign Minister fired a shot across our bow during a bellicose media doorstop.

I would grow to respect Bill Hayden as I travelled with him overseas; or rather, tagged along with the media pack into foreign parts, on stories I can't always remember. But my feelings of dread and determination still spark across the years to touch a particular memory into life, the memory of his press conference on our Philippines story. There was nothing in Hayden's public life, before or since, that suggested a vindictive man, yet at this Canberra press conference he turned verbal bovver-boy, or at least that's how I recall his words, relayed sharply down the line from colleagues on the spot: there would be 'strategic consequences … if *Four Corners* gets even one fact wrong'.

We made sure we didn't. The threat of litigation is like a cattle prod to journalists. So we started to sift through what was hard-sourced fact, what was gleaned from conversations on and off the record, what had been confirmed in interviews and by the camera's keen eye. Seven months in the making, this hour-long documentary held attributable facts that had been tested over time by researcher, journalist and producer. I worked through the night confirming their attribution. What had grown on us as fact had to be proved again, a defence against an irritated government. It wasn't needed. The indefatigable Alan Hall drove home the edit, with Jonathan like a hot but totally supportive breath on our necks.

The report was awarded the Gold Walkley; Australia stripped aid money from Filipino army roads and promptly transferred it to clearer humanitarian projects.

Deeper satisfaction came later. In February 1986 the world watched a 'velvet' revolution in the Philippines. I was at the ABC Melbourne news desk by then, so found myself presenting nightly reports from our correspondent in Manila of a sustained non-violent protest that eventually tipped Marcos and Imelda from their thrones. I saw again calm on the faces of silent citizens in serried rows before government tanks. Not so many farmers this time but the priests were there, standing with a well-heeled congregation of the middle classes and students in school uniform. Nuns in crisp white habits prayed the Catholic rosary.

When the doomed president finally fled in a military helicopter — he with bags stuffed with gold, his wife with bags stuffed with shoes — they left a presidential palace with corridors of rooms devoted to storing their indulgences. Another dictator plundering a hungry nation.

At its best, journalism seeks the truth. It is often an inconvenient truth for governments balancing multiple objectives, as I now keenly appreciate after seven years as a state government minister. Certainly *Four Corners* exposing the foreign aid duplicity of Marcos made for an uncomfortable realignment in Canberra. Yet I don't remember any political dissembling. Rather Hayden, his department and the government responded with a clear policy shift and the issue was over. It was good, smart politics and a useful public-benefit symbiosis of politics and journalism.

Looking at our doco nearly three decades later I am comfortable with its balance, though it is almost tropically languid in its pace! There is solid evidence of Jonathan's quest for, and belief in, hard facts and revealing pictures. What strikes me though, in this soggy era of spin and obfuscation, is the directness of the interviewees. There are no weasel words in these interviews; no PR flaks steer an Aussie road contractor away from speaking of aid dollars sticking to the fingers of local officials, or a former Philippines senator from bluntly declaring the cost of corruption to his country, or even the chuffed local governor happily admitting himself a 'freeloader' on the Australian gift.

But until I clicked onto the *Four Corners* archives recently, I had forgotten the benefit to our report in the timing of a tragedy. Six days before our documentary was aired in the familiar *Four Corners* time slot, Filipino opposition leader Benigno Aquino was assassinated on the tarmac in Manila. Returning home from exile, the admired senator and Marcos political prisoner had spoken to reporters aboard the plane with him about the risks. 'I suppose there's a physical danger because you know assassination's part of public service.'

Minutes later he was dead on the runway, surrounded by soldiers and a supposed 'lone gunman'.

These prescient words from a martyred man formed the platform of moral outrage against Marcos and his cronies that cushioned our case for review of aid used by his government.

Good journalism, the journalism I have long admired on *Four Corners*, often captures a current, a wave of indignation or inquiry that connects with community instincts. Our report definitely rose on the revulsion of the killing of a patriot.

Sometimes journalism operates at a juncture, a small turning point that is read later as a fulcrum. Aquino's assassination and Marcos's gormless lies about who actually did it were the beginning of the end for the despot. It certainly was the end of the Marcos gravy train of Australian aid. It took three years of persistent people power to force him out, led by the widow Cory Aquino, who was elected president in 1986. Their son took the same office in 2010.

Four Corners over its 50 years has hammered out Australian journalism's template for identifying social trends, picking the turning points, throwing small pebbles into large ponds and often being surprised at the magnitude of the ripples — from feminism to chronic Aboriginal disadvantage to the dark arts of politics. I put my toe in the water also that year with a look at the emerging überscience of in-vitro fertilisation. Understanding how the law lagged doggedly behind the crusading scientists and cries of the childless, we called the report 'In Vitro; In Limbo' — another of Jonathan's pithy titles.

Journalism's annual awards gala is held each year in a different capital city. In 1983 we had to cross the continent for it and I missed the plane. (There was an unfortunate symmetry in this; I had also missed the plane to the Philippines, which set me back a day behind the team who jetted off, incredulous, without me.) Getting another flight to Perth had me only a few hours behind Allan and other colleagues' celebrations. I didn't mind missing the speeches. I knew nothing of the Gold until it was announced. That task, as it happened, fell to the soon-to-be Australian envoy to the Vatican and not much later guest of Her Majesty's prison in Perth. But these were still the glory days of WA Inc and the political zenith of Premier Brian Burke.

I should have stayed longer at *Four Corners* but another fantastic opening came along, to the accompaniment of the siren song of the new and untried. The great ABC innovator Ian Carroll had dreamed up a sort of magic carpet role of flying current affairs reporter covering Asia, a peripatetic addendum to the bureaux sited in Asia, which at that time were quarantined to news. Paul Keating had not yet arrived as PM, with his Asia focus, but ASEAN was new and shiny, Japan was challenging as our top trading partner and China was stirring.

Another opportunity of a lifetime.

Clockwise from top: 'French Connections': The sinking of the Greenpeace vessel *Rainbow Warrior* in Auckland Harbour, 1985, was a world exclusive for Chris Masters; 'Banned Aid' (1985) brought the conflict and famine of Ethiopia into Australian living rooms; 'The Big League' (1983): sensational revelations about how NSW officials ran the game of rugby league nearly toppled a state premier.

7

THE BIG DIG

by Chris Masters

I have long felt I did not so much find the subject of corruption as it found me. There was more than a trace of naivety accompanying my arrival at *Four Corners* in the early 1980s. Not long down from the country I was, remarkably, recruited by a new English Executive Producer, Jonathan Holmes, who wanted a more local sound and feel to the program.

So I came through a side door, from the Rural department. This probably meant I carried less of the 'can't do' baggage that comes with the territory in big city newsrooms. Something else I carried, not so much my own as the product of forebears, was a sense of duty.

It may be false memory but I can still conjure an image of myself at the feet of my parents in the early 1960s as they watched this brand-new current affairs program, *Four Corners*. There is no doubt they would have been avid viewers of the 'landmark Box Ridge program' broadcast in September 1961; the family home at Lismore being not far away, Mum being a journalist, and both of them connected to the plight of fringe-dwelling Aboriginals.

It was impossible to have anything but respect for the work of Michael Charlton, Bob Raymond, John Penlington, Mike Willesee, Allan Hogan, Caroline Jones and others. There was and is an understood responsibility to honour the record and seize an unusual opportunity in journalism to go the extra distance.

That partly sets the scene for my first report, 'The Big League', produced with Peter Manning and Jonathan Holmes in 1983. A mild enough inquiry into dirty dealings around the sporting field led to an explosive investigation of judicial corruption. The subsequent Street Royal Commission returned a mixed result, finding against rugby league boss Kevin Humphreys and former Chief Stipendiary Magistrate Murray Farquhar, and exonerating NSW Premier Neville Wran.

What the investigation revealed for me was the tawdry façade of governance and rule of law in modern, civilised Australia. This was a time when it was easy for people in the know, journalists included, to have speeding fines torn up; for prosecution briefs to go missing; for evidence to be routinely invented; for criminals who are 'right for it' put away despite having been nowhere near the scene of the crime; for Drug Squads to sells drugs; Armed Holdup Squads to organise armed holdups, and worse.

There was also a sense the public did not care too much as long as there was a good meal at the end of the day and the wheels of industry continued to turn. Many appreciated the flexibility of rules that could be ducked by insiders. Around the concept of public order had grown a fringe industry dedicated to avoiding compliance, with which many citizens gratefully engaged.

What journalism can do at a time like this is form the narrative so the public can be informed to a point where they care. The truth should not be confined to mavericks and victims unlucky enough to be bashed in a cell or die from a heroin overdose sold by a police-franchised trader.

The report that for me best told this layered story was 'The Moonlight State', made again with Peter Manning and other *Four Corners* treasures, Shaun Hoyt and Deb Whitmont.

The investigation began in 1986 with a tip-off from a Canberra police intelligence contact. He told me of a Queensland colleague in a jam because he had been bribed by a superior to suppress the passing of intelligence on organised crime to national policing agencies.

When we poked our noses in further, the reek of systemic corruption intensified. A system common enough in pre-war Australia was still intact — of underworld bagmen collecting for the bosses who secured a fringe benefit by protecting more benign crimes, such as illegal gambling and prostitution.

Queensland Police Commissioner Sir Terence Lewis had followed the lead of his predecessor, ensuring he retained a cut in the same way he had by standing over working girls in his early days on the beat. He and Lady Lewis would receive their brown paper parcels of cash funnelled via a former colleague, Jack Herbert, as they sat down to tea at one of the better Brisbane hotels.

Lewis had powerful protectors such as Premier Sir Joh Bjelke-Petersen, who continued to defend him as law enforcement in Queensland began to spin out of control. Subordinates were furious about either being beaten to promotion by a slippery colleague or missing out on their cut.

The old rationale for copping a quid for turning a blind eye to 'victimless' crime, for accepting a dividend for society's dirty work, was also becoming harder to justify as a burgeoning post-war drug trade encroached on old territory. Senior cops who said they would never take a sling from a drug dealer were doing just that. Once they licensed the crime bosses they could not then arrest them without endangering themselves.

In the early months of 1987 our small team, armed with no power to compel testimony or tap telephones, put in some unmerciful hours. By May 1987 we had gathered enough facts to make a case of entrenched and systemic police corruption as well as accompanying political blindness. 'The Moonlight State' triggered another judicial inquiry as well as long overdue reforms to policing and governance that would spread beyond Queensland. Following the Fitzgerald inquiry, Sir Terence Lewis was jailed and the long reign of the notorious Bjelke-Petersen government ended.

For *Four Corners* and myself, however, the experience of making the program was then eclipsed by a death by a thousand courts. It was not until the turn of the century before the last searing tentacles of litigation fell away.

The trial of defending the program turned out to be greater than the trial of making the program. And making it had been difficult. I was away from home for over three months. The underworld and their corrupt cohorts became nasty when they saw us getting close to the truth. Cameraman Chris Doig and sound recordist Guntis Sics were roughed up and our camera smashed by hoods in Fortitude Valley. In investigative journalism you don't expect a painless path to the truth.

While the path to resolution proved more tortured, it was also eased by the ABC Legal Department. If a program so demonstrably in the public interest had been found wanting, it would have been a blow not only to the ABC but all media. So an effective defence was called for and thanks to the likes of lawyers Bob Mulholland QC, Michael Sexton, Judith Walker and many more, the battles were finally won.

The program had made a difference. Queensland and Brisbane, released from other clawing tentacles, raced to the new century. The sophistry of Bjelke-Petersen's 'can do' regime became more apparent. Corruption has more than moral consequence. Cronyism bestows favour on the unworthy. In 'The Moonlight State' gaudy property developers were preferred to credible rivals. Ethical police officers lost ground to amoral colleagues. Talent shrank from the tertiary sector. Joh's 'can do' system was a political estate built on mud and mangrove.

Time and tide found it out. An inevitable swelling of grievance from all those failed yet worthy competitors had for us fortuitously coincided with the May 1987 broadcast.

Within *Four Corners* the program also had ongoing influence. The 'big dig', as we call it, became more defined than random. It is unusual in journalism to apply so much time and resource to a single subject. Investigative journalism had always been a feature of the program. But it was never all we did. *Four Corners* is a healthy melange of storytelling forms, encompassing interview-based profiles, lyrical films, long-form essays, history documentaries and so on.

Now we were applying more resources to the prospective 'big dig', with a focus on corruption, and most particularly police corruption. It was clear the Queensland system, termed 'the joke' by insiders, was operating elsewhere, if in varying forms.

In 1991 Neil Mercer made 'Police Story', an early *Underbelly*-style profile of one of the kings of Kings Cross, Louis Bayeh. It was a clever character portrait and economic profile of how the business of organised crime works in New South Wales. Kings Cross has always had its Mr Bigs. Over time the system was being finessed to a point where they were becoming untouchable. By being seen to be powerful you can, like a feudal lord, informally tax your subjects without getting your hands dirty.

As it turned out, Big Louis's finessing proved deficient. In 1996 before the Wood Royal Commission he admitted to bribing 41 police. In 1997 Bayeh received four years' jail for perverting the course of justice. In 2000 he faced a different court — of peers — falling wounded before a hail of bullets outside the El-Bardownie restaurant at Narwee. In 2001 he copped another three years for supplying drugs and demanding money with menaces from brothel proprietors. By then the Kings Cross throne was vacated and swiftly re-occupied. Indeed the newest King of the Cross, John Ibrahim, later celebrated in the tabloid press, had featured briefly in 'Police Story'.

My later program, 'Academy of Crime', broadcast in June 1995, had connections to both Neil Mercer's report and 'The Moonlight State'. It focused once more on Kings Cross, relying substantially on work generated by the Wood Royal Commission and a team that had learned some valuable tricks in Queensland.

Gary Crooke QC, who had been counsel assisting Tony Fitzgerald, now took on a similar role with Justice James Wood. By now commission personnel such as Crooke had learned to avoid recruiting from the ranks they were investigating. They had also seen the value of roll-over witnesses. In 1994, a team largely from the Federal Police, derided by NSW colleagues as 'plastics', began covert observation at the broad and gaudy intersection of Kings Cross detectives and crime landlords.

Hundreds of meetings were videotaped and recorded. In one I recall the NSW detectives who saw themselves as the toughest in the land pledging loyalty to the brotherhood. 'We'll never roll over like all those little cowboys in Queensland,' declared the ruler of the roost, Inspector Graham 'Chook' Fowler.

Chook did not know his good mate Sergeant Trevor Haken had done just that. The public would be entertained with images of Chook's hairy legs and pungent prose as he pocketed wads of cash. A tiny camera and microphone had been secreted forward of the passenger seat in Haken's Toyota. 'Crotch cam' joined its sporting equivalents 'stump cam' and 'helmet cam' in the lexicon, as the public eavesdropped on the detectives' ingenious orchestration of the F word into every sentence. 'That's out the fuckin' window, mate … fuck me dead I'm fuckin' bleeding … I'm not even fuckin' going near him.'

The listening devices revealed the local villains adopting the same codes used in England. Haken and Fowler called $500 a 'monkey' and $1000 a 'gorilla'. In New South Wales the Queensland 'joke' became 'the laugh'. Taking a bribe was known as 'a drink', which was close to the truth; a huge amount of the monkeys and gorillas were supporting prodigious consumption.

Chook further delighted the public with his brazen denials of wrongdoing. He sought to avoid the court by taking the 'psychiatric express', claiming a hurt-on-duty exemption from giving evidence. Chook pretended to slip on a spilled milkshake. The B-grade subterfuge was caught on tape.

The program, made with Sue Spencer, my favourite producer, reached beyond the entertainment value that the underworld can use to disguise their core business of exploitation, ugliness and pain. Sue brought hard work, measure, good sense and a big heart to the slippery slopes of the Cross.

With strong material from the Wood inquiry to build on, we further sought context and meaning. It is easy to think these stories are about their key elements: prostitution, police, politics and so forth. But most of all they are about people.

In all journalism there is nothing like getting out of the office and going to the evidence. Sue and I trawled Kings Cross, stepping tentatively beyond the glitter. We joined our film crew for midnight excursions with the NSW Ambulance Service. The ambos' routine following an overdose case was to inject Narcan at $85 a shot, more money than the fit of heroin that had reduced their patient. There had been 1201 overdoses in the area in the preceding year, and 28 deaths by overdose. We witnessed an angry user railing at us as 'hyenas' while the ambos laboured over his inert girlfriend. We watched the ambos later carry from a shabby boarding house a corpse of one they could not save.

We spoke to demoralised business owners as the last menswear store in the area closed its doors. Most memorable was a conversation with a teenage prostitute who spoke of heartache and helplessness. Her story was that overwhelmed by the pressure of finals exams she had taken the train to the city, where she met a man who introduced her to heroin and a new, old profession. She said she missed her family but it was too late to go back. She was the age of my daughter. We tried to stay in touch but soon lost contact. I often wonder about her.

Like so many of these reports, 'Academy of Crime' exposed an unnatural order. The job of the Kings Cross detectives should have been to protect that young girl rather than facilitate her destruction. Kings Cross had long been a breeding ground of mischief with police officers such as Trevor Haken learning the tricks of the wrong trade and becoming more like a crook than a cop.

I later got to know Haken, who came to regret not only his corruption but rolling over to the Royal Commission. He remained proud of and continued to identify with the brethren he betrayed. Like Jack Herbert, the Queensland bagman, who also rolled, he had done us all a service, and as with Jack there was no way of turning back. Trevor missed the long lunches and the camaraderie. He continued to believe that despite the abject corruption, his ex-mates were law enforcement's A-graders, the true hard men. I wondered how they could have got anything done after 2pm, by which time they were generally swimming in alcohol as well as self-delusion.

The reform process is not easy. The Fitzgerald and Wood commissions were confronting generations of neglect. Too much had been for too long in the too-hard basket. Overdue reform is hurtful and there was inevitable and regrettable bruising of the undeserving, alongside a purging of the impious.

While the news cycle demands instant change, reality works at a different pace. Unless police acquire the skills necessary to do their work ethically, the point of their work becomes meaningless. A generational change was through these decades becoming more visible. Police Services started taking greater advantage of science and technology. They improved self-education. More often the cops went home to wives or to the gym rather than sliding into pubs. And to the grand frustration of many a boozing predecessor, they also began to demonstrate greater effectiveness.

The fact that this time *Four Corners* had worked somewhat 'inside the tent' was itself telling. The program would not have been made without the cooperation of the Wood Royal Commission investigators, who I presume saw value in public education. This arrangement would not have been possible a decade earlier, when working 'outside the tent' was the only viable option.

By the 1990s anti-corruption agencies were entrenched in most states, with Victoria a notable exception. Gangland wars blighting Melbourne soon advanced pressure for another Royal Commission. The Victorian government stubbornly resisted, giving rise to a presumption they were fearful how far the investigators might reach. Their Police Minister denied the existence of endemic corruption, rejecting the Royal Commission option as 'an expensive wigfest'.

By the turn of the century I began to wonder whether the political community was no longer seeing credit in reform; the pain and ugliness being such, the more that was revealed, the more they got the blame.

In 2004, as Victoria's gangland death toll climbed to 22 after six years, my old boss, Jonathan Holmes, began working on 'Speed Trap' with the help of a young gun reporter, Nick McKenzie, and producer Sarah Curnow.

Drug law enforcement remains the most volatile frontier in policing. The cops can make little impact on demand. A bulk of the clientele are otherwise respectable citizens, many of them our own sons and daughters. Removing one drug dealer creates space for another. Profits beat other forms of criminal enterprise hands down. A young detective on a raid can pocket the deposit on a house for simply looking the other way, with little likelihood of protest from the victim.

What we have seen from Brisbane to Baltimore is a kind of 'greenlighting', with selected dealers allowed to operate in exchange for information that keeps competition down and statistics up. Some in the Victoria Police Drug Squad were now further refining the system in keeping with an advancing underworld business model. The old drugs of choice started giving way to synthetic competitors. Methamphetamine in varying forms and names — 'ice', 'ecstasy', 'speed' — were cheaper to purchase and easier to produce. Indeed it took little skill and enterprise to buy the chemicals and equipment, such as a pill press, and then subcontract the cooking. Otherwise ordinary street-corner hoods from the Williams and Moran clans began disporting themselves as crime barons. Throw in some otherwise ordinary cops eager to strengthen their pension plans and you had a crime wave.

'Combined chemical delivery' was the trick. The cops bought the precursor chemicals with government money from legitimate suppliers, handed it on to the underworld and waited for the cut. Their moral justification: 'You don't catch grubs without getting your hands dirty.'

Jonathan, Sarah and Nick, in profiling the business model, brought to light the glaringly obvious — that not too many grubs were getting caught. Jonathan even managed to interview one of them. Carl Williams, who had taken a bullet in the stomach fired by a rival from close range, did something of a Chook Fowler in professing mystification about the identity of his assailant.

The crooked cops in Victoria were demonstrating a keener sense of entrepreneurialism than many colleagues in other states. And while it might be true there was a touch more sophistication to their dirty work, they were also confronting improved anti-corruption forces.

I had seen the proposition that you need to be dirty before you make clean disproved by tough and honest cops such as Bob Inkster in New South Wales, who arrested the multimillionaire murderer Andrew Kalajzich. In Victoria there were others: Ron Iddles, Peter de Santo and a remarkably impressive detective, Gavan Ryan, who ran the Purana Task Force, then investigating the gangland killings.

I am pleased to say I much later interviewed Gavan, as did my colleague Liz Jackson. But at this stage, when telephoned by a reporter, he would hang up. Strange as this may seem, I could not help being impressed. Unlike the faux *Sopranos* gangsters, Gavan was not attracted by limelight.

A year after Jonathan's report aired, *Four Corners* returned to the subject, although work had actually commenced at the end of 2004. What most separates investigative journalism from daily journalism is time. You need time not merely to uncover facts but build trust. I had by now learned to try to position the 'big dig' at the end of the year, as we had done with 'The Moonlight State', to allow additional research time over the summer months while the program is off air.

Another distinguishing feature of investigative journalism is a lesser reliance on long-term contacts. A problem with building stories on the word of well-placed sources is a narrowing of the information horizon, and an increased danger of being used.

The same team to work with Jonathan now joined me. Nick McKenzie and Sarah Curnow had good Melbourne connections to the usual secret assembly of police and underworld contacts. But of course we needed to go further.

It tends to work better if you can put the story ahead of the issue, and the story that captured us, which gave rise to the issue, was the May 2004 murder of Terence and Christine Hodson. Terry Hodson was a registered police informant who in 2003 had been arrested with a cop while attempting to rob a drugs safe house. Hodson then turned on his associates, giving evidence against Detective Senior Constable David Miechel, and an alleged conspirator, Detective Sergeant Paul Dale.

Eight months later the Hodsons became victims 27 and 28 in the Melbourne underworld 'war', clinically executed in their own home at Kew while under witness protection. The case synthesised the morbid entanglement of organised crime and police corruption as well as underscoring the seriousness of Victoria's law enforcement crisis. While the Victorian government might reasonably argue corruption was not systemic, in a sense it was worse. There was not just franchised drug trafficking but, it seemed, orchestrated murder on their watch.

On 23 November I called the victims' son Andrew and asked to meet and talk. He was good enough to agree, but at this stage, much as anticipated, was reluctant to further cooperate. Daily journalism regularly crashes at this barrier. You need time to build cooperation. *Four Corners* had not much to offer but a keenness to tell the story with as much depth and insight as we could muster.

Over the Christmas break Andrew took the opportunity to think. Trust, which is always mutual, had grown a touch, and by the New Year began to extend to his siblings, Mandy and Nikki. They were as much in the dark about who had committed the murders, but could tell what they did know and help us better understand their world.

The Hodsons were career criminals, with their children accordingly inducted, much the same as if they had grown up on a farm or above a grocery store. They were also a loving family. Terence Hodson doted on his grandchildren. Nikki had just given birth to Dylan, whom Terence dubbed 'the villain'. The grandparents had been looking forward to a family gathering when, deep into a Saturday evening, they were ordered to their knees and each twice shot in the back of the head.

We called the program 'Melbourne Confidential', an homage to James Ellroy's novel *L.A. Confidential*, which had profiled a similarly vicious and amoral landscape. *L.A. Confidential* was based on a true incident — a police bashing in California in the early 1950s that became a catalyst for wholesale reforms.

In all probability the Melbourne murders also had a deeper provenance. While corruption did not so clearly reach up as in Queensland, a range of bad habits and unholy alliances maintained a lantana-like grip. The longer-form 45 minutes' single-issue programming gave us the scope to colour in this background, with the help of cameraman Andrew Taylor and soundo Jerry Rickard. We were also able to interweave candid interviews with the younger Hodsons and home video material that took us inside that Kew home. We broke some news that demonstrated dangerous connections between Hodson's police handlers and criminals who, in the parlance, Terry had 'lagged'.

In other crime programs reported up to then I had seen how corrupt police had the power to eliminate dangerous criminal allies by tipping off their adversaries. It so happened that information reports from Terence Hodson, registered informant number SCS4/390, had been freely dispersed in the underworld.

I was pleased with the work of our team as the report worked at many levels: as a revealing film and story with strong interviews and breaking news. I don't know how much of a difference it made. You can measure the number of people who watch, but not so much the impression that is left.

Paul Dale was charged with the murder of the Hodsons but the charge was later formally withdrawn.

Former detective Dale was subsequently charged with misleading the Australian Crime Commission about his dealings with the late Carl Williams. Prior to his murder, Williams gave statements to police linking himself and Dale to the Hodson murders. It was reported in the Melbourne *Age* that Garry Livermore, counsel for the ACC, observed: 'People who assist in endeavouring to prosecute Paul Dale have got a pretty poor life expectancy.' Dale proclaims his innocence, and without telling evidence to prove otherwise, deserves to be so considered.

So the mystery and an important watershed case remain, at the time of writing, unresolved. Victoria never got its Royal Commission. I came to ruefully lament that instead we got a miniseries. The *Underbelly* franchise would also follow the blood trail in Victoria, with a different approach to public education. 'Melbourne Confidential' had shown the world of the gangster as far from glamorous. On that Saturday night in May 2004 what mattered most, love and family and life itself, was extinguished forever.

As if at the hands of a master forger, the outline of organised crime constantly adjusts. In 2010, Nick McKenzie would make the program that for me best exemplifies the way it was again transforming. 'Crime Incorporated' shadowed Operation Hoffman, a multi-agency inquiry led by the ACC which was investigating large-scale drug importation and money laundering.

The hoods of Kings Cross, Lygon Street and Fortitude Valley stand small before the barely visible transnational crooks targeted by that inquiry. While the Australian gangsters openly blaze away at one another for the sake of territory and market share, others never on the police radar, perhaps never even entering the country, could in a single deal make profits that a Kings Cross nightclub would not see in a lifetime.

The latest business model saw Chinese triads collaborating with Dutch chemists, Australian bikie gangs, Vietnamese money launderers and waterfront insiders to import container loads of drugs. One scheme became visible through the antics of an Australian crook of Turkish heritage, Hakan Ayik, who was savvy enough to draw these players together. Traditionally, criminal syndicates have been loath to step outside trusted familial and ethnic networks. Now transnational criminal networks, like other big businesses, were globalising.

Perhaps it simply goes with the territory that Ayik would be revealed through the modern portal of social networking. Ayik became something of a Facebook gangster, unable to resist showing off the high-life trappings of flash watches and exotic cars.

But one element of the operation belonged very much to the past. The Hoffman inquiry exposed an old guard of corruption still intact on the waterfront. Australian ports were just as porous as the massive coastline. Between Customs, federal and state police jurisdictions were gaps you could sail a supertanker through.

The story demonstrated that crime and corruption would continue to provide material for investigative journalists like Nick. After a quarter of a century it was time for me to move on. I can't say I ever found the subject inspiring. It often felt like that bag I carried around. When I was on a big dig my shoulder bag swelled as documents collected. In the early years, property and company searches, court records and the like were obtained by turning up at a registry and filling in a form. As I uncovered important documents I found it safer and easier to hang on to them. And that bag could become a burden.

Now you access all manner of data online, one of many examples of how investigative journalism should be easier today. Defamation reform has made the court process far less punishing. And as I came to notice, the investigative reporter now has more allies. When we did 'The Big League' there was no formal support. When we did 'Academy of Crime' 12 years later, it was in cooperation with one of many new anti-corruption agencies that were nonexistent when *Four Corners* debuted. Nick McKenzie's 'Crime Incorporated' also showed law enforcement bodies had gathered trust to a point where they were pooling inquiries, a circumstance unthinkable in the old days.

A telling example of change can be seen in a report by Sarah Ferguson in 2009. 'The Dishonouring of Marcus Einfeld' told the story of a Federal Court judge from an upper tier of power and influence, disgraced after being unable to escape a $75 speeding fine. Who would try these days what not so long ago was routine?

A contrast demonstrating the roller-coaster nature of corruption reform emerged in another *Four Corners* program, 'Standen — The Inside Man', reported by Marian Wilkinson in 2011. Mark Standen was one of many police insiders I spoke with over the years. So it was a shock to me as well when the Assistant Director of the NSW Crime

Commission was charged and later convicted of attempting to import 300 kilograms of pseudoephedrine.

As police get closer to the true Mr Bigs there is also an exponential increase in the size of jackpot gains and consequent temptation. Drug law enforcement also increases its vulnerability to corruption as a new generation familiar with recreational drug use is recruited. But in general, undeniably, the skill levels and integrity of policing have improved.

When I look back on *Four Corners*' 50 years I see a similar incremental rising standard. And in doing so I sight the faces of wonderful colleagues now departed. Andrew Olle presented 'The Moonlight State' and proved a true friend at a difficult time. Cameraman Brett Joyce and editor Des Horne were part of the esteemed labour force on 'Academy of Crime'. Sandra Harvey, completely uncontaminated by all those years covering the underworld, was a valued partner on the 2005 prisons' profile, 'Supermax'.

When operating principles awkwardly adjust to a tumultuous online revolution, *Four Corners* also defines an important industry standard. If it comes to it, citizen journalism will be, in my view, a pale successor. Investigative journalism requires institutional support; it calls for researchers and lawyers as well as reporters.

Four Corners is a treasured archive of both modern history and working journalism. A core asset is primary research. While others shrink behind computer screens and recycle evidence to conflate opinion, *Four Corners* gets out there chasing facts. And instead of milking the headline it forms the narrative. The program takes the time, now too often surrendered, to tell the story.

Celebrating 30 years of a program no one thought would last. Chris Masters and Executive Producer Peter Manning lift their glasses at a *Four Corners* party.

8

THE ADRENALIN YEARS

by Peter Manning

Nothing was more pleasurable than being in the back of a camera car constructing a story for the mighty *Four Corners*. I have two images. In the first, Chris Masters and I, two close mates, are being paid due disrespect by cameraman Chris Doig and soundo Tim Parratt, driving through Melbourne, the day's main interview having just fallen through. Mere reporters and producers sat in the back, of course. When the Carlton Tennis Club came into view, Doig ('the dog with one eye', Chris would tease him) impishly said, 'Tennis anyone?' Chris and I exchanged grins and said, 'Why not?' We had been working round the clock for days, without much luck, on a story about the impact of the Costigan Royal Commission into the Painters and Dockers Union. For the next two hours, the most ferociously competitive match saw us play each other to a standstill. Beers were called for, so we retired to a pub in Lygon Street. Then followed a good Italian dinner, more drinks and finally the sleep of the just.

In the second image it is 1983 and I am anxiously waiting for Chris Masters, cameraman John Hagin and soundo Bob Peck to come through the arrivals gate at Hanoi airport in Vietnam. As producer, I have been here for a week, setting up interviews and film locations. I had learned that it was best to understate the amount of currency we were bringing in for the three weeks of filming ahead; currency rackets at Customs were fleecing Westerners. How could I get an effective message to Chris through the gate? Over a large crowd of Vietnamese, all waving and shouting to their friends and relatives, I spotted Chris approaching the well-dressed military guard at Customs. I yelled, 'Chris! Chris!'

He stopped right in front of the guard. He looked over at me. He could see my distress. 'What's up?'

I couldn't tell him the truth in plain English. I had to think quickly how to explain. I said, 'Mate, fudge the dough!'

'What?' he said.

'Fudge the dough!'

'Oh!' he said. 'Which way?'

'Down!'

'Okay.'

He came through and we killed ourselves laughing. Aussie vernacular had saved the day.

There are many, many such memories: of long lunches at La Stazione in Artarmon the Tuesday after a show went to air; days and nights slaving over hot Steenbeck benches in the edit rooms of master craftspeople like Alec Cullen, Des Horne and Julia Wright, fighting the good fight to get stories to air. It was a magic time.

It was also the time of the Hawke Labor government, the best years of *60 Minutes* and the second (and last) decade of the Fairfax Press's investigative weekly, the *National Times*. And it was the decade of Margaret Thatcher and Ronald Reagan.

I was a slightly despondent newcomer to the *Four Corners* team in January 1982. I had been happy enough on the ABC's then daily program, *Nationwide*, breaking stories as an on-air senior reporter in

1980 and '81. I'd covered the first man to escape from the notorious maximum security Grafton jail, Raymond John Denning; interviewed Peter Baldwin MLC the day after he was bashed in his Marrickville home for taking on the Labor Right's stranglehold over Sydney's inner-city ALP branches; and, with Paul Murphy, investigated the Nugan Hand Bank for shonky dealings.

But I was not your traditional ABC reporter. I had not come up through the ABC News system, instead doing my journalism cadetship at Fairfax's *Sydney Morning Herald*. My first appearance on ABC TV was on *This Day Tonight* (*TDT*) in 1972 and '73, and that happy band of *TDT* firebrands (think Mike Carlton, Stuart Littlemore, Bill Peach, Peter Luck, Richard Carleton, Paul Murphy and Kerry O'Brien) was always viewed slightly askance by the nabobs of the ABC. To make matters worse, at *TDT* I had worked on investigative, muckraking programs. They included reports on the Premier Bob Askin's corrupt police and their protected gambling parlours, crooked building societies ripping off small investors and strange land deals in the then outer Sydney suburb of Menai. My return to the ABC in 1979 was to the 'radical' youth radio station 2JJ; my year there didn't help my image either.

So when I was called up to see Peter Reid, the Head of TV News and Current Affairs in late 1981, I had a sense all was not well. He told me he had created a field producer position on the weekly current affairs program *Four Corners*, and wanted to transfer me there. This was not a choice but a direction. With a young family to feed, I complied, but it truly felt like being sent to Coventry.

Four Corners at the time was mocked as 'the House of Lords'. Reid had been its longest serving Executive Producer during the 1970s, and Caroline Jones its iconic presenter. But most of my colleagues, including Reid and Jones, felt its best programs were well behind it. Many felt it had not long to live. The only colleague I admired there was Paul Lyneham, whose investigative programs on the coal industry and Queensland Premier Joh Bjelke-Petersen stood out from the pack.

In the way of *Four Corners* of 1981, an 'issue' was required to head out filming and 'both sides' of the issue were to be sought and aired. Also, as a producer I now required filmmaking skills. This was foreign country for me. After more than a decade in journalism, I was confident of my journalism but not of filmmaking — especially in the long form needed for this program.

The first 'issue' I investigated was the rapid loss of trade skills occurring in Australia. In a string of factories I talked to metal workers, carpenters, car mechanics, leather workers, plumbers and electricians about the effect of computerisation on their trades. The accompanying pictures were mainly of lined, sweaty faces, deft handwork and threatening machines pumping out abstract plastic and metal shapes and crushed-wood kitchen cupboards. I did too many interviews and took too many pictures. Whereas the normal ratio of footage shot to footage used was at most 10 to 1, mine was probably 20 to 1. I arrived in the edit room of Alec Cullen with tins and tins of film. When Alec looked appalled, I became red-faced. A week later, though, Alec's rescue job was a sight to behold. Here was a 'rough cut' — with acres of unused footage on the cutting-room floor — that looked like it had a structure and some film sequences, awaiting my script words of wisdom.

'How did you do it?' I asked Alec, a cockney Englishman.

'I used Kraftwerk; heard of them?'

I hadn't, but pretended I had. The minimalist electronic sound of the German band acted as the perfect background for visuals of machinery devouring old craft skills. All I had to do was add a few words, let the interview grabs speak for themselves and, hey presto, a reasonable film. I was entranced.

Lesson Number One about *Four Corners* staff: the upper structure might be forbidding, but the film crews and film editors would save your bacon (if reluctantly).

Gradually, I found myself enjoying this place *Four Corners*. But I was still somewhat verboten with the old stagers of the unit.

I approached Peter Ross about doing a story on coal mining. Soon we were in the back of one of those camera cars, uncovering the pros and cons of this industry. At Mount Kembla, near Wollongong, we found a village that had seen a series of mine disasters over the previous century. The cemetery told the story — lines of graves from tragedy after tragedy. Peter seemed unimpressed. I thought we should walk to the village next door on a hunch that the families of the dead miners would still be there. We did, and they were. Peter's initial reluctance turned to enthusiasm as families told their stories. 'Coalface Facts' was my first proper *Four Corners* report.

And then a bombshell hit the quiet office. The ABC had advertised for a new Executive Producer and the chosen candidate was a BBC producer with a Cambridge background, now working on our sister program in Britain, *Panorama*. Since we already had an English EP in John Temple, this would not seem a change. But when he arrived, change — and immediate change at that — was exactly what he represented.

Jonathan Holmes was precisely what the program needed. Young, straight-talking, intellectual, with a sharp wit and a beautiful Swedish wife, Ann, he sliced through the torpor at *Four Corners* like a knife through butter. In a talk with staff he made it clear the most unforgivable of sins for *any* program was to be boring. He wanted a new staff, with Australian accents, committed to good journalism but also good filmmaking. He would, he warned, be open to ideas but harsh in the cutting rooms when called to see the 'fine cuts' of the films before they went to air. Film sequences would dominate storytelling from now on, and the less voice-over talk the better, too. No more 'issues'.

Happily, I was working on a good story with a respected member of the 'old guard', Jim Downes. I could deliver for this exciting new boss, and fast. We had research showing that an Australian businessman was illegally making money out of his back-room connections in Fiji with the Prime Minister, Ratu Sir Kamisese Mara. Jim and I set off, facts at the ready, to seek an interview with the 'Father of Fiji'. Mara agreed to the interview, and even though no allegation of direct corruption by him was suggested, he savaged Downes live to camera, outraged that his honour had been questioned. His overbearing anger was something to behold. I saw Jim's hand shaking. The Prime Minister walked out mid-interview.

I was delighted. Jim was stunned. I remember thinking, 'This is the new *Four Corners*.'

When Mara lost many seats at the 1982 election, he took his anger out on *Four Corners*. A Royal Commission was called into 'Australian interference' in Fiji's affairs. But its findings vindicated the program.

Next came 'The Big League', Chris Masters and my Australian bombshell. Jonathan had made it plain he wanted a program that would re-establish the name of *Four Corners* in the popular mind. Neither Chris nor I had any knowledge at the start of our research into rugby league that this would be it. There were two different initial strands: a smell around league refereeing decisions, especially when Manly was playing; and a suggestion of something wrong in the case of Kevin Humphries, Rugby League boss, in a magistrate's court some years earlier. Neither seemed connected. We set off, following up on leads independent of each other. *Four Corners* stories normally take at least six weeks to turn around (two weeks each for research, shooting and editing) but in this case both of us could see we were not hitting pay dirt, even after we'd been researching for a month. Getting people who normally don't talk to the media to put their faces on the ABC's national program to allege corruption of a treasured sport, thereby risking their own careers, was proving difficult.

The story behind 'The Big League' has been told many times; suffice to say we got there. Remarkably, through persistence, not taking no for an answer and appealing to fundamental social values, the right people spoke out. In the end, Humphreys was convicted and the offending magistrate, Murray Farquhar, went to jail.

I was hugely impressed with Chris. Viewing the program today, I see the same honest face that so impressed our fragile sources. Chris's serious honesty, dedication to detail, concern for the ordinary man and Aussie self-deprecation was a winning combination. We became great friends. We needed to be.

Not surprisingly, the program had a huge night in the ratings, beating its commercial rivals for the timeslot. This was *Four Corners* back from the dead! But the political cost to the ABC was long-reaching. Accusing Labor Premier Neville Wran of involvement in the Humphreys case earned not only Wran's ire — followed by the Street Royal Commission, which cleared him — but the wrath of the entire right-wing faction running the Party for the next decade. Quite apart from the personal abuse Chris and I received from Labor supporters, the anonymous packages of forged documents about us sent to commercial radio stations, television commentators alleging pro-Liberal bias and the friends who quietly dropped off, Labor leaders used the program as a stick to beat the ABC with at every opportunity. A paranoia developed about 'these people' out to 'get' the Hawke government.

Incidents followed which involved pressure on the ABC from Labor: over Jenny Brockie's program on uranium mining the next year; over Marian Wilkinson's program on transport boss Peter Abeles (a mate of Bob Hawke) in 1987; and — as late as 1991 — over the First Gulf War and the ABC's news and current affairs coverage. The powerful leader of the right wing in New South Wales, Senator Graham Richardson, told an ABC executive in February 1985: 'We've no problems with management. The problems are Manning, Holmes and Masters.' By that date, Labor had installed a clutch of candidates on the ABC Board. I anticipated retribution by the new Labor-appointed Chair. Fortunately, that didn't happen.

Denied the opportunity to apply for the Walkley Award later in 1983 for legal reasons (Wran sued the ABC for defamation; he settled later), Jonathan organised for a tongue-in-cheek office awards ceremony. The whole *Four Corners* staff — 60 or so of us — had gone through the terrors and excitement of the program (Jonathan's secretary, Nadine Connor, had even taken documents home in case we were all arrested) and we needed some acknowledgment. In a solemn ceremony, Jonathan presented a framed 'Clayton's Award' for Best TV Program 1983 to Chris and me. We patted ourselves on the back; it had been a baptism of fire.

Far easier was a program shot in late 1983 with Jenny Brockie as reporter and me as producer. It looked at whether the 'safeguards' on the Hawke government's export of uranium were working in Canada, the United States and Europe. Jenny and I had formed a close relationship, soon going beyond work. Then, over northern Ontario, in search of a nuclear facility fabricating Australian uranium, our light plane got lost. In driving snow, over white mountains and under heavy cloud, all Jenny and I could see was white every which way. The pilot said he would search for the nearest airport and to keep calm. Jenny and I got closer fast. We held hands as we scanned the terrain for anything not white. Finally, a small airport reared up before us as the plane skidded to a stop at a hangar manned by Indigenous Canadians. I proposed at a small restaurant in Paris, on our way to a German facility near Hamburg. The so-called safeguards, of course, were more rhetoric than reality and, of course, the program angered the Foreign Minister, Bill Hayden, and Hawke, yet again. Jenny and I would marry the next year and have our beautiful daughter, Thea Manning, now working for ABC Radio News!

The work–life balance was a constant issue on a hardworking program like *Four Corners*. Long hours in the office (sometimes editing until early morning), long periods on the road filming, intense pressures in the office mixed with plenty of alcohol tested just about all relationships. Sometimes it was easy to feel we were one big team and we alone understood the stresses and strains. I remember Kerry O'Brien suggesting we would all end up in the same nursing home together!

The impact on our families struck me in 1983, after leaving Vietnam with Chris Masters. When we finally made it to Bangkok, there was a lovely handwritten letter at our hotel from my 13-year-old daughter, Megan, from my previous marriage. It asked me gently to please stop travelling so much and spend some time with her and my son, Paddy. She wanted and needed me. It had an immediate effect. I decided to seek an office job in Sydney and be around more for my teenage young adults. When Jonathan said he needed a new Associate Producer, I applied. For the next year he and I operated as a smooth double act: I supervised the researchers and story selection; he did the post-production. It worked extremely well.

Robyn Smith, Sue Spencer (now Executive Producer), Shaun Hoyt, Virginia Moncrieff, Penny Lysaght, Deborah Whitmont, Monica Attard and Kate McClymont were researchers over my seven years. They were all meticulous, cautious journalists, with an investigative edge. Penny and Deb were both lawyers; Deb had arrived as a casualty of the law, wanting something more public-spirited.

There was usually a staff of three researchers at any one period. They were not there as fact-checkers for 'star' reporters but were the engine room for *Four Corners*: the ones who sniffed out stories, chased them down and then 'sold' them to the Engine Driver (AP or EP). Reporters were often in cahoots with them, trying to get first dibs on an upcoming scoop. For many years, Sue, Shaun and Deb made up a core that drove the investigative agenda from the ground up, appearing as unsung heroes in the credits that went to air each Monday night. They were a delight to work with.

Being a second-in-charge was good for me. Jonathan was nothing if not fully committed to the independence of the program. I watched as he fought upper management when Allan Hogan's program 'Borderline' brought down upon *Four Corners* the full wrath of the Papua New Guinea government of Michael Somare. Hogan had interviewed James Nyaro of the Free Papua Movement in a program about PNG. Indonesia would not be pleased. PNG and Australian governments would not be pleased. And, behind the scenes, our very own News department, often at odds with Current Affairs, feared that their correspondent in Port Moresby would be asked to leave. All of that came to pass — including Sean Dorney in Moresby being expelled. But the Free Papua Movement had had its voice heard on Australia's national program.

One curly-haired young reporter from Radio Current Affairs (*AM* and *PM* in those days) stuck his neck out too. He did a program about the pressures on *Four Corners* inside the ABC to buckle and not air their report. His name was Tony Jones. Jonathan called him across to do a report on 'youth today'. But when he applied for a job later that year, he was beaten by another young candidate, Sarah Walls. Jonathan might have felt we needed a better gender balance. I remained a firm believer in Jones. I waited my chance to hire him.

My chance to shape the team came after a year as Associate Producer when Jonathan decided to move to the United States to produce documentaries for public TV. By then he had become a mentor and a friend. He had changed *Four Corners* forever, restructuring its filmmaking, beefing up the program producer's power, giving it a public profile, good ratings and a reputation for reliability and independence under pressure. When I won the Executive Producer position in mid-1985, I was beside myself with happiness. I set myself the task of taking the program to another level. It would be marked by journalistic excellence, bravery, more investigations, risk-taking and currency, and all with a more Australian feel.

In particular, I wanted to sharpen our focus to finally eliminate 'issues' stories. Only those that broke fresh angles or revealed fresh information would make it to air. The best, of course, would be where the program itself *was* the news. But that couldn't happen every week because big stories didn't come that often but, in the meantime, we would develop something we later called 'over the horizon radar' — stories that broke news on the day, they were aired in reaction to an event we knew would happen. But the programs would have taken six weeks to produce (and looked great).

And from now on we would occasionally jump out of the six-week cycle mode and put together a program in a week, just to show *Four Corners* was the place to go on your dial each Monday night if you wanted to know what was happening. Reactive stories would juggle with blockbusters.

And, finally, we would do special documentaries on Australian stories — like the last generation of Australian soldiers from Gallipoli — that not only recorded precious voices from our past but picked up on Australian themes. My childhood had been spent at Bondi Beach and Parramatta, two iconic places of Australian history. I was a proud fifth-generation Australian on both sides of my family. I was confident I knew how Australians thought. A side-bar to this reasoning was also to encourage the reporters who did the big stories to take off a block of time after the program and bring out a compelling book on the subject, thereby inserting *Four Corners* into Australian culture. Bestsellers about Alan Bond and Kerry Packer stand as testimony to that.

For me, the key element in this mix was having the bravery to back my own judgment and take risks. Only by taking the risk to commission unlikely stories, and to make snap decisions, could some spectacular journalistic successes come our way. This kind of leadership was new to me — even though I had been editor of the national weekly *Nation Review* in the mid-70s, not that 'The Ferret' was like *Four Corners* — but with our excellent reporters, producer, researchers, crews and editors, I felt we could achieve anything.

The challenge struck in my first week as Executive Producer. Two bombs exploded in the Greenpeace vessel *Rainbow Warrior*, berthed in Auckland Harbour, on 10 July 1985. Many thought it was unremarkable, the unfortunate actions (a photographer was killed) of some crazy New Zealander. I didn't. Greenpeace had been sending ships to protest French nuclear tests in the French Polynesian island of Mururoa earlier in the 1980s, and its ship seemed likely to have been headed back to that island. Checking out French government movements seemed a reasonable bet. In the background, I had no admiration for French actions in Algeria and had no illusions about their military penchant to strike with maximum force. Within hours I'd sent Chris Masters as investigative reporter and Bruce Belsham as his Kiwi researcher and producer.

It paid off. Within days Chris and Bruce returned with evidence of the French trail, plus pictures. I despatched Chris to Paris for interviews with French Intelligence agents and experts. Within a month we'd broken an international scoop: French terrorism had struck in friendly New Zealand. The story went to air on 16 August and sold like hot cakes around the world. It set off its own series of bombshells: the jailing of the terrorists; the resignation of the French Defence Minister; and, ultimately, the admission that the French President, François Mitterrand, had ordered the bombings. 'French Connections' became a classic. And my nose for a good story was in fine shape!

David Marr soon joined *Four Corners* as a reporter. We were friends from our days on the *Bulletin* magazine in the early 1970s but by now he was a seasoned investigative reporter from the *National Times*. A month after 'French Connections', David's searing story of how the West Australian Police had treated four Aboriginal prisoners in custody hit the headlines. The WA Police Union stood by the appalling actions of their members, torturing Aboriginal men to death — by strangulation, leading to heart attack. The Labor Police Minister said he was 'disgusted' by the program. The union banned interviews with ABC reporters.

I also moved quickly to hire that young radio journalist Tony Jones (now of *Q&A* and *Lateline*). It was important to me to achieve a balanced staff structure at *Four Corners*, both by age and gender. The 'old' *Four Corners* seemed to me to be full of senior men. Sarah Walls joined Jenny Brockie and Clare Petre as members of the team. And Tony Jones would join Chris Masters and David Marr (and then Kerry O'Brien for a year).

Jones hit the ground running. He'd heard whisperings about alleged strange dealings at the croupier's table at the Palace Casino by contacts of the famous bookmaker Bill Waterhouse. One source was a sometime uninvited visitor to the *Four Corners* office, Sydney bouncer and private eye, big Tim Bristow (who looked like Chesty Bond and knew the worst cops in town). Another was Valerie Murphy, sister of criminal defence barrister Chris Murphy. Robbie Waterhouse was then facing charges over the Fine Cotton/Bold Personality 'ring-in', but these stories Jones was hearing were unrelated. Jones came to me alleging Bill Waterhouse was involved in illegal gambling, running a casino and paying off the NSW Deputy Police Commissioner, Bill Allen. I urged him to continue the research, checking fact on fact with first, second and third sources. Jones's report also covered the internal battles of the Waterhouse clan — between Bill and his brother Martin's grieving widow.

As the program came together, Bill Waterhouse, also a powerful man in Sydney's police and political world, was letting it be known he would stop it going to air. 'Horses for Courses' became the subject of a legal injunction. It went to the Supreme Court and was defeated. One of the judges remarked on how truly defamatory the program was, but that the ABC had the right to broadcast it: on 10 November 1986 it went to air. It was then the subject of criminal defamation action by Bill Waterhouse in which not only the ABC were named but so were Jones and myself. Tony and I pictured ourselves sharing cells together in Long Bay jail. NSW Police came raiding our offices at Gore Hill (we filmed them). Tony remembers us sitting in court near Bill and his son, Robbie Waterhouse. Their trousers were pulled up, displaying silk socks. When Tony looked up at the Waterhouses, their braces were pulling their trousers up. He started thinking Alcatraz. Luckily, they lost their case. I had felt genuinely scared, both to be criminally charged and to be up against the powerful Waterhouse family. It underlined that this bravery act of mine was fragile and close to bravado. It had what US judges called 'a chilling effect'. Nevertheless, I appeared on news broadcasts singing the praises of freedom of speech.

Around this time two major changes in staffing took place, both due to have big implications for the program. This year — 1985 — Andrew Olle had been appointed by Jonathan and me as presenter of a new-look program, complete with a studio component and a weekday timeslot. Backed by top News Director Glyn Patrick and her feisty and humorous director's assistant, Mandy Hasler, we now had the capacity to tackle a political crisis in minutes. Andrew was a colleague of mine from way back — as a *Nationwide* reporter and, long before that, on *This Day Tonight* in the '70s. His urbane, calm, fair-minded attitude to everything made him a natural presenter. He was on good terms with all across the political spectrum. He lived near Gore Hill and, within a block, was Opposition leader John Howard. They were friends.

Olle's funniest interviews were always with Queensland Nationals' Premier Joh Bjelke-Petersen. Old Joh loved Andrew because he was a Queenslander and would let him know that in on-air interviews. On the other hand, Joh didn't like being questioned. He'd blame Andrew's curly questions on his being corrupted by his time down south in Sin City, full of lefties and communists. It used to reduce me to stitches. I never had any idea of Andrew's own politics.

Having a studio component forced me to get on with appointing my own Associate Producer. I chose Martin Butler from Channel 10's *Good Morning Australia* program. Martin had a thick English working-class accent and a degree from Oxford to his name. He sold himself on his studio skills but we did a deal: he would be allowed once a year to go on the road as a producer. He would later team up with Mark Colvin (one of the ABC's great foreign correspondents) to head off to New Caledonia to interview leaders of the Kanak Liberation Front about an alleged atrocity by French police in a cave where militants were hiding. As with 'French Connections', I followed my hunch and, in under an hour, ordered the team off to catch the moment. The program 'Murder a la Carte' was a terrific opening salvo for the Butler and Colvin combination.

We took our upgraded studio capability to Sutherland Town Hall in southern Sydney to look at the Grim Reaper campaign, designed to combat the HIV virus (then called AIDS). Under Olle's deft questioning of a suburban audience, the full gamut of opinion was aired about this disease, now disproportionately affecting Australia's homosexual community. The first known cases had emerged only two years earlier but already HIV was the subject of this full-scale national health campaign. I was proud of our ability be part of Australian community education.

Meanwhile, Chris Masters was again on a research-intensive burrowing mission. He'd told me in late 1986 that a police contact of his had been offered a bribe by a superior in the Queensland Police Force and that it related to a criminal who wanted the freedom to run brothels in Fortitude Valley in Brisbane. Now *this* sounded promising! I assigned one of our top researchers, Shaun Hoyt, who I'd also encouraged to go out on the road producing, to head towards Queensland. The result is now well known as the award-winning

'Moonlight State' — the program that brought down not only the Police Commissioner, Terry Lewis, but also the Premier, Joh Bjelke-Petersen and, after the Fitzgerald inquiry into police corruption, the whole era of Nationals' domination of Queensland through rigged electoral boundaries.

I was conscious that Chris, my close friend, was deeply tired even before he headed north on this story. His work rate had been stunning. On a couple of occasions, I travelled to Brisbane to help out Shaun and Chris on what I thought was a dangerous story for both of them. Once, when Chris seemed to be losing heart, I pushed him to keep following the leads to the top of the tree, past the expected sleaze at street level. When the story went to air on 11 May 1987 — heavily legalled by our latest ABC Legal Department leaders, Bruce Donald and Judith Walker — it had the same effect on Queensland law and politics that 'The Big League' had done in New South Wales.

But it was far from over. For Chris and the legal team, it was the beginning of a decade of court appearances defending the program, including court appearances for Chris and me in Cairns. Donald and Walker were part of the 'new' ABC now run by David Hill, Managing Director since October 1986. Donald and Walker came with a novel legal philosophy: the job of defamation lawyers is to ensure good programs get to air, not to stop them, and all practical steps would be taken to support them. From here on, program-makers worked closely with the lawyers before broadcast to stiffen up their research, scripts, witnesses and documents to ensure we would win the inevitable defamation case in the years ahead. This, in turn, involved support 'upstairs' from my new head of TV News and Current Affairs, Bob Kearsley (and later, Derek White), and all the way up to David Hill. Hill was fully committed, including with the budget to run the cases until we won.

In the same month as 'Moonlight State', we also hit our straps in the reactive mode I wanted. I had recently hired Marian Wilkinson from the *National Times*, and among her contacts was a source in Suva. Fijian politics had been volatile since the departure of Ratu Sir Kamisese Mara, and when Marian was warned that a 'move' to bring down the democratically elected Fijian government was imminent, I despatched her with a crew. We wanted to be there on the spot when it happened. Within days military strongman Major-General Sitiveni Rabuka struck, invading Parliament and locking out the politicians and media. Producer Andrew Clark barely had time to fly in to join the team. Within a week we had pictures of Marian, sleeves rolled up, knocking on the gates of military HQ, as well as exclusive local interviews and analysis. Marian had turned the story of the coup d'état around in a sixth of the normal time.

Marian's appointment was itself a coup for *Four Corners*. She came with a sky-high reputation for investigative reporting from the *National Times* and, before that, with pieces from Queensland in *Nation Review*. Later the same year she would produce the story on Sir Peter Abeles so hated by the Prime Minister. And, along with researcher Monica Attard, Marian would expose the inner workings of a plot to destroy Liberal Opposition leader John Howard and install Andrew Peacock. Marian's and Monica's persuasiveness in getting reluctant politicians to publicly parade their egos and Machiavellian skills was truly extraordinary in 'True Believers'.

The year 1987 started extremely badly for me. Late 1986 had seen rumblings in the world of media giants. Channel 10 had been bought by a company belonging to one of Australia's richest men, Frank Lowy, owner of the Westfield chain of shopping centres. He, too, wanted to dabble in media and, in particular, in current affairs television. He started *Page One* and began a search for top reporters. A group of *Four Corners* staff, including Chris Masters, would walk out the door for the big bucks offered in commercial land.

Through 1987 and '88 I moved fast to fill these holes, keeping sacred 'the format', with Andrew Olle as presenter, and continuing the run of hard-hitting stories. I raided Fairfax again. In the footsteps of David Marr and Marian now came investigative crime reporter Neil Mercer, news reporters Kate McClymont and Deborah Snow and librarian Kate Owen, the latter to start our own News Clippings Library when Fairfax closed theirs in 1987. I had kept the wonderful Nadine Connor as secretary when Jonathan left, but when she departed two years later, I was able to secure Rosemary Meares (now Newell) from Fairfax, too. It was a quality journalism transplant. But all, like me, faced learning filmmaking from scratch. Once again, our great producers, crews and editors would step up to the mark in an informal training program.

One hole I felt *Four Corners* had was coverage of business stories. No one on the program knew how to read a corporate balance sheet. Enter Paul Barry to the rescue. Paul was a reporter and presenter for the BBC who was seriously itching to bring his wife and family to Australia. He rang about a job. With his Oxford background, good looks, presentation skills and fire in his belly, he was perfect.

Paul made an immediate impact, taking *Four Corners* to new heights (while *Page One* failed to hit the mark). He did a program on Margaret Thatcher and how her neo-liberalism was transforming Britain and its economy, wrapping new ideas in a current affairs format. His first expedition into corporate behaviour was a highly emotional report about blue asbestos mining in Western Australia. With the help of producer Sue Spencer and researcher Kate McClymont, he found one of Australia's top-tier companies, CSR (Colonial Sugar Refining Co Ltd), was involving its Wittenoom mine workers and their families, who lived nearby, in practices the company executives knew were likely to give them the deadly cancer mesothelioma. The program, 'Blue Death', used all *Four Corners*' latest documentary skills to expose the corporate crimes being committed. Cameraman Wayne Harley and Paul found themselves in tears several times during and after the report.

And in 1989 Paul targeted another of Bob Hawke's business mates, Alan Bond. This time the tone was forensic rather than emotional. Barry's back-room dissection of Bond Corporation's tax avoidance was relentless. I threw money at his project. He flew to the Cook Islands to chase down some of Bond's tax-haven accounts and catch contacts unawares. From there, he visited Hong Kong to gather documents proving Bond's tax dealings. And finally he turned up in front of Bond's Chief Financial Officer, Roger Oates, for what I regard as the best interview of my period. We added an extra camera to record the CFO sweat as Paul went head to head with him about the balance sheet detail of how the company was illegally avoiding tax. Between camera rolls, Paul spoke not a word to Oates, although they sat metres apart. When the verbal battle was over, Oates was demolished. Bruce Donald advised doing interviews from a Sydney accountant to back up Paul's reading of the figures. When 'Bondy's Bounty' went to air, it kick-started legal proceedings that brought down one of Australia's high-flyers (and hero of the America's Cup win) and put him in jail.

The week after this program came another game-changer: 'Frozen Asset', about proposals to introduce mining in the large Australian chunk of pristine Antarctica. Martin Butler had been following the debate in the federal parliament and convinced me *Four Corners* needed to be part of it. Could he take Tony Jones and cameraman David Maguire and soundo Eric Briggs to film what was at stake? Yes was the answer, though the story would take many more weeks than normal to bring to air. The result was not just stunning cinematography (including an iceberg that spectacularly rolled over in front of the crew in its dinghy far from the Russian mother ship) but a powerful moral case for saving this wilderness. Following the program, both Environment Minister Graham Richardson (an unlikely greenie) and Opposition leader John Howard declared their total opposition to any mining in Antarctica.

In the space of two weeks *Four Corners* had put to air two programs that would change Australia. For the last seven years it had made that kind of impact, with major programs several times a year. We had won a score of individual Walkley Awards, the most prized by the journalist community. And in 1988 and again in 1989 we won the Logie for Outstanding Achievement in Current Affairs. My pride in my team was overwhelming when I walked to the stage in 1989 to pick up the Logie from *60 Minutes* and *A Current Affair* star Jana Wendt. We had achieved mixed results with ratings but made an enormous impact.

Four Corners had developed its own format, too; a way of telling stories that marked us out from our commercial rivals. We didn't just air allegations or market 'exclusives', we insisted on chasing down allegations and proving or disproving them. This took more time, more manpower and more money, but the rewards — for us personally and for Australia — were greater too. We earned our credibility.

My memory is we also had a good time. The esprit de corps in the office was very high. The passion and adrenalin always seemed to be running. Three of my favourite editors came to me at a recent *Four Corners* celebration and said, 'Thanks for making us feel like we were all equals on your program.' I could not have received a greater compliment. I think 'leading from behind' marks out an Australian management style, from the military to corporations to the public service. We made the ABC proud, too. I remember Board member Sister Veronica Brady dropping in one day and saying, 'How about lunch?' We usually went to the Great Northern Hotel in Chatswood. I asked if she cared for a barbecued steak. 'Sure,' she said, then jumped in a camera car and off we went. We enjoyed her company immensely. Likewise that of big Tim Bristow. And Paul Keating on the blower shooting the breeze about Pay TV. And John Howard in the studio Green Room with Andrew and me, complaining about Asian immigration.

Ah, what a privilege. I think the key for us journalists was that we all enjoyed each other's successes. And the key for our viewers was that we were accountable to them as taxpayers, not to shareholders and advertisers. Long may it last.

'This fringe group assumed because I was pregnant, I would be sympathetic.' Jenny Brockie on the trail of the pro-life movement in the United States.

9

HANDLE WITH CARE

by Jenny Brockie

I arrived at *Four Corners* in 1983, hot on the heels of 'The Big League'. It was a great break for a 28-year-old, and didn't I know it.

I'd been recruited from the ABC's daily national TV current affairs show *Nationwide*, where I'd been a reporter for more than four years in a talented and headstrong team which included Mark Colvin, Andrew Olle and Paul Murphy. We were a tight bunch, and took our journalism, and sometimes ourselves, pretty seriously. *Nationwide* had been a wild ride, a hothouse of journalistic intensity and long lunches typical of the late '70s and early '80s. I forged lasting bonds of friendship with many of the people there, but after more than four years, I was growing frustrated with daily current affairs and ready to move on, having exhausted the patience of successive executive producers with my agonising over scripts and desire to do longer and longer stories.

I'd wanted to join *Four Corners* for at least a year, naively believing there couldn't be that much difference between doing a 20-minute story (which I occasionally got away with on *Nationwide*, though the program preferred shorter pieces) and a 30–50 minute one. When I tentatively inquired about a move I was told I was too young, that if I went to *Four Corners* too soon I'd have 'nothing to look forward to'.

At the start of the '80s the program was unkindly dubbed 'the elephants' graveyard', a place where older journalists saw out their final reporting days. Despite a much respected 20-year history, its languid, ponderous style had become clunky and dated. *60 Minutes* had burst onto Australian television screens in 1979 with a faster pace and more engaging storytelling. Channel 9's brash new offering was much maligned by ABC diehards, but its Executive Producer, Gerald Stone, had lured some of television's best journalists to his stable, and they were delivering some strong stories. *Four Corners* needed to lift its game.

As I sat tight at *Nationwide*, trying to work out how to age faster, I was also warned that *Four Corners* was 'difficult' for women. No one could really explain why. Caroline Jones shone as a woman of talent and grace who'd deftly managed to navigate the flagship, but she looked like an exception. Mary Delahunty had done well, but it seemed to me the few other female reporters in the program's long history either hadn't stayed or, if they had, were often described by colleagues in terms of personality and temperament rather than the quality of their work. *Four Corners* had reported on the rights of women, but it didn't have a stellar history of hiring or keeping them.

By 1982 though, there was an appetite for change. An Englishman had been imported to give the show a shake. His imminent arrival was anticipated with a predictable journalistic cocktail of blind hope and knee-jerk suspicion. Jonathan Holmes had a fine reputation as a producer with the BBC's *Panorama* program, but what on earth would he know about Australia? It might be just what *Four Corners* needed. Oh, God, why do they always think the Poms will do a better job? *Panorama* was terrific, lots of investigations. But wasn't the ABC trying to get away from being so British?

My then boyfriend, Peter Manning, a Bondi-loving, cricket-playing enthusiast for all things Australian, had been moved to *Four Corners* as a producer, and was unofficially tasked with making Jonathan feel welcome. Peter's approach was to plot a quick program of cultural re-education for the very English Mr Holmes. He would win Jonathan over with Australia's irresistible charms. Jonathan would quickly shed his Englishness and embrace all things Australian — the sun, the sand, the gum leaves.

Days after the new EP's arrival, friends had invited us to a picnic at Mount Wilson in the Blue Mountains. It wasn't exactly Bondi, but Peter figured it would be the perfect transition, with a friendly game of cricket and plenty of nice deciduous trees. Familiar. Unthreatening. We invited Jonathan to join us and he accepted.

As we headed up the Great Western Highway, Jonathan asked from the back seat when we would be seeing some trees. 'Those are trees,' I said, vaguely waving at the intermittent eucalypts en route. 'But trees are green,' he replied firmly.

Once we'd arrived and found a perfect spot for our picnic, we laid out the blankets. The new *Four Corners* EP remained resolutely on his feet. What was likely to be making those small rustling sounds under the fallen gum leaves? He'd read that a lot of things in Australia could kill you.

Then a crow squawked nearby.

'What's that!'

'A bird Jonathan, it's a bird.'

'That's not a bird. Birds go tweet tweet.'

It didn't help that he was quickly bowled, twice, when we played cricket.

I suggested Peter should just take him to dinner.

Fortunately Jonathan enthusiastically embraced Australia and set about overhauling *Four Corners*. When he offered me a reporting job, he made it painfully clear he wasn't at all sure I was up to it. Privately, neither was I.

At 28, I was keen and ambitious but quick to doubt myself professionally, believing I'd somehow fluked my way into journalism and would one day be unmasked as a complete fraud. My journey through the ABC to that point felt like a combination of lucky breaks and bizarre obstacles. During my cadetship at ABC News I'd been told by an executive to forget my dreams of political journalism because women's voices weren't authoritative enough. I was crushed, but somehow made it to the Canberra press gallery within a year. Another executive confided to me at a party — he was very drunk — that I would never be appointed overseas because the ABC didn't want homosexuals in foreign postings. I was completely dumbstruck. So was my boyfriend. So wrong, in so many ways. And hardly reassuring to know the executive was paid handsomely to safeguard standards of fairness and accuracy. There were some truly strange people in the ABC in the late '70s and early '80s.

Mark Colvin, Jim Middleton, Paul Lockyer and others had been beacons of support as I stumbled through those early years, and John Penlington's offer to join the *Nationwide* team in 1979 had been a godsend. But some of my experiences had made me overly defensive about my work and wary of people in charge, often when I didn't need to be. More importantly, despite some solid work at *Nationwide*, I still had a huge amount to learn.

Ironically, I probably got the job at *Four Corners* in large part because I was female and young. Jonathan wanted to change the show's profile, but he didn't have many young women journalists to choose from. I knew I was riding a very lucky break. So I sailed into *Four Corners*, ambitious and scared, hoping the winds of change would be kind to me.

Instinctively I knew what I was good at — interviewing and getting to the nub of a story. My big weakness in those days was structure. I regularly struggled to assemble the masses of raw material gathered for a lengthy television story into a compelling narrative. I would pore over scripts for hours, getting stuck on detail or looking for the perfect segue, rather than pulling back and embracing the story as a whole. That was a quality I'd seen in Andrew Olle, who was notorious for continually changing scripts until the very last minute. I've often wondered whether some journalists reduce stories to black and white, not necessarily because it's their preference, but because it's so much easier than capturing nuance.

Four Corners was hard. Structure was all-important to the new EP and he was clearly appalled by what he saw as a dearth of it on air. We were urged to be storytellers, to film sequences, to use words cleverly and sparingly. Jonathan had a remarkable skill. He could sit through a one-hour 'rough cut' (first edit) of a story, take no notes, then clinically take it all apart almost frame by frame. His love of the craft of making television resulted in tortuous scripting sessions and fierce arguments in the cutting room and beyond. There was resistance from reporters, editors and crews. The urgency with which he viewed the task of improving *Four Corners*' standards sometimes led to him so thoroughly taking over stories, they no longer felt like our own. Rewritten scripts occasionally bore the hallmarks of an Englishman abroad. He would rip apart our 'films', as we liked to call them, until they were barely recognisable, then reconstitute them and occasionally, in an exasperating moment of his own self-doubt, wonder aloud whether they might have been better before. They invariably weren't.

My early stories at *Four Corners*, though respectable enough, were far from what I wanted to achieve, but towards the end of my first year, I began to gain some confidence. I missed the more collegiate atmosphere at *Nationwide* but decided to put my head down and absorb as much about making television as quickly as I could. The editors provided much valuable advice, in particular the legendary Alec Cullen and wonderful, gentle Des Horne.

Four Corners had built much of its early reputation on social documentary, but now the focus was on hard-edged investigations, the stories that would create headlines. Swirling around us all was the fallout from 'The Big League'. A Royal Commission had been called and there were continual accusations that *Four Corners* was 'out to get' the Australian Labor Party. It's hard to convey the depth of the ALP's animosity towards *Four Corners* in those days. It was raised continually by Party loyalists and sympathisers everywhere we went. When the following year I did a story investigating international uranium safeguards, I felt it firsthand.

Uranium mining in Australia was highly contentious in the early '80s, and due to be debated at the ALP's annual conference in 1984. The Labor government argued a stringent international safeguards system ensured none of our uranium could be diverted into producing nuclear weapons. We decided to investigate the safeguards system and found elements of it wanting.

In a one-hour special, 'Uranium: Handle with Care', we followed the path of a typical shipment of Australian uranium to Canada, the United States, Germany and France, exploring the safeguards at every stage. One key element of the program was an interview with a nuclear physicist and former International Atomic Energy Agency safeguards inspector, Roger Richter. Richter had travelled the world inspecting nuclear facilities. He'd resigned from the IAEA and had given evidence to a US Senate Committee claiming diplomacy was compromising the safeguards system.

Richter had refused many international requests for interviews. To my delight and astonishment, he agreed to mine, in part because he had a soft spot for the Antipodes and was thinking about a move to New Zealand. Richter claimed it would be 'extremely easy' to fool the IAEA. 'I think the public would be very surprised just how cursory our inspections are.'

Coming less than a year after 'The Big League', the government saw our story as further proof *Four Corners* was anti-Labor. Several days after 'Uranium: Handle with Care' went to air, Prime Minister Bob Hawke told his caucus, 'We have enemies in the media', referring to the ABC and the *National Times* newspaper. Foreign Minister Bill Hayden called the ABC a 'second rate organisation' and Energy and Resources Minister Peter Walsh, who'd been equivocal in his interview on the program, attacked *Four Corners* in the senate.

Hayden's attitude towards me and *Four Corners* eventually softened. A year later, after an interview for another story, the Foreign Minister smiled and handed me an unopened bottle of Nepalese apple brandy on his desk, which I read as some kind of peace offering (though I did inquire, not knowing what was in the bottle, whether he might be planning to knock off ABC employees one by one). It sat on my desk as a memento until I left *Four Corners* later that year, when I bequeathed it to my roommate, Kerry O'Brien. Apparently it tasted just fine.

Even in 1990 when I returned to *Four Corners* briefly as a guest reporter, it was clear some Labor ministers still held a grudge. During a break from filming a moderately tough interview with Gareth Evans about the disposal of chemical weapons in the Pacific, the then Foreign Minister, knowing the camera was turned off, rose to his feet, arced across his desk towards me and bellowed, 'Fucking ABC, I should have known you'd do this!' He then continued to rant about *Four Corners* and how he was fed up with us.

The crew and I were stunned. The outburst was ridiculously disproportionate to the mistake I'd picked him up on in the interview, but it betrayed a deep level of animosity. It also reduced his press secretary to a near foetal position on a chair in the corner of the office.

Making *Four Corners* programs in the '80s swamped many of our lives. Social events would be cancelled, dinners left cold, friends stood up, then at some stage we'd register the ABC cleaners vacuuming around us as we slaved away on a script or edit into the wee hours.

It was toughest for the editors, stuck on a crazy rat wheel of program after program — structured, restructured, scripted, rescripted, viewed, reviewed, over and over. Often it was tempting to contemplate sleeping in the office rather than dashing home for a few short hours. It was no way to live, and took a heavy toll on relationships. On one overseas trip I remember Guntis Sics, a talented sound recordist I'd travelled with a lot, looking at me over breakfast and declaring, 'You know Jen, I've just figured out I've probably shared more meals with you than I have with my wife.' We both found that disturbing.

And a word here for those wives at home, waving their husbands off to exotic locations and countless nights in the office. Bills would have been unpaid, clothes unwashed, parent–teacher nights unattended were it not for these remarkable women. And it was mostly women. Their stories may never be documented as part of *Four Corners*' illustrious history, but they put up with hell. They'd often say the worst time was when their husbands returned from a filming trip, only to spend night after night in an editing room. 'He's home, but he's not home.' I can't begin to describe how regularly I wished, in my few years at *Four Corners*, that I had a wife at home.

There were, of course, countless compensations for the punishing hours. We were working on arguably the best current affairs program in the country, able to travel, and do proper research. It was a gift, and it substantially shaped my thinking about journalism and my professional life. Lack of time is a true enemy of good journalism. *Four Corners* gave me the opportunity to wrestle with ideas, hone my skills, explore the depth in people's arguments. I began to distrust black and white, became deeply wary of ideologues and much more interested in the intersection of power and human frailty. It eventually led me away from a purely adversarial style of journalism.

Some of my fondest memories of my stint at *Four Corners* are moments of sheer hilarity, shared with producers and crews in ludicrous situations on the road, especially internationally. Typically it was when journalistic naivety met real life. There was the boat trip in Hawaii to watch villagers use their traditional deep-sea fishing technique — a huge hook and bait lashed to an enormous rock with thick rope, then hurled overboard to the ocean floor. Of course they quickly hauled in a giant fish — then promptly shot it through the head with a pistol. Or the long trip to a remote island in Palau to film villagers at a traditional dance ceremony, only to have the dancers emerge wearing Nissan T-shirts and chanting 'hup, two, three four', a dance clearly shaped by ancestral contact with soldiers during World War II. With time to properly explore anything, there are myths to explode, lessons to learn.

By the beginning of 1985 I was 30, engaged and thinking about having a child. We began the year with our usual ideas meeting and I proposed a story in the United States, where abortion clinics were being bombed with alarming frequency. US President Ronald Reagan had put his name to an anti-abortion book, and looming changes to the Supreme Court could lead to a change in the law. Jonathan wasn't convinced; the story was interesting but would be expensive. We agreed to keep an eye on it.

By the middle of the year, there'd been 40 bombings or attempted arsons at abortion clinics across the United States in 18 months. A radical anti-abortion activist from Chicago had been in Australia, promoting his book and geeing up the movement here. Joseph Scheidler said he didn't condone violence; he didn't think it worked, but he was well and truly on the fringe of the anti-abortion movement, harassing people and using inflammatory rhetoric. Chapter titles in Scheidler's book included 'Infiltrate Abortion Clinics', 'Use Private Detectives', 'Get Information from License Plates' and 'Warn the Garbage Man You're Hauling Corpses'. He called doctors who performed abortions 'murderers' and didn't care that abortion was legal. Scheidler would later tell me, 'It's an unjust, immoral law, and I'm obliged to break it every chance I have.'

Jonathan asked me if I still wanted to do the story. Of course I did, but by then I was pregnant. He checked again a few days later, looking mildly alarmed. Was I absolutely sure I wanted to do this? It never occurred to me to say no, partly because I didn't want to be seen as incapable of doing my job. Anyway, it was shaping up as a strong story.

I arrived in a steamy Washington summer five months pregnant and set about looking for madmen and women who might think bombing an abortion clinic to make a political point was a good idea. The alleged bombers were either facing charges or in hiding and disinclined to talk. It wasn't looking promising, but I didn't factor in my appearance. While I didn't mention my pregnancy to anyone, it was pretty obvious, and doors began to open. It's a measure of the sophistication of extremist thinking that this fringe group probably assumed because I was pregnant, I would be sympathetic.

In Pensacola, Florida, I tracked down a classic southern belle, 19-year-old Kaye Wiggins, who with her fiancé, Matt, and another couple had been involved in bombing three local medical centres that provided abortion services. Kaye had bought the gunpowder for the bombings, but was appealing her conviction on the grounds she hadn't really been in on the action. Kaye said she loved Matt so much, she was worried that if she told on him she'd be throwing away the rest of her life. She said Matt and his friend Jimmy were just 'ordinary American guys … always pullin' somethin' … they're crazy guys they're always doin' strange things'. The bombings had been carried out on Christmas Eve. Matt had told her, 'What better gift could Jesus have received on his birthday than no abortions being performed, no children being killed?'

Down the road with his ragbag of followers, John Burt, a former member of the Ku Klux Klan, was picketing the home of a local doctor who performed legal abortions. Did he support the bombings? 'I understand the bombings and if the Lord told me to bomb a building, yes I would.' The Pensacola doctor was scared.

Mr Burt carried a bucket and midway through our interview pulled out what he claimed was a late-term foetus, covered in formaldehyde, to make his point about babies being killed. It looked a bit like a bruised rubber doll to me, but Burt was adamant he'd been given it by 'a pathologist that's very pro-life' who had 'intercepted' it at a Midwest hospital before it was sent to the incinerator. It struck me that John Burt had a curious approach to valuing human life. Even shoving a supposedly aborted foetus in front of a pregnant reporter hardly seemed, well, thoughtful.

As we packed up after filming, cameraman John Hagin and sound recordist Tim Parratt asked if I was okay. I said sure, no problem, but I felt sick to my stomach. Hagin paused, put his arm around me and said the heat was terrible, and that he felt pretty awful too. There's a touching, understated empathy on the road. You see some dreadful things and Hagin, the kindest of men, knew me well. It was his way of saying, 'That was hideous; it's perfectly okay for you to fall in a heap now, and if you do, we won't tell anyone back at the office.' I didn't, but I probably should have. All I wanted was to get back to the hotel and be alone with my baby.

I'd planned to stay on at *Four Corners* until the very end of my pregnancy, but my daughter had other ideas. By midway through the seventh month I was sneaking into the first-aid room every lunchtime, locking the door, sleeping for an hour, then emerging as though I'd just ducked out for a little while. I've only realised writing this that I may have been the first *Four Corners* reporter to work through a pregnancy. I did everything I could not to be different to the other reporters — so ridiculous, looking back now. I knew it was time to go when I wanted to stay on that first-aid bed all afternoon.

On the evening my daughter, Thea, was born, I lay in the delivery room at Sydney's Women's Hospital in Paddington, exhilarated but totally exhausted. When a phone beside me rang, I automatically picked it up. It was editor Julia Wright and she was at a party with some of the *Four Corners* gang. They knew I was in labour and had decided to check how I was going, never imagining they'd bypass the system and get through to me directly. When I told her I'd had a baby girl minutes earlier, a cheer went up in the background. I cried. My life had changed forever. I hadn't even told my mother yet, but *Four Corners* was all over it.

A year's maternity leave made me realise I didn't want the *Four Corners* lifestyle with a small child. I also became interested in a different type of investigation, one which explored people — their motivations and moral boundaries — and institutions. When the ABC asked me to help set up a new Documentary department, I jumped at the chance.

I returned to *Four Corners* as a guest reporter in subsequent years, each time aware how much it, and I, had changed. Production values continued to improve, and there were a lot more women. Visiting was great but I'd moved on, and was enjoying telling stories in a different way.

Ultimately I found my voice outside *Four Corners*, in documentaries, on ABC morning radio, in interview series, and hosting *Insight* on SBS. But the time I spent in the early to mid '80s trying to hold a demanding audience for up to an hour, gave me confidence to take risks I may never have embarked on otherwise. *Four Corners* taught me a lot about journalism and myself. May many more journalists be blessed with such an opportunity.

'It's difficult because of the gap between what has been reported and what should be reported.' David Marr's story on alcohol use in Aurukun, Queensland, was one of a line of ground-breaking reports on black Australia.

10

REPORTING BLACK AUSTRALIA: THESE STORIES AREN'T OVER

by David Marr

'This is Box Ridge,' said Michael Charlton looking like a man from another planet come to Earth in Coraki, New South Wales. 'Just over here is a cemetery, a cemetery for the dead. And what Bishop Davies has called "a cemetery for the living" is all around us.'

Four Corners was three weeks old and filming on location for the first time. Behind Charlton was a cluster of humpies denounced a few days earlier by an Anglican bishop. As the camera roamed, Charlton listed the horrors of the place: more than 100 people living in a dozen shacks, one water point, no light and no power. He said, 'We are going to talk now to some of the people who live here at Box Ridge.' With this implacable simplicity, *Four Corners* began reporting black Australia.

At that time, pale children were still being stolen from their Aboriginal mothers. Aborigines could vote in neither federal elections nor polls in Queensland and Western Australia. Nearly everywhere, the Country Party held a veto over all reform of laws touching Aborigines. Black stockmen worked for their keep. Bush schools were usually segregated. Missionaries had absolute authority over blacks on reserves. 'Full bloods' were forbidden to drink and sly grog was rife across most of the nation. Police and magistrates could always rely on Aborigines pleading guilty. There were no black graduates, playwrights, filmmakers or politicians. Appalling clusters of humpies like those at Box Ridge stood outside hundreds of country towns. Aborigines were thought to have entirely lost ownership of their customary lands. Native title was not yet the daydream of Eddie Mabo and a couple of Melbourne QCs.

All that changed. *Four Corners* reported and at times helped provoke those changes. In the early days of television, we took cameras to places like Box Ridge where cameras had never been taken before. We challenged what the Aboriginal leader Pat Dodson calls the 'placidness' of Australia: its belief that 'the destiny of Aboriginal people was to live in squalor and to live on the margins'. The reporting of Indigenous stories was driven by both anger and high hopes, but over time *Four Corners* showed itself to be sceptical of simple solutions. Complexity and contradiction were acknowledged from the start. Disappointing outcomes in black Australia drove *Four Corners* further, but not always swiftly, into the difficult territory where black and white Australians struggle with race.

Bob Raymond came home and created *Four Corners* after working in West Africa 'at a time when colonialism was coming to an end, when the Gold Coast was becoming Ghana'. So often in the years that followed, the reporters keenest to investigate black Australia were those returning after years away — or coming here for the first time — and seeing these old, familiar scandals through foreign eyes. They saw the stories with a clarity often denied to the locals. It was inevitable, really, that Raymond would soon take Charlton somewhere like Box Ridge. But the story did not unfold in quite the heroic manner, nor did it have the decisive impact on *Four Corners*' reputation Raymond would claim.

'I saw,' said Raymond, 'a little item in the *Sydney Morning Herald* where the Bishop of Newcastle had described an Aboriginal settlement at Box Ridge near Casino as a living cemetery. I said to Mike, maybe we should go and see what he's talking about.' The bishop's remarks were front-page news and the *Herald* had immediately despatched a reporter and photographer to Coraki. There followed a fine story in the paper, with heartbreaking photographs and a thundering editorial: 'Must the public be confronted year after year with reports of this kind?' In the NSW parliament the somnolent minister ultimately responsible for the scandal, Gus Kelly, was fielding questions for days. All this had happened before Raymond and Charlton flew north. A familiar pattern was being set here: the collaboration of newspapers and television in the reporting of black Australia. But Box Ridge was pioneering. 'In 1961, news crews and television stations didn't go anywhere near Aboriginal settlements,' said Raymond. 'There wasn't any story there.'

He took a journalist so impeccably turned out, so intelligent, so decent, a man with a voice of such authority it seemed not only Australia but the whole British Empire was seeing this scandal. Charlton's questions were perfect: 'Mr Kapeen, why do you live in this tin shack?' In nearby Casino he had an exchange with a rather tubby Anglican priest that still reverberates 50 years later. 'Why have we only just heard about places like this?' Charlton asked. 'The indifference of people,' replied the priest. 'Usually when people read something about Aborigines they just turn over the page to the next item and look for something sensational. It is only when someone in authority such as a bishop makes a startling statement that people really sit up and take notice. But these things have been said over and over again but people have just ignored them.'

And television audiences flinch. 'Black–white relations are a blind spot with Australians,' says Peter Manning, Executive Producer in the

1980s. 'They don't want to know about it in their hearts.' Liz Jackson, who made a number of key stories on Aboriginal issues in the last 20 years, was warned every time she proposed another that the ratings would crash. That was only one of a number of formal difficulties *Four Corners* faced when bringing black Australia to television. 'It's difficult because it's expensive,' says Jackson. 'It's difficult because it is a difficult culture; difficult because a lot of Aboriginal communities don't want white film crews in their parts if they are going to focus on what they call "shame jobs". It's difficult because of the gap between what has been reported and should be reported. We are closing that gap.'

We don't know how many people watched 'Box Ridge' when it went to air on Saturday 9 September but it caused quite a stir. 'If we were shocked when we saw what was happening there, so were the viewers,' said Raymond. 'People all over Australia were outraged and the New South Wales government was deluged on Monday with all kinds of protests.' The Minister for Justice flew north to inspect the shanties. After cabinet the following Tuesday the elderly Premier, Bob Heffron, declared: 'Here and now I tell you we are going to give them a new deal in housing.' The *Herald*'s 'Onlooker' columnist was amazed to see the government shaken out of its torpor: 'Wonders will never cease!'

Legend has it that 'Box Ridge' made *Four Corners*' name at a single blow. Not really. It was ground breaking. It showed how television could reignite interest in an old scandal. Even 50 years later it is remembered with gratitude. But *Four Corners* first caught the imagination of its audience by filming a beach inspector throwing a woman in a bikini off Bondi. 'I do not want to see anything indecent on the beach,' was the war cry of Abe Laidlaw, the gnarled guardian of decency on that stretch of Sydney's coast. The *Herald* reported filming the expulsion of that woman 'rated more newspaper space' than anything *Four Corners* screened in its first weeks. And reform came swiftly: by the end of October, the government had announced the repeal of the ordinance mandating neck-to-knee costumes on all

Sydney beaches. No *Four Corners* report from black Australia has ever provoked such a clear-cut response.

For 40 years, injustice was almost the sole focus of these reports. *Four Corners* was not blind to troubles in Aboriginal communities. The first years of the show were the last years of alcohol bans and their impact was examined in 'The Right to Drink' (1964). But drink, violence and illiteracy hardly seemed to matter at *Four Corners* in the face of the neglect, dispossession and exploitation of black Australia. There were not many Aboriginal reports — only one or two every couple of years — but they added to the provocative reputation *Four Corners* was winning. 'People wanted to watch it, because it was telling them things about the country that they hadn't really come across before, or hadn't thought deeply about before,' said John Penlington, a reporter in those years. 'Things like Aborigines in humpies in the back streets of some country town in New South Wales, seeing a Communist interviewed during the Cold War on the ABC, seeing people talk freely about sex …'

Those early years saw so many humpies and so much squalor on *Four Corners*: Marble Bar (1962), Palm Island (1970), Walgett (1971), Alice Springs (1972), Redfern (1973), Brewarrina (1973). None of these reports had the impact of Peter Reid's 1969 'Out of Sight, Out of Mind', which the then trainee priest Pat Dodson thought 'absolutely fantastic' when it went to air. 'Whilst there are horrifying things said in some of that program, the central thing about the poverty, the injustice that Aboriginal people were living in was graphically portrayed.' This was not in a newspaper but on television 'coming into the lounge rooms of many, many Australians'.

The scene was Cunnamulla in Queensland, where Nancy Young had lived with ten children in a shack on the edge of town. Young had been jailed for manslaughter after the death of her baby. The scene was appalling. There were only four water taps for dozens of shacks. Disease was rife. The camera pans over boils, rashes and sores on the pitted faces of children playing where Cunnamulla's sewage pours into the river. Reid acknowledges that the inhabitants of these shanties could eat better and drink less, but the conclusion of his report is that they were being deliberately left to live in these wretched conditions. 'To my way of thinking they are certainly not an underprivileged section of the community,' said Cunnamulla shire president Jack Tomkins. 'Something for nothing is their motto. And they don't get much for nothing, that I'll admit.'

Four Corners took Young's case to Australia. 'Out of Sight, Out of Mind' went to air as a phalanx of doctors, clergy, lawyers and university students were working to spring her from prison. Embarrassing evidence had emerged that scurvy was killing children in the Cunnamulla camp. The Queensland courts found a technicality on which to quash her conviction. One of the law students caught up in the cause was Geoffrey Robertson, who says Nancy Young's case was his 'first inkling about how often justice only gets done when someone takes notice'.

The '60s saw *Four Corners* begin to report black Australia's struggle for land, which was to be a great theme of the show for nearly two decades until the land rights movement ran into the sand in the early years of Bob Hawke's government. These reports began in 1966 with Frank Bennett's impeccable report of the Gurindji walk-off from Wave Hill Station, a corner of Lord Vestey's pastoral empire in northern Australia. 'The Price of Equality', broadcast when the strike was only a couple of months old, is full of complexity. Bennett didn't assume for a moment all would be well once blacks were given wages rather than flour, tea, tobacco and pocket money. An urbane Vesteys manager he interviewed standing on the wing of his plane warned of 'disemployment' among black stockmen 'when the award wage comes on and the native is in direct competition with the white man'. Bennett pointed to what lay deeper than the conflict over wages and conditions at Wave Hill: 'The Aborigine's inherent lack of property rights in his own country is the crux of his unrest.'

Land rights took *Four Corners* to some of the most remote and beautiful stretches of Australia. Never have so many didgeridoos been heard on television. Hardly questioned were the high hopes that drove Aborigines, their white supporters and, over time, many of the governments of Australia. More than justice was involved here: something like salvation was said to be at hand. In a dozen or so reports across a vast landscape, *Four Corners* pursued the enemies of land rights. Mike Willesee took on developers in New South Wales in 'A Place in the Sun' (1969) and Tony Jones went back for more in 'Coast Mortem' (1988). Others on the list were the mining giant Nabalco in Brian King's 'Gove: Land Rights and Wrongs' (1969); the British Ministry of Defence in David Flatman's 'Maralinga' (1972) and in Bob Hill and Noel Norton's 'Maralinga Sequel' (1980); Rio Tinto mining uranium in the heart of the Kakadu National Park, in Peter Ross's 'Northern Land Story' (1979) and Kerry O'Brien's 'Battle for Kakadu' (1986); and Joh Bjelke-Petersen's Queensland implacably opposing any form of land rights within its borders in Jim Downes' 'Palm Island' (1970), Maryanne Smith's 'Aurukun' (1978) and Jack Pizzey's 'Why Are They Marching?' (1982), which covered the demonstrations that put the struggle for land rights before the press of the world gathered in Brisbane for the Commonwealth Games.

But the late '70s and early '80s were not the finest years of *Four Corners*. 'It was a fairly prosaic operation,' Peter Ross recalls. 'It didn't have money and didn't have real purpose. You simply reacted to stories. It was a machine operation. It lacked gravitas.' That changed in 1982 with the appointment of Jonathan Holmes as Executive Producer. This young man from the BBC reinvigorated the show but moved cautiously in the reporting of Indigenous affairs. He had no direct experience of black Australia. Holmes says he put his energy in this area into 'scratching round to find ways of doing Aboriginal stories that might appeal to people'.

The formal structures of discrimination had all but disappeared by this time. Aborigines could vote, drink and were, everywhere but in Queensland, paid much the same wages as whites. Black graduates were coming through the universities. There were Aboriginal lawyers, doctors and teachers. Charlie Perkins, an Arrernte man from Alice Springs, was about to be promoted to Secretary of the Department of Aboriginal Affairs. Traditional owners had been granted title to half the Northern Territory and a swathe of South Australia. Bob Hawke came to office promising uniform land rights across the rest of the country but capitulated in the face of opposition from the miners, pastoralists and Labor government of Western Australia, as David de Vos reported in his obituary for land rights, 'Labor's Landmine' (1984).

But 25 years of change had only tempered the profound disadvantage of black Australia. Each reform had brought its own disappointment. Old problems along the black–white divide persisted. One of these was the violence by white officials which Alan Hall and I examined in 'Black Death' (1985) after a number of Aboriginal men, often drunk, died following beatings by police and prison warders in Western Australia. Our target was a system and a state of mind that saw no one punished, not even reprimanded, for these killings. A black prisoner having some kind of psychotic episode — he had just cut his wrists — was beaten by warders in the yard of Freemantle Prison. Twenty prisoners watching from their cells would give evidence that batons were used, that the prisoner was kicked and punched. They were all disbelieved. The chief forensic pathologist — who told me he had never in 20 years' service found evidence of assaults by warders or police — couldn't find a cause of death. A private autopsy in South Australia established swiftly that the young man was killed in a headlock. The warders were commended for their restraint.

We did not break the deaths in custody story. *Four Corners* was once again giving form and substance to worries already in the air. The response from the west was visceral: outraged denials, threats of defamation, and a complaint by Hawke to the ABC board. But Pat Dodson credits 'Black Death' with waking police, judges and policy-makers to the existence of this 'gaping sore' and argues *Four Corners* was 'absolutely essential' to the establishment of the Royal Commission into Aboriginal Deaths in Custody, on which he sat. But that did not come swiftly. A couple of years and a dozen more deaths followed before Hawke established the inquiry. And the deaths didn't stop, as reported by Deb Richards in 'Who Killed Mark Quayle?' (1987) and Liz Jackson in her very fine investigation 'Who Killed Mr Ward?' (2009) into the death, essentially by slow roasting, of a Western Desert man being driven to Kalgoorlie in a van without air conditioning to face a drink-driving charge.

In 1985, Holmes handed over to his deputy, Peter Manning, who looks back with regret at the failure of *Four Corners* to drive change for Aborigines in these years. 'We brought down governments, we brought down police commissioners, we put people in jail but with Aboriginal Australia we stopped nothing.' Manning believes too many Indigenous stories were done by *Four Corners*, not because they had much to reveal or anything to add, but because they *should* be done. 'It might have been better to decide stories on merit alone,' he says. 'I think audiences can smell an obligation story from a must-be-told story instantly.' The stories made were heart-rending but correct. Much bad behaviour was forgiven because the problems of black Australia were sheeted home to centuries of white occupation. Little was heard on the show of those voices calling for Aborigines to do more to haul themselves out of their troubles by being more disciplined, better citizens.

Manning suspects *Four Corners* was pointing its cameras too often in the wrong direction. 'I think in retrospect we needed context stories, stories that went deeper than the shock–horror scenes and looked back at our own white racism and maybe how we all are the problem, not just the easy targets of country yokels, cruel cops and mayors of shires.

Maybe we should have dug deeper into white Australia to address the problems of black Australia?'

Outside the ABC, the reluctance to report the dark side of black Australia, the fear of feeding racism by reinforcing old stereotypes, was breaking down. On leaving *Four Corners* to join *60 Minutes* in 1984, Jeff McMullen made a famous report from central Australia. 'An Aboriginal woman in her twenties, completely out of her mind sniffing petrol drained from a nearby car, lurched towards the crew waving a wheel wrench and screaming,' he wrote in his memoir, *A Life of Extremes*. The filmmaker David Bradbury followed McMullen across the line in 1988 with 'State of Shock', about drinking and death in Weipa. This was not a report from Kerry Packer's Nine Network but a film from the heart of the left, and its impact on the new Executive Producer of *Four Corners*, Marian Wilkinson, was profound. Bradbury's film convinced her that the show's old hesitation to investigate drink and violence in black communities had to end. 'The issue was too critical.'

She despatched Martin Butler and me to Cape York to make 'Six-Pack Politics' (1991), a study of grog's destructive impact on the contradictory little settlement of Aurukun. 'It's grim but a kind of paradise,' I told the camera. 'It's a black community that's never had so many whites running it. It presents a united face to the world but it's a town divided by old feuds. Fighting has always been part of the culture here. Nothing much gets done. In the end we have to ask the difficult question: is Aurukun today precisely as they want it?'

The old were mission-trained and spoke their minds; the young were illiterate and tongue tied. Far from resenting white policing, the senior women of Aurukun were demanding more arrests and more men to be thrown into the cells. One of the locals told us, as we filmed six tonnes of beer being unloaded from a barge, 'This is the main stuff. The piss.'

Butler and I decided only blacks would reproach blacks in our report. Marcia Langton did so with magnificent eloquence: 'In 15 years the conditions in Aboriginal communities have deteriorated beyond belief simply because of alcohol. And standard Aboriginal ways of behaving have simply gone for the younger generation because they see people rolling around on the ground drunk, behaving abominably.'

This was *Four Corners*' second visit to Aurukun. A pattern was being established of returning from time to time to see what had happened to people and their communities after those early reports. As a result, *Four Corners* was building a unique television archive of material on Indigenous Australia. Most of these return stories are in a little genre of their own: reporting rays of hope in black Australia. There would be three visits to Box Ridge (1961, 1967 and 1993), two to Walgett (1967 and 1971), at least three to Alice Springs (1972, 2006 and 2010) and three to Aurukun. Butler and I weren't looking for rays of hope in 1991 but when Matthew Carney went back in April 2011, he found a community now officially dry and an encouraging number of kids turning up at school. But the Aurukun story isn't over — none of these stories is.

'Six-Pack Politics' did not see a profound shift in *Four Corners*' reporting of Aboriginal Australia. Through the 1990s, under Ian Carroll, Paul Williams and John Budd, the show continued to focus on questions of justice. The High Court's Mabo decision brought land rights back in the new guise of native title. That in turn revived old disputes with mining companies and state governments. The stolen generations made a late entry with Liz Jackson's 'Telling His Story' (1996), about the life and suicide of the activist Rob Riley, who had spent his childhood at the appalling Sister Kate's home for 'nearly white' children in Perth. A lawyer not long back from London, Jackson drove the show's reporting of efforts to find Indigenous punishments to fit black crimes, beginning with 'Payback' (1994). Her powerful 'Go to Jail' (2000) — provoked by the suicide in prison of a 15-year-old boy from Groote Eylandt jailed for stealing a few marker pens and a tin of paint — helped feed protests across Australia that led to the softening of the Northern Territory's mandatory detention regime.

Bruce Belsham became Executive Producer of the show in 1999 with a renewed determination to investigate the dark side of Indigenous Australia. A New Zealander, Belsham had absorbed the message of personal responsibility in the writings of Alan Duff, whose novel *Once Were Warriors* was filmed in 1994. He came to *Four Corners* having just made *Frontier*, a television series about Australia's 150-year land war. The discovery that white Australians were acknowledging even back then the wrong they were doing reinforced his belief that it was time for black Australians to do the same now, in particular to take responsibility for violence and abuse in remote black communities.

On Groote Eylandt to film the mandatory detention story, Jackson realised most of the people waiting in court weren't kids about to be slotted for petty theft but victims of domestic violence. 'We are doing the wrong story,' she thought. She had also been reading the anthropologist Peter Sutton's exasperated challenge to the old discourse of white guilt and black independence in the remote communities. 'When so many lives are being lost,' he wrote in early 2001, 'when three-year-old children are found suffering from gonorrhoea, when Indigenous women are 45 times more likely to be victims of domestic violence, when local action on severe problems is not working, does not the wider community have to recognise its responsibility by supporting a more interventionist approach?' Jackson's response was 'The Shame' (2001), which revealed the scale of child sexual abuse in black communities. Sutton's blast had not only shattered white illusions but, Jackson believes, encouraged black leaders to break old taboos and speak about this on camera for the first time. Dodson was one of these and he took a particularly grave view of the situation: 'The survival of the Indigenous people of this country is at stake.'

Under Belsham and his successor, Sue Spencer, *Four Corners* has pursued ruthless art dealers; examined the reform agenda of Noel Pearson and the progress of John Howard's Northern Territory intervention; reported yet more deaths in custody, the sad fate of bilingual schooling and the continuing breakdown of black communities. 'The Road to Nowhere' (2006) led Jackson to Impanpa, a settlement in complete collapse, only a few kilometres from Alice Springs. Michael Charlton was sure Box Ridge could be fixed. But this cemetery for the living left Liz Jackson with no such confidence. 'Tonight,' she said, '*Four Corners* travels to one small remote community — not notorious, not in the news — to witness the results of the failure of Indigenous policy over the last 30 years. It's time to ask the hard question — do communities like this have a future?'

The old sense of obligation to take television cameras into black Australia has not left *Four Corners*. The focus has shifted. Old hopes have died. New problems have arisen. But the underlying ambition of the show hasn't really changed in 50 years. *Four Corners* can boast bringing clarity to a subject that's difficult for television and appallingly hard for Australia. So much has changed but the obstacles to change remain formidable. Peter Manning identifies the deepest of them all as 'the persistent, horrible reality in Australian life which is called racism'.

Despite numerous clashes on air, Liz Jackson profiled the Prime Minister John Howard on several occasions. The tension between the two never abated.

11

COMFORTABLE AND RELAXED: ENCOUNTERS WITH JOHN HOWARD, 1994–2007

by Liz Jackson

JACKSON: **Do you like television?**
HOWARD: **Love it.**
JACKSON: **What do you watch? What's your favourite show?**
HOWARD: **Ah, well, I watch the news and current affairs** [laughs]. *Four Corners*, **I always watch** *Four Corners*.

[*Four Corners* interview, 1996]

I had never met John Howard before the first time I interviewed him back in 1994. He'd been a Member of Parliament for 20 years, I'd been at *Four Corners* about eight weeks. It was for the first *Four Corners* program I'd ever made, and the first of many with Howard over the next 16 years.

When I moved into my new ABC office, pinned above my desk was a scrap of paper on which someone had written, 'No-one ever died from being asked a question.' I took the anonymous message to heart as I interviewed John Howard over those years, following his ascension to power, his time as Prime Minister, through to his final downfall, watching his capacity to duck, weave and deflect questions grow as his power and authority increased.

The program was also my introduction to the potential for *Four Corners* to be a player in the political events of the country. The morning before the show went to air, the National Party leader, Tim Fischer, told his colleagues: 'I note the *Four Corners* program tonight. It will be very interesting to see what happens in the aftermath of that *Four Corners* program.'

The program was 'Bishop's Move', where the Bishop was Bronwyn and the move was against the then Liberal leader, Dr John Hewson. My assignment was to investigate the depth of leadership tensions in the Liberal Party after Dr Hewson lost the so-called 'unloseable election' in 1993, handing then Prime Minister Paul Keating what he called 'the sweetest victory of all'. It was a loss that galled political professionals within the Liberal Party, who felt that Keating didn't win on ideology but because Hewson was a political novice. 'We should have beaten a government that had been there for ten years in the middle of a recession, with a million people out of work,' John Howard told me, and pointedly added, 'We have to make sure it doesn't happen again.'

From the moment of Hewson's loss, Howard was after his job, and a year later he had not given up. But there was a new contender, Senator Bronwyn Bishop. She had surprised many colleagues by emerging in the polls as a serious leadership rival, a populist conservative who was doing an efficient job of destabilising Hewson. But would the party choose her as a replacement? Or John Howard, Peter Costello, Alexander Downer or even Peter Reith?

It was not a good time for Howard. Five years earlier he'd been dumped as Liberal leader, famously conceding that his return to the leadership would be 'like Lazarus with a triple bypass'. He was well aware that a return to him would be regarded by many of his colleagues and much of the media as a return to the past.

Before our interview with Howard began, while the crew set up the camera, he took me and producer Mick O'Donnell aside. His tone was urgent. The message he wanted to impress on us was that he was again a serious leadership contender, that we would be wrong to write him off as yesterday's man. He would, he assured us, ride out the nay-sayers. It was a combination of dogged self-belief and vulnerability that I hadn't expected, born of an awareness that how *Four Corners* presented him would matter.

We did the interview in his office in Sydney, where his minders had left a high-backed upholstered swivel chair for Howard to sit in. Swivel chairs do not work well on camera so we swapped it for an ordinary office chair, the same kind and level that I would be sitting in. When he saw what we'd done, Howard would have none of it. It was the high-backed chair or nothing he insisted, and made us change it. The appearance of authority was crucial, and he didn't trust us.

We sat down to do the interview. I asked two questions about Bronwyn Bishop; his answers were, 'Next question' and 'I'm not going to talk about Bronwyn, I'm not.' In those days *Four Corners* used ten-minute rolls of film, so every ten minutes we needed to stop the interview and reload the camera. I moved on to the more important questions, about Howard's own leadership ambitions. I had spoken with Bill Taylor, a Queensland MP and an old Howard loyalist. He had told me that Hewson had to be dumped, but that he had switched his support to Bronwyn Bishop. Howard, he said, had 'missed the boat' as he would be seen as 'a recycled leader'. Taylor added that as a friend he had told Howard this, and agreed to say so on *Four Corners*.

I needed to put this to John Howard, and it was a delicate question. This was, after all, an unexpected arrow from a friend into his Achilles heel.

'John,' I said, with the camera rolling, 'I have spoken to some of your parliamentary colleagues who voted for you in the last leadership ballot, and they are saying that they have said to you, you must publicly bow out. You must accept that you have missed the boat, that you will never be the leader of the Liberal Party.'

Before Howard had a chance to respond the cameraman informed us we were out of film. He needed to reload the camera. It took around two minutes; it seemed like ten. We sat in our set positions, facing each other, in more or less silence. He was stony-faced. Small talk seemed inappropriate somehow; he didn't offer any so neither did I. The camera was reloaded, and I started again.

'John,' I repeated, as if nothing had happened, 'I have spoken to some of your parliamentary colleagues ...' and continued to the bitter end '... you will never be the leader of the Liberal Party.'

'Well,' he responded, having had two minutes to think about it, 'I haven't had any such conversations so they must have mistaken me for someone else.' I pushed on.

JACKSON: **And why don't you?**
HOWARD: **Why don't I what?**
JACKSON: **Why don't you say publicly, 'I will not lead the Liberal Party. I do not —'**
HOWARD: **Look, I have said to you before and I will say it again that the question of the future leadership of the Party is a matter for the Party room. I am not really required, nor am I going to say anything more on the subject.**

The following morning the *Four Corners* program was front-page news. The gist of the headlines was that the public disloyalty to Dr Hewson showed his leadership position was weakening: 'Liberals Hit Hewson Again' (*Sydney Morning Herald*); 'Outspoken Libs Turn

Up Heat on Hewson' (*Australian*). A statement from Paul Keating's office described it as Hewson's 'slow death by television'.

Within four months Dr Hewson was dumped. The Liberals initially replaced him with Alexander Downer, but within a year John Howard had won the Liberal leadership. One year later he would be the Prime Minister of Australia. So much for being yesterday's man.

* * *

JACKSON: **Are you the most conservative leader the Liberal Party has ever had?**
HOWARD: **Probably, you'd have an enormous debate on that.**
('Average Australian Bloke', *Four Corners*, 19 February 1996)

I met John Howard again at the Adelaide Oval in January 1996. Australia was playing the third Test against Sri Lanka. The leader of the Opposition was in a good mood. The first Newspoll of the year had just put the Coalition ahead of Labor by 10 percentage points, and Prime Minister Paul Keating had lost his lead over Howard as to who would make the better PM. Things had picked up since I'd last seen him two years earlier; John Howard was smiling.

We sat together side by side and did our best to engage in convivial chatter about the cricket for the camera. We'd been given about six minutes to film with Howard before he headed off. *Four Corners* was making profiles of both Howard and Paul Keating as a federal election was due to be called in the coming days, and I was on the Howard story. The sun was shining in Adelaide, and it was batsman David Boon's last Test for Australia. My cricket knowledge was shaky but I chanced it with, 'Is that Boon out there?'

'Yes,' was Howard's reply.

'Have you got a particular affection for him?' I continued.

'Oh, yes,' he said. 'He's just been one of the bulwarks and the mainstay. When we went through that difficult period in the mid '80s, he and Border between them held the show together.'

It was a good response for us, enabling *Four Corners* to use the cricket pictures to talk about Howard's own difficult time in the '80s. Like Boon he had been dropped by his team, but had persisted and returned. Howard was happy with politics and cricket analogies, and gave his view on their shared winning strategies:

HOWARD: **Persistence over a long period of time, that sort of thing.**
JACKSON: **Yes. The sort of thing that you might see yourself as having a strength in, John?**
HOWARD: **That's for others to judge, but I think sticking at it and being dogged is part of the game.**

But John Howard's long and familiar history was a problem as he approached the upcoming election. It was not so much the image of a recycled leader anymore; he'd dealt with that. It was that in his political history there were things he had said and positions he'd taken that he would prefer to put some distance behind him. Back in 1987, in a *Four Corners* program, Howard had stated, 'Anyone who knows me knows that I am the most conservative leader the Liberal Party has ever had.' His self-description as an ultra-conservative made political sense in 1987; back then Howard was threatened with an electorally lethal split among the conservatives, caused by the Queensland Premier Joh Bjelke-Peterson's short-lived campaign for Canberra, and Howard needed to hold the conservative vote. But it was the wrong image for 1996. It was clear from early in the '96 campaign that Howard was repositioning himself on the safe middle ground as an unthreatening alternative to Keating, whose big-picture policies such as engagement with Asia, reconciliation and support for a republic were regarded as having little resonance outside the urban elites. Howard, by contrast, pitched himself as being in touch with mainstream Australia; so much so that when I asked him to describe himself he offered the following: 'I'd like to be seen as an average Australian bloke. I can't think of a nobler description of anybody than to be called an average Australian bloke.'

Not too radical and not too conservative either, just 'an average Australian bloke'. It crossed my mind that saying he could think of nothing 'nobler' was laying it on a bit thick, but maybe not for his purpose. As the campaign progressed you couldn't help but notice a more middle-ground man in language and policy than the John Howard of old. He had been known over the years as proposing radical industrial relations reform, as a staunch monarchist, a defender of the traditional family and an opponent of Medicare, which he had branded 'a total disaster'. What had happened to this John Howard, and when? These were questions I needed to put to Howard, and I thought carefully about how to frame them, so that his repositioning was clear.

> JACKSON: **I'd like to run through a few of the issues —**
> HOWARD: **Sure.**
> JACKSON: **— that will be big in this debate; Medicare being the first. When did you change your mind about Medicare?**
> HOWARD: **What part of it?**
> JACKSON: **Well, for instance, that it was a total disaster. When did you change your view that Medicare was a total disaster?**
> HOWARD: **I have accepted, for some years now, that the Australian people like Medicare and they want to keep it.**
> JACKSON: **When did you change your view that bulk billing was a rort?**
> HOWARD: **Once again, the Australian people made a decision that they wanted to keep bulk billing, and they therefore — look, on all of these sorts of issues, anybody who has the same**

view year in and year out, irrespective of the expression of public opinion, is stupid.

JACKSON: **So you changed your view on bulk billing and Medicare generally because of public opinion?**

HOWARD: **Public opinion played a very major part on both of those issues, yes.**

JACKSON: **What do you think of the view that 'politicians should stand for what is right, not what is popular'?**

HOWARD: **I think on most occasions that is absolutely correct, but it must also be tempered by the recognition that if people express a definitive view, you have to accept that their right to make the decision is superior to yours.**

JACKSON: **So those are your words in 1986, that a politician should stand for what is right, not what is popular —**

HOWARD: **I remember them.**

JACKSON: **But you've now changed that view to accommodate —**

HOWARD: **I remember them very, very clearly. There's really no inconsistency.**

Over a period of three weeks we followed John Howard around the country, filming him on the campaign trail. In and out of cars, on and off planes. He and I never really struck up an easy rapport. He went about his job, trying to ignore us; we went about ours, trying to get our camera and sound gear to pick up every move he made, every word he uttered. He was polite but abrupt, and naturally wary of me and Janine Cohen, the producer of the story. He didn't know us the way he knew the Canberra press gallery, and there was for him a lot at stake in coming on *Four Corners*. This election was his best and last chance to become Prime Minister of Australia.

At one point, in Victoria, John Howard and I were sharing a car and the camera wasn't running. To my surprise, out of the blue, he said as if to reassure me, 'Liz, we are not going to cut the ABC's funding,' and then repeated it: 'We are not going to cut your funding.' I don't remember what I replied, just that I was thrown by this. After all, the Liberal Party's election platform promised there would be no cuts to the ABC. Why was he saying this to me at this particular time? If I'd been older and wiser, I'd have asked him that — then and there. But we just continued to the next destination, a factory where he would be filmed for the evening news talking to workers and management about industrial relations. I used the same interview approach as before:

> JACKSON: **I'd like to talk about industrial relations. Do you accept that you've changed your view on industrial relations?**
> HOWARD: **Where?**
> JACKSON: **Certainly your policy position has changed. Would you accept your policy position has changed?**
> HOWARD: **No, I don't. You tell me where I've changed.**
> JACKSON: **Do you not accept that the policy —**
> HOWARD: **No, no. You are putting to me that I've changed, and I say no. Now, I'm asking you to tell me where I have changed.**
> JACKSON: **In 1993, you advocated a $3 youth wage. Have you changed your view about that?**
> HOWARD: **I have on that.**

The issue of immigration was the most sensitive to raise. In 1988 John Howard had floated the idea that Australia should slow down its rate of Asian immigration, 'if it is [seen] in the eyes of some in the community that it's too great'. In 1995 he apologised for his comment, the same year Pauline Hanson was pre-selected by the Liberal Party as a candidate for the '96 election. She had, at the time of our interview with Howard, just been disendorsed after writing of Aboriginal people that 'Government showers them with money, facilities and opportunities that only these people can obtain, no matter how minute the Indigenous blood that is flowing through their veins.'

But another new Coalition candidate was also causing Howard embarrassment. Bob Burgess was a member of the National Party and had just proclaimed that the sources of Australia's immigration input should be skewed more towards European migrants. What did Howard think of this view? He was edgy.

> HOWARD: **We have a non-discriminatory immigration policy, full stop, and he won't be saying any more on that subject during the campaign.**
> JACKSON: **Does it make it difficult, though, for you to discipline somebody for saying that when you, yourself, raised the same issue in terms of the sources of our immigration?**
> HOWARD: **Well, he's a National Party member.**
> JACKSON: **He's part of the Coalition.**
> HOWARD: **There's a Liberal candidate in that seat, so really it's a matter — I mean, you talk about discipline; I've not even spoken to him. I've never met the man.**
> JACKSON: **You don't feel, 'Here's an echo from my past come back to revisit me?'**
> HOWARD: **No.**

It was hard to feel I was getting closer to the man. Even with personal questions, his answers appeared political, in conformity with the new pitch: 'I am less conservative than you might think.' I tried asking if he had any favourite music. He nominated 'many of the so-called protest songs — Bob Dylan and Joan Baez, I liked them immensely'. I was surprised; he'd never shared the views of the protest generation. When I remarked on this he was defensive. 'You shouldn't be so politically correct that somebody who may not necessarily share the views of the vocalist can't enjoy the music.'

It was not until towards the end of the interview that I asked John Howard the question that produced his most revealing and remembered answer. It was a 'soft question', an open-ended invitation to spell out his vision for the year 2000 to voters. His answer contained the catch phrase that would dog him for years.

> HOWARD: **By the year 2000, I would like to see an Australian nation that feels comfortable and relaxed about three things: I would like to see them comfortable and relaxed about their history; I'd like to see them comfortable and relaxed about the present; and I'd also like to see them comfortable and relaxed about the future.**

It struck me at the time as a little underwhelming, with a touch of *Brave New World*. The vision of a nation of people all feeling 'comfortable and relaxed' about their past, present and future.

> JACKSON: **Do you think that's a dynamic enough vision to inspire Australians as they move into the next millennium? Is that dynamic enough for Australians?**
> HOWARD: **I think people do want to feel comfortable and relaxed.**
> JACKSON: **They don't want to feel excited?**
> HOWARD: **Well, you can't possibly hope to feel excited about something unless you feel comfortable and familiar with it.**

The show went to air two weeks before the election. The commentators and cartoonists jumped on the weakness of the Howard vision, highlighting the phrase 'comfortable and relaxed'. The secretary of the union movement, Bill Kelty, publicly mocked Howard, calling him 'the Captain Snooze of Australian politics'. Journalist Pamela Williams would later reveal what Howard's senior adviser, Graeme

Morris, wrote in his diary the day the program went to air: 'Gaffe over tax policy; foot fault on Laws. *FOUR CORNERS*. LOSS — BIG TIME.' Williams wrote that Howard's advisers later 'dismissed the program, calling it a typical ABC hatchet job. They expected nothing better and some privately vowed revenge when they got into government'.

But maybe the bland reassurance of the vision we aired was precisely what the electorate was craving after the unease and overexcitement of the Keating years. On 2 March 1996 the Coalition swept into power in a landslide victory, and John Howard would be the Prime Minister of Australia for the next 11 years.

Six months after taking office, John Howard cut the ABC's budget by $60 million. It turned out the commitment not to cut the funding was 'a non-core promise'. *Four Corners* colleague Jonathan Holmes joked darkly that the ABC should send me back to Canberra with a placard around my neck declaring: 'YOU CAN HAVE HER. GIVE US BACK OUR $60 MILLION'.

* * *

INTERVIEWER: **Would you ever agree to come back on *Four Corners* for a profile?**
HOWARD: **Yes, I think it's an important program. I'm the Prime Minister, and the ABC's an important Australian institution, and if I'm ever invited for that kind of program of course I would agree [pause] I might argue about the conditions but I'd certainly agree.**

[Interview for *Four Corners*' 40th anniversary program, 2001]

The next time I interviewed John Howard he was the Prime Minister of Australia, and there were conditions imposed; conditions that arguably *Four Corners* should not have agreed to. The story we were making was 'Too Good to Be False', a forensic account of who knew what and when, in relation to the Children Overboard affair. It went to air in March 2002, five months after the Prime Minister had told Australians that asylum seekers heading for Australia had thrown their children into the sea when intercepted by the navy. This shocking claim exploded into the 2001 election campaign, in which border protection was already a passionate and critical issue, and community reaction was huge.

> PHILIP CLARK, RADIO 2GB: **I was horrified, I think every parent would have been, about the image you had at the weekend of boat people throwing their children overboard. What was your reaction?**
> JOHN HOWARD: **Well, my reaction was I don't want in Australia people who throw their own children into the sea.**

Three days after the alleged incident, pressed for evidence that it had indeed happened, the Defence Minister, Peter Reith, produced two photos. They showed women and children in the water being assisted by navy personnel, but that was all. That night the photos were shown on the ABC's *7.30 Report*, and senior naval officers were aghast. They knew immediately the photos had been taken the day after the throwing of children was alleged to have occurred, and that they were in fact photos of women and children being rescued, after their boat had sunk. The Chief of the Defence Force, Admiral Chris Barrie, later told a Senate Estimates Committee that he personally phoned Peter Reith the next day and told him the photos were wrong, and that senior officers had doubts the incident had occurred at all.

Three weeks later the *Australian*'s Natalie O'Brien reported: 'Christmas Islanders allege that naval officers told them that claims that asylum seekers had thrown children overboard during a confrontation last month with HMAS *Adelaide* were untrue.' In addition to the photos, the government had talked of there being a video, but Defence Minister Reith knew it contained no evidence to back the claims. The day the O'Brien article was published the acting Chief of the Defence Forces, Air Marshal Angus Houston, rang Peter Reith to make it clear that 'fundamentally there was nothing to suggest that women and children had been thrown in the water'.

Later that day Peter Reith phoned John Howard. The content of this call is critical. Did Reith tell Howard that he'd been advised by Defence 'there was nothing' to back the allegations that children were thrown into the sea? Howard and Reith say no. Months later Howard would agree, however, that Reith had raised doubts about the photos: 'He indicated to me that there was some debate about whether they were the one day or the next ... He just said there was doubt about it.' The next day, at the National Press Club, two days before the election, the journalists knew nothing about these phone calls. But the ABC's Fran Kelly put it to Howard that Defence sources were saying the photos were of people 'in the water because the boat was sinking, not because people had been thrown overboard'. There was nothing in Howard's answer indicating he knew of any doubts or debate about the photos; in fact he said nothing about the photos at all.

Five months later the content of Air Marshal Houston's phone call to Reith finally became public. It was in this context that *Four Corners* sought an interview with Prime Minister Howard.

But there was a problem. The PM would not agree to an interview unless we agreed to his conditions. First, we would have exactly ten minutes of his time. Second, he would not do the interview until four days before the show was due to air. Third, we could not cut his interview into the show: it had to stand alone at the end of the program. Fourth, we had to run it all, uncut. Fifth, if we did run over time we could not cut it down unless his press secretary, Tony O'Leary, agreed the cut was 'fair'.

We'd refused requests like this before. *Four Corners* makes documentary-style programs — that's the distinctive format of the show — with interviews edited into them. If we agreed, our acquiescence would set a dangerous precedent. But at the same time we felt it was critical that we include Howard, in fairness and because the show raised questions that needed to be answered. Reluctantly we agreed to the terms, and it drove home the power that Howard had now gained. Opposition leaders have to work hard to get media coverage while Prime Ministers can pick and choose who they want to talk to, and how.

We began the interview and the clock started ticking down. It didn't start well. In my first question I asked the Prime Minister if Peter Reith had told him there were doubts about the photos at their 'meeting'. It was a slip; it had not been a meeting but a phone call, and I knew that. Howard corrected me and continued: 'Mr Reith indicated to me there had been no advice contradicting the original advice. The main subject of our discussion at that time was the release of the video.' Nothing about the photos, so I followed it up:

> JACKSON: **But you've indicated that you did discuss the photos.**
> HOWARD: **Yes, I indicated there was an allusion to the debate — to the discussion about the photographs, yes.**
> JACKSON: **To their doubtful nature?**
> HOWARD: **Look, I just repeat what I've said before.**
> JACKSON: **Was it indicated to you there was any doubt that they were the wrong photos?**
> HOWARD: **Look, I can only repeat what I've said before.**

I knew the Prime Minister had previously admitted that Reith had told him there was doubt about the photos, and I was surprised, perhaps naively, and increasingly frustrated that he would not now say this. It was important.

JACKON: **Well it's an important issue, isn't it?**
HOWARD: **Yes.**
JACKSON: **Because you were asked —**
HOWARD: **That's why I am very careful in what I am saying because it is an important issue.**

I asked five times about the photos and was still getting nowhere, but I couldn't resist just one more try.

JACKSON: **Fran Kelly put it to you that Defence Forces were saying they were the wrong photographs. Why didn't you indicate at that stage that you'd discussed the photographs the night before and the issue had, in your words, 'been raised' with you?**
HOWARD: **Well, the reason, the reason why I'd moved on from the photographs —**
JACKSON: **But she was asking you about the photographs.**
HOWARD: **No, I'm sorry.**
JACKSON: **I mean, you might want to move on, but the whole of the Australian —**
HOWARD: **No, what I'd like to do is to be allowed to answer your question and not constantly interrupted. The reason why I gave the answer that I did to Fran Kelly was that in my mind, the important thing was the release of the video. And I don't have anything to regret or retract about the answer that I gave to Fran Kelly.**

At the end of the interview Howard was tetchy, but Tony O'Leary was pleased. Nothing had been clarified, let alone conceded. The ten minutes had been eaten up by going over the same ground or off at a tangent. I had interrupted too many times to try and stop this, and the look was bad. We'd gone a minute or two over the allocated time, but O'Leary didn't care, as long as we did not cut out the start where I had made the slip. The Prime Minister insisted on that.

The reaction to the interview from viewers on our website forum was polarised:

> Subject: **Interview of John Howard** post id: 1730
>
> The person interviewing John Howard in this evening's programme was treating John Howard in the same way that a lawyer would treat a criminal being charged with some offence — utterly disgraceful. The woman should be taught a few manners.

> Subject: **Liz you're a dynamo** post id: 1194
>
> Thank you for doing what I suspect many would like to do is pin the PM down & make him answer the question directly, that he didn't just shows his culpability in the whole affair.

I was disappointed. Not because I agree the encounter was a win for John Howard; that's not the point. But because, despite my persistence, I never managed to get an answer to what still remains an unanswered question: What did Howard know about the photos? Why didn't he disclose this? That was all I wanted to know.

* * *

> JACKSON: **Mr Latham has acknowledged that you're a formidable opponent. He's described you as 'wily', 'cunning' and 'tough'. How would you describe him?**
> HOWARD: **Inexperienced.**
>
> ['The Contenders', *Four Corners*, 5 October 2004]

Two years later, in 2004, we were back on the election campaign trail with Prime Minister Howard. We were in a Christian bookshop in Howard's electorate, with his now familiar press secretary, Tony O'Leary. O'Leary told me there was no way *Four Corners* would get a Howard interview unless it was on the same conditions as the last time: an uncut interview played 'as live' at the end of the show. It was just as we had feared; the interview from 'Too Good to Be False' was cited as a precedent.

I explained it wasn't possible, that that had been a one-off agreement. Furthermore it wouldn't be fair to Opposition leader Mark Latham. The discussion got loud and heated, and other journalists were listening in. O'Leary was saying, 'Well, you can't have Howard then.' I was saying that was a shame, as we were getting access to Latham for an hour and a half and so he'd be all through the show. It was typical minder-versus-media brinkmanship. The final outcome was as follows: We could have the interview with the PM, for 20 minutes. We could cut the interview into the program, but it had to be in an agreed number of unedited segments, up to a maximum of four. Deal done.

One of the major issues to be covered was the war in Iraq. Since I'd spoken with John Howard two years before, his government had sent Australian troops to fight in Iraq, in the face of opinion polls that showed the majority of Australians were opposed. Howard justified this commitment in an Address to the Nation, stressing the need to rid Iraq of its weapons of mass destruction: 'Not only is it inherently dangerous for a country such as Iraq with its appalling track record to have these weapons, but if Iraq is allowed to get away with it, other rogue States will believe they can do the same.'

By the time we did our interview it was clear to the world that Iraq had no weapons of mass destruction, and the question of when our troops would come back had become a major election issue.

JACKSON: **You told Australians that you knew that Iraq had chemical and biological weapons. Do you think it's time, now, to tell Australians you were wrong?**

HOWARD: Well, the intelligence assessments haven't been vindicated, but I made my statement based on the intelligence assessments.

JACKSON: I'm not disputing that. I'm just asking if it's time, now, to say to Australians, 'Look, looks like I was wrong.' Can you say that to them?

HOWARD: Well, the intelligence assessments have turned out to be inaccurate, and I've said that, and I don't intend to add to that.

JACKSON: You don't intend to actually say, as Tony Blair has to the British public, 'Look, I was wrong about it.'

HOWARD: I don't know —

JACKSON: Don't find — you can't come at that?

HOWARD: The most recent thing that Mr Blair has said, but I make my own decisions based on my own assessments, much and all as I like Mr Blair, irrespective of what he says —

JACKSON: Can't say, 'I was wrong on that'?

HOWARD: [Does not answer question]

'Does not answer question' is what the interview transcript records, and it's literally what happened. There was silence. John Howard simply sat there: not just declining to answer the question, declining to speak. He was displeased. It was tense as I sat and waited. Twelve seconds passed and he was still immobile and silent, so I moved on to another issue. When we put the rough cut of the show together, I included the full 12 seconds of silence. I thought it was compelling and revealed a man unable to concede an error. When the show went to air it was cut back to four seconds. The majority view, and the Executive Producer's decision, was that it stood out too much, and opened us up to a charge of bias.

Two years later, the Prime Minister and I returned to the subject of Iraq, for a show timed for broadcast five years after the terrorist attacks on 11 September 2001. Howard had been in Washington on the day and I was keen to know if he had ever thought there was any link between Iraq and 9/11. His response was meandering and evasive.

> HOWARD: Well, when something like this happens you are looking for immediate information to try and fill in the picture; you're looking for some kind of immediate explanation. I mean, I had seen President Bush the day before, and we had not talked about terrorism, and that's an indication of how unprovoked it really was. I mean, let's understand one thing very plainly — that this was the beginning of the world in which we have lived over the last five years.
> JACKSON: But can I just re-ask the question, which was did you at any time think there was any —
> HOWARD: Well, I've given you, I've given you my answer.
> JACKSON: Yes, but specifically, did you at any time think there was any link between Iraq and the attacks on 9/11?
> HOWARD: When this attack took place, as I said to you a moment ago, you look for immediate information and explanations.

For my sins I kept trying, but the ensuing exchange hit the edit room floor:

> JACKSON: At any point in the next —
> HOWARD: No, no, no, well, well I'm, you can ask that question any time, any way you like, I'm giving you my answer.
> JACKSON: Which is?
> HOWARD: The one I've just given you.
> JACKSON: Was that 'a link' or a 'no link' answer?
> HOWARD: It was the answer I gave you.

It was the classic Howard stonewall: stand by an irrelevant answer, and then act as if it's out of order for the interviewer to continue to question him on the subject. Sometimes, I concluded, the best you could do in a John Howard interview was to highlight the questions he would not answer, as a way of revealing the issues on which he could not concede he was wrong.

* * *

HOWARD: **I accept full responsibility for the Coalition's defeat.**
[John Howard's concession speech, 24 November 2007]

It needs to be said that to his credit, Prime Minister John Howard almost always agreed to be interviewed on *Four Corners*. He was generous in his praise for the show. Many other politicians — Kevin Rudd and Paul Keating come to mind — were not so amenable. The only program I was involved in where he refused to take part was the last major show we made about him, 'Howard's End'. It went to air in early 2008, after John Howard lost not only the 2007 election but his own seat of Bennelong — a humiliating outcome. He spoke to no media outlets at the time.

On election night we were at the Wentworth Hotel in Sydney, and by 9pm the result was clear. We waited ready to film Howard arriving to give his concession speech. He appeared, riding up the elevator, a fixed smile on his face, his wife, Janette, by his side, and strode head high into the ballroom. The crowd of supporters closed in on him as he made his way to the podium, past the banner which said 'JOHN HOWARD FOREVER', where the 'A' in Howard was a love heart. Voices called from the throng, 'We love you, John ... we love you, Johnny.' He raised his arms and lowered them, to hush the crowd.

Men and women wept as he spoke about how much the job had meant to him, the honour and the privilege of leading the country for so long. He ended by assuming responsibility for the devastating election loss, but as a captain who goes down with his ship, not as the man whose inability to let go of the leadership had cost his party so dearly. As he stepped down the chanting started, 'How-ard, How-ard.' He circled the room for nearly an hour accepting accolades, consolation and homage. One senior Liberal woman appeared to kiss his hand. His supporters comforted and embraced each other, as if they were at a funeral. There were trays of champagne and I took a glass, but quickly and awkwardly put it back. There were pointed hostile looks, as if to say, 'You think there is something to celebrate?' Some people were drunk by now and getting aggressive. Several were looking at the journalists around and muttering, 'You're to blame.' It was unclear whether this was directed at the media generally, the ABC or *Four Corners*.

* * *

Postscript: John Howard and I did meet again when I interviewed him for a *Four Corners* profile of new Liberal leader Tony Abbott. Howard, private citizen, was still wary. I always found him so. He treated the interview as before — like an innings of cricket, where controlling the play, holding your ground and winning is what it's about. I remain of the view that accountability is what it's really all about, and that no one ever died from being asked a question, even five times.

'The Network' (2002). The story that changed a life: Sally Neighbour on the trail of Al Qaeda in Bali, Indonesia.

12
'THAT AWFUL BLOODY PROGRAM'

by Sally Neighbour

It was early 1996 when I fronted up at the ABC's rambling Sydney headquarters for my first day at *Four Corners*. Paul Keating was in his last few weeks as Prime Minister, John Howard was storming towards the Lodge, and I was just back from a three-year posting in Hong Kong and Beijing as ABC TV's Asia correspondent. I would have been feeling fairly pleased with myself as I announced my arrival to the ABC's commissionaire, as the guy on the front desk was grandly known, accompanied by my partner, journalist Michael Doyle. I figured I had come a long way since my first TV job as a news reporter at GLV8 in Traralgon, Victoria, and a subsequent stint at Channel 10's *Good Morning Australia*, where my assignments included a live cross to an attempt to make the world's longest sausage and a report on a new pet boutique, where I paraded my friend's bull terrier in and out of the dressing room in a succession of ridiculous outfits.

'We're starting today at *Four Corners* and *Lateline*,' I announced to the commissionaire.

'Are you here for work experience?' he enquired.

I might as well have been. As an ABC TV foreign correspondent, I was already accustomed to relentless deadlines, gruelling hours and Third World working conditions. But the work ethic at *Four Corners* was something else again. Executive Producer John Budd had a sofa in his office which doubled as a bed for whichever reporter, producer or editor needed to snatch the odd hour's sleep as they worked, sometimes around the clock, to get their programs to air on a Monday night. 'You're only as good as your last story' was a phrase I heard very soon after I arrived, and often over the years.

The legendary programs of the 1980s — like Chris Masters' 'The Big League', Tony Jones's 'Horses for Courses' and Paul Barry's 'Bondy's Bounty' — had set the bar so high it was almost impossible to reach. But reaching it was what we were there for; if you couldn't, there was no guarantee you would last at the program. Two reporters — both fine journalists and popular, hard-working, dedicated staff members — had just been sacked; another two would be dismissed later that year.

The social documentaries which had been *Four Corners*' specialty in its early years were now out of fashion (to the program's cost, some would argue); hard-hitting investigative exposés were expected. There wasn't time for much office camaraderie, except for the occasional post-program Tuesday lunch (and, as I would later learn, the Christmas party, which generally wound up in some grimy pub in Oxford Street at about 4am). The pressure to find a story and then get it to air to meet the preset deadline was intense. I was horrified to learn that reporters were assigned air dates before they even had topics to fill them. Once you had a story, the working title would appear on Budd's whiteboard next to your name and date; if you hadn't found one, there would instead be the initials FBH, which stood for 'fucking black hole'.

When I joined, *Four Corners* was fighting to keep its coveted 45 minutes and its Monday night slot from 8.30 to 9.15, which it had occupied since the early '80s. Ratings were in the doldrums; some media commentator had written an article headlined, as I recall it, 'Has *Four Corners* lost its edge?', a perennial question asked about the ABC's much-vaunted flagship. A show like *Four Corners* will inevitably have its quiet patches, but too many months without making front-page headlines, snaring awards or prompting government inquiries, and the questioning starts again. Has *Four Corners* passed its use-by date? Should it be cut back, dumped or relegated to a late-night time slot?

Also at play were long-running tensions between the powerful News and Current Affairs department (known as NewsCaff), and the omnipotent Television department, which controls scheduling. Often throughout the ABC's history, Television has felt NewsCaff has had too much influence, resources and air time, and has pushed to shift the balance to more impoverished program departments such as Drama, Comedy and Documentaries. Budd had resisted the move to encroach on his turf, but the message was clear: perform or lose your prime-time slot and your precious 45 minutes. The tensions were further exacerbated by the knowledge that John Howard's Liberal–National coalition was on its way into government, intent on bringing the recalcitrant national broadcaster into line, and budget cuts loomed.

In truth, none of this bothered me much. Like the rest of the journalistic staff I was fixated on filling the dreaded FBH next to my name on the whiteboard, and content to let management deal with loftier concerns like budgets, scheduling and the future of the program.

I quickly figured out what I wanted to do as my first story. Returning from abroad to my hometown Melbourne, I'd been struck by the inexorable growth of the city's new landmark, Crown Casino, which now dominated the skyline, and by the cosy relationship between Premier Jeff Kennett's Liberal government and the casino's proprietors, Hudson Conway, run by Kennett's friends: businessman Lloyd Williams and his partner, Ron Walker, who was also federal treasurer of the Liberal Party. Championed by Kennett as 'a beacon of light in this state's revival', the casino had been exempted from normal planning laws and had doubled in size since being approved. The casino contract had proven a veritable licence to print money; Walker, Williams and their partner Kerry Packer had already made a combined profit of more than $500 million on their casino shares.

There were questions being asked about whether the casino tender had been independent, fair and free of political influence. Rival tenderers were claiming information about their bids had been leaked to Crown. There were also questions about whether Hudson Conway was 'of good repute' as required under the Casino Control Act, having recently been found liable in the Federal Court for deceptive and misleading conduct over an earlier property transaction, and being subject to an ongoing investigation by the Victoria Police Fraud Squad over yet another deal.

Embarking on the story brought us into immediate conflict with Kennett, who, since his landslide election win in 1992, had adopted a policy of unbridled contempt towards the media outlets he considered most inimical to his government: the *Age* newspaper — which had lampooned him as a 'buffoon' 13 days into his premiership and which he in turn had reviled as 'absolute crap' — and the ABC. Kennett's policy, from a journalist's perspective, was to deflect scrutiny by attacking the media, discrediting individual journalists, continually claiming political bias and boycotting the outlets he considered hostile while favouring those that gave him an easy run. It seemed to me that through sheer tactical aggression, Kennett had succeeded in cowing elements of the media into submission.

'The Crown Deals' was a typical *Four Corners* 'big dig'. Producer Mark Maley and I spent weeks reading everything we could find that had been written about Crown, including hundreds of pages of court transcripts and company records, and ringing everyone who knew anything about the casino, which meant speaking to about 200 people. It's a laborious and tedious task: ringing dozens of wrong phone numbers before finding the right one; knocking, after hours, on the doors of strangers who, not surprisingly, often close them in your face; trying to persuade people that it's in some amorphous 'public interest' for them to give you information, when they could face punishment for doing so. As is so often the case, there were plenty of people prepared to talk off the record but none willing to go public, given the powerful connections of the casino operators. The other obstacle we faced was the sweeping secrecy provisions in the Casino Control Act, which made it a criminal offence to divulge any information about 'the establishment or development' of the casino. Some of the insiders we spoke to had been explicitly warned they would face criminal sanctions if they spoke out.

Midway through our research we got the break we were looking for when we found a former staffer of a key government agency who, amazingly, was willing to talk. And her account was explosive. 'M' (I am still bound by my promise to protect her identity) told us that during the tender for the casino, government ministers had been given regular briefings on the rival bids. She described how she had personally on several occasions placed this information in sealed envelopes to be sent to the members of a certain Cabinet sub-committee. The revelation was a bombshell, directly contradicting Premier Kennett's insistence in parliament that 'the government [had] no knowledge of the content of the bids, nor [did] it seek that information'. Even better, M was willing to go on camera.

But our jubilation quickly evaporated when we consulted the ABC lawyers about the forthcoming interview, in one of the numerous legal sessions that always precede such a contentious program. The head of the legal department, the eminent Judith Walker, believed we were ethically bound to advise M of the clause in the Casino Control Act which exposed her to a possible criminal conviction and a fine of up to $5000 if she breached the secrecy clause. I admit now with some embarrassment that I was aghast at having to let ethics get in the way of such a great story. I knew without having asked that M must not be aware of the criminal sanction and that if we told her she wouldn't go ahead with the interview. Surely we were not obliged to tell her, I argued. Surely it was up to her to weigh up the implications of talking to us. To her credit, not mine, Judith prevailed. I informed M of the risk, and she pulled out of the interview. She did, however, allow us to use her as an anonymous 'inside source'. And she also agreed — again at the request of the lawyers — that in the event of legal action being taken over our report, she would appear in court as a witness to support us. Without this assurance, the lawyers indicated they would not allow the information to be aired.

The pre-show legal dramas took a new turn at 4pm on Monday 18 March 1996, a few hours before 'The Crown Deals' was due to go to air, when a fax arrived at the *Four Corners* office from the Commonwealth Director of Public Prosecutions. The DPP was seeking an injunction to prevent the show being broadcast because it contained a 30-second reference to a person associated with the casino who was due to stand trial on unrelated charges in Victoria. At 5pm, three and a half hours before air time, the ABC lawyers were in court fighting to get the program approved. When *Four Corners* agreed to delete the offending 30 seconds, the injunction bid was dropped.

Kennett's response to 'The Crown Deals' was colourful even by his own rhetorical standards. He blasted *Four Corners* as 'a great leech sucking the blood out of society', asserting that our program was the result of 'months' of work by 'dozens' of people, at a cost of 'hundreds of thousands of dollars' to the taxpayer. (We calculated it cost about $15,000 excluding staff wages and the use of ABC production facilities.) The program prompted a senate inquiry into Crown. The Kennett government, however, refused to cooperate with the inquiry, which caused the senate committee to eventually abandon its public hearings and recommend a full judicial inquiry or Royal Commission, 'enabling issues relating to probity and the confidentiality of the tendering process to be investigated'. No such inquiry was ever held. Apparently Victorian voters were unfazed; on 30 March 1996 Kennett was re-elected with a 32-seat majority.

The following year we took on Premier Kennett again to examine his family's share dealings in a company called Guangdong Corporation, which had been the first Chinese firm to list on the Australian Stock Exchange. Majority-owned by China's richest provincial government and spruiked as 'an investment vehicle for you to share in the growth of China', it had been one of the hottest floats of the year in 1993. Kennett and his wife, Felicity, had snapped up 50,000 shares, several days after an announcement to the market that due to overwhelming demand the company was 'unlikely to accept any further application for shares'. The investment had been revealed by Channel 7's *Today Tonight* in a report which was temporarily — and sensationally — pulled from going to air in May 1996 after Kennett phoned the station in a rage just before it was due to be broadcast.

When *Four Corners* asked the Premier for an interview and then submitted a series of written questions, Kennett's office responded in characteristic style: 'We do not wish to be interviewed by the *Four Corners* program, or answer the inane questions you supplied, as the ABC continues to justify its appalling bias and waste of public money.'

In the absence of an interview, broadcaster Neil Mitchell allowed us to film in his studio at 3AW during his weekly session with the Premier. Kennett walked in with an airy greeting to Mitchell's crew — 'Good morning, team; are you all well?' — then spotted our camera. 'We have an intruder. Do we not have an intruder?' he demanded. Mitchell told him it was the ABC, then Kennett turned on the hapless ABC cameraman who'd been seconded for the job.

KENNETT: **ABC? Is this for local ABC, or is it for that awful bloody program? Who are you working for?**

CAMERAMAN: [deliberately mumbles] ABC.
KENNETT: Yeah, which part of the ABC?
CAMERAMAN: [almost incoherent] 4 Cs.
KENNETT: Who?
CAMERAMAN: 4 Cs.
KENNETT: Four Corners. This is this what's-her-name's program …

As the camera rolled, Kennett fumed, 'I think I'd close the bloody ABC; it's a waste of time,' then sat down at the microphone with Mitchell and continued his attack on air:

> It's come to my attention in the last few weeks that Sally Neighbour, who runs a lot of what I call distasteful programs on the ABC, inasmuch as they're all negative and they're very personal, is putting together a program on our five years in office, which comes in October. You can expect from Sally Neighbour an hour of slime.

Kennett's 'hour of slime' punchline (notwithstanding my protestations that it was only 45 minutes) was incorporated into a promo, aired ahead of the program, which director Janie Lalor reckoned was one of the best *Four Corners* ever had. It certainly didn't hurt the ratings.

Kennett's campaign against us continued with a letter to the ABC's Managing Director in which he accused us of 'stalking' the boss of the underwriter Sino Securities, Richard Li, who had approved his shares. The complaint followed our visit to Mr Li's home in suburban Melbourne, where we had set up our camera on the footpath outside, and producer Janine Cohen had gone to the door and told him we were there to get footage of him for *Four Corners* and would stay as long as it took. What Kennett considered 'stalking', we thought was a reasonable approach to getting the pictures we required.

The big break came this time when Kennett's former press secretary, Stephen Mayne (later of *Crikey* fame), agreed to go on camera and reveal the inside account of how Kennett had obtained his shares.

> MAYNE: **Jeff came around and asked if I'd heard about this Chinese company that was floating [and] he said, 'Oh, I want to get into this Chinese company, I think it's gonna be a good investment ... The shares are hard to get,' and you know, all the signs were, he was saying, that, it was going to be a good thing to get into.**

Mayne described how he was with Kennett in his office when the Premier rang Richard Li to ask about the float and request 100,000 shares. He ended up with 50,000, issued to his wife.

> MAYNE: **He came around three or four days later, I think, and he was very excited, and he told me that as it turned out he got an extra 30,000, or Felicity got an extra 30,000 shares.**

When the company debuted a week later, almost a million shares changed hands and the price climbed from 78 cents to $1.15, giving the Kennetts a paper profit of $18,000 after a single day's trading. Kennett hosted an official reception for the company's directors at Parliament House and joined them at a fancy Melbourne restaurant that night to toast their success.

Mayne's revelations were dynamite. We were sure we had a great story. But the ABC's lawyers were not so impressed. After we screened the 'rough cut' of the program, their verdict was, 'You can't run this. It's defamatory.'

The lawyers were understandably jumpy. A few months earlier we had aired a show called 'Packer's Power', about Australia's richest man, Kerry Packer, focusing on his successful push to win control of the Sydney casino and his bid to take over the Fairfax newspaper group. Packer had sued for defamation, with what was widely seen as a 'stop writ' to prevent other media reporting on his activities. The case would drag on for six years, until it was settled at Packer's instigation in 2003, when the ABC released a statement saying, 'The ABC has accepted a proposal put forward by Mr Kerry Packer to settle his defamation action over a 1997 Four Corners program, *Packer's Power*. After six years, this legal action is now concluded.' In the end, the ABC decided to pay Packer a token sum in order to end a case that had already cost it a small fortune and would cost very much more if it continued to trial.

Although I could see the financial rationale, I was appalled by this decision. I had a strong urge to resign in protest, but was pacified when these crucial lines were included in the ABC's statement: 'The ABC continues to stand by the program, which was an important investigation into casino licensing and business transactions involving companies associated with Mr Packer. The ABC makes no apology for the broadcast and does not retract any of its content.'

All this was yet to play out back in 1997 when the lawyers were vetting our exposé on the Kennetts' share dealings ahead of its broadcast. But with one major defamation case looming, they were loathe to risk another. Hence their advice that we should not run this.

I was shocked. The fact that a piece of journalism is defamatory doesn't automatically mean it can't run. Investigative journalists publish stories that damage people's reputations all the time. The decision on whether to publish is a calculated risk which takes into account the truth of the allegations, the level of public interest, the likelihood of the person suing and whether they will persist, the strength of the evidence obtained by the journalists, and their efforts to corroborate it. The burden of proof can be extremely high because what journalists end up having to defend, at least in some jurisdictions, is not what they actually report but the imputations that arise from it.

The lawyers' view in this case was that the Kennett shares story would be simply too hard to defend.

But Mark Maley and I weren't willing to accept that as the final word, and nor was our EP, John Budd. So we set out to re-make the program, switching the focus from Kennett's personal behaviour to the style of governance in Victoria. We called it 'Kennett's Culture', and summarised it in the program précis: 'We examine the political culture that's grown under his rule and a state that is run like a business [and] investigate questions over the Kennett family's share dealings, intimidation of the media and the growing reputation of Victoria as a "mate's state", where favourable deals are made with businessmen close to the government.' We got it to air in September 1997. No one sued.

* * *

My run-ins with Jeff Kennett in Victoria were trifling compared with the battles being fought between the ABC and the new Howard government in Canberra. Three weeks after Howard became Prime Minister in March 1996, the government announced a restructure of the ABC board, abolishing the role of staff-elected director (later reinstated) 'in line with modern principles of corporate governance'. A few months later, it slashed about $60 million from the ABC budget.

In July, Howard appointed his friend the Liberal Party loyalist and Opera Australia CEO Donald McDonald as Chairman of the ABC. Staff were horrified; their apprehension borne out when McDonald gave a personal public endorsement of Howard during the 1998 federal election campaign. Over the years, however, McDonald would emerge as a staunch champion of the national broadcaster, lauded by some as the most independent Chairman the ABC has had.

There was much less affection for the succession of ABC directors appointed during the Howard years, such as arch-conservative historian and cultural warrior Keith Windschuttle, News Limited columnist and vociferous ABC detractor Janet Albrechtsen, Liberal Party powerbroker Michael Kroger and Queensland anthropologist and 'ideological zealot' (in the words of then Shadow Communications Minister Lindsay Tanner) Ron Brunton. Political stacking of the ABC board was by no means new; the Whitlam government had replaced the entire board, and governments before and since then have sought to mould the board to suit their own ideological bent. Seldom, however, have new appointees been so palpably hostile to the organisation they are being tasked with helping to run.

But the most controversial appointment in the Howard era was that of a little-known Australian-born former Baltic TV executive, Jonathan Shier, to the role of Managing Director in January 1999. Shier's ascension — famously marked by an address to staff in which he pranced about with a microphone crowing, 'I've got the gig' — ushered in three years of chaotic management, indiscriminate hiring and firing, falling ratings, and the dumping of popular shows such as *Quantum* and *Media Watch*, later restored by popular demand.

For *Four Corners*, the nadir of Shier's reign came with his intervention in the broadcast of the program 'Party Tricks', made by reporter Andrew Fowler, producer Quentin McDermott and researcher Peter Cronau in 2001. The program documented how a disgruntled businessman with a grudge against the Commonwealth Bank worked with senior Liberal Party figures to unearth bank documents of dodgy provenance that were used to attack former Prime Minister Paul Keating over his investment in a Hunter Valley piggery. The show was potentially damaging for the Howard government as it named the NSW Cabinet Secretary, Senator Bill Heffernan, and former Liberal Party president Tony Staley and reported that $18,000 had been laundered through Indonesia to pay for allegedly stolen Supreme Court documents used to discredit Keating.

Like all *Four Corners* programs with potential legal ramifications, 'Party Tricks' had been scrupulously vetted by the ABC lawyers and independent counsel and approved for broadcast on 16 July 2001. But Shier, himself a former Liberal Party staffer, pulled the plug, announcing he wanted yet another legal opinion before the program could air. The decision caused uproar. Staff were outraged and Opposition Leader Kim Beazley declared, 'The political independence of the ABC is on trial.' The lobby group Friends of the ABC said it was more evidence the board had become politicised. Donald McDonald retorted that the only political pressure was coming from the Opposition, the Friends and the unions, and insisted 'these decisions are made free of political pressure'. Three days later, after getting another legal opinion, Shier announced that 'Party Tricks' would go to air the following week, stating, 'I am satisfied that all the relevant issues have been addressed [and] that all reasonable steps have been taken by *Four Corners* to verify the accuracy of information contained in the program and to corroborate every allegation.' The director of News and Current Affairs, Max Uechtritz, added, 'The story has not been diluted or diminished in any way.'

Shier's intervention ensured that 'Party Tricks' was the highest rating *Four Corners* of the year. The *Sydney Morning Herald* reported that the alleged theft of Supreme Court documents revealed in the program had been referred to the NSW Police and the Independent Commission Against Corruption.

Three weeks later, on the night of Sunday 12 August, 600 people — including pioneers Bob Raymond, Michael Charlton and John Penlington — crammed into a cavernous TV studio at Gore Hill to commemorate *Four Corners*' 40th anniversary. It was the closest the ABC gets to putting on a glittering occasion, and it felt like high time for a celebration after a year and a half of internal ructions under Shier. (I had missed part of it, having taken maternity leave in 1999 for the birth of my son, Oscar, then moved to *Lateline* for a brief stint as a presenter before returning to *Four Corners* in 2000.) Executive Producer Bruce Belsham, who steered the program through that whole fraught era, employed his best diplomatic skills in the speech he delivered to an audience that included Chairman Donald McDonald and MD Shier:

> *Four Corners* **is a program that will always throw up stories that embarrass influential people and institutions. It's the nature of the beast … And our kind of program can never be comfortable for senior managers or the ABC board … But the hallmark of any good public broadcaster has to be courage and a willingness to be disliked from time to time, and a willingness to fight for good journalism.**

Later in the evening, *Four Corners* researcher Linda Larsen and producer Quentin McDermott, who produced 'Party Tricks', introduced themselves to Shier. An Englishman whose exquisite manners can be deceptive, McDermott asked Shier what he had thought of the program. Shier responded that he thought it had been a 'non-event' in which the Australian public wasn't interested (despite the high ratings) and that 'heads would roll' if the allegations in it didn't stand up. The encounter became heated when Shier called McDermott, according to the latter's record of the conversation, 'the stupidest producer he had ever come across in his entire career' and said he would be speaking to his boss. Before storming off, Shier rebuked Larsen for having introduced them and told them, 'You have ruined my evening.'

But Shier's evening wasn't quite over. Liz Jackson, who had witnessed the encounter, decided to find out what was going on. So she confronted the rattled MD, introduced herself, and announced that 'as a journalist' she felt obliged to ask him what the argument had been about. Still angry, Shier fumed that he would 'not stand for' the likes of McDermott contradicting him 'just to impress the blonde' (a reference to Larsen), that McDermott's rudeness was not acceptable, and 'he would not be around the ABC corridors for much longer'.

In fact, it was Shier's days that were numbered. Two months later, to the enormous relief of ABC staff and supporters, his departure was announced in a statement from ABC Corporate Affairs. He had finally lost the support of the board, although in the ABC's time-honoured tradition of giving face to people it is sacking, the statement announced: 'The Chairman of the ABC, Mr Donald McDonald AO, thanked Mr Shier for his services to the Corporation' and so on. The *Australian*'s media writer, Amanda Meade, was much closer to the mark when she wrote, 'Personal style aside, Shier's restructure was chaotic and wasteful, and produced little of broadcasting quality and a historic slide in ratings.' For years afterwards when people would ask, 'How are things at the ABC?' my standard reply was, 'Compared with the Shier era, things are just fine.'

* * *

Towards the end of 2001, an event occurred that eclipsed the ABC's internal tumult and re-focused our attention on events further afield. The terrorist attacks of 11 September 2001 were followed a year later by the Bali bombings of 12 October 2002, which killed 202 people, including 88 Australians. For me personally it was the latter atrocity that proved more momentous, sending me on a personal journey that would occupy much of the next nine years, taking me from Bali through Southeast Asia on the trail of the Indonesian terrorist group Jemaah Islamiyah (JI), to the torture prisons of Egypt and the dusty streets of Kabul, Afghanistan, where it had all, in a sense, begun.

On the morning of 13 October 2002, I was preparing to board a plane in Kuala Lumpur with *Four Corners* producer Morag Ramsay, cameraman Neale Maude and sound recordist Jerry Rickard, when the phone rang. It was the *Four Corners* office in Sydney. There had been an explosion in Bali, I was told, and two nightclubs had been destroyed; the cause was unclear, it might have been a gas main. The Department of Foreign Affairs was saying two Australians were confirmed dead, about 40 injured and 'a large number' remained missing.

As it happened, we were on the trail already. My friend Margot O'Neill, a reporter at *Lateline*, had been at me to investigate a mysterious Indonesian group, JI, which was led by a little-known cleric, Abu Bakar Ba'asyir. The previous December, two months after 9/11, authorities in Singapore had uncovered a plot by the group to conduct a series of bombings aimed at targets that were said to include the Australian High Commission. Detained suspects had named Ba'asyir as their ringleader, and there was talk of connections to Osama bin Laden and Al Qaeda. At first I was sceptical. Police and intelligence agencies in the highly policed island state were notorious for exaggerating security threats to help justify draconian laws which allowed for indefinite detention without trial. But I needed a subject to fill my looming 'FBH', and this one seemed worth investigating.

By the time I got the phone call on the morning after the Bali bombings, we were on our way from KL to Jakarta to interview Sidney Jones, an analyst from the International Crisis Group, who knew more than anyone about JI. She believed the group was the most likely suspect behind the bombings, although it would take months for Australian and Indonesian police to gather the evidence to prove it. Suddenly our assignment took on a new urgency. We took the next available flight to Denpasar and drove straight to Kuta Beach, the site of the demolished Sari Club and Paddy's Bar.

Sometimes, years later, when so much has been written and said about an event, it can be hard to summon an authentic memory of it. What I do recall strongly is the deathly silence as the four of us tramped down Jalan Legian towards the bomb site, the road having been closed to traffic. Barely 24 hours after such a catastrophe, I had expected there would still be wailing sirens, earth-movers digging through rubble under searchlights, weeping relatives waiting for news of loved ones. But there was nothing; just blackness (the lights were out) and the sound of glass and rubble being trodden under our feet. The streets were strewn with smashed glass — it seemed every pane for hundreds of metres around had shattered — and, as we got closer, splintered bits of timber, corrugated iron, discarded thongs and sandals. The other thing I remember is the smell, the foul stench of burned remains. The bomb site was deserted. The structures of thatch, timber and corrugated iron had been so flimsy they had crumpled and burned to cinders. The bodies and the charred survivors had already been removed.

Next we headed to Denpasar's Sanglah Hospital, where the scene could not have been more different: open-air corridors with rows of bodies, dozens of them, covered in sheets; a room which one of my colleagues glimpsed briefly, containing a pile of limbs; wards like those in a war zone, with burned survivors hooked up to drips, comforted by friends clearly in shock. A footy player from the Coogee Dolphins, Eric de Haart, was searching for his mates, six of whom he would soon learn had died. Another enduring memory is of a nurses' station filled with apparently ill-trained young women in starched white uniforms, who stood or sat idle, sometimes giggling, utterly at a loss over what to do, while volunteers from Australia and other foreign countries tended the wards.

From the hospital we drove to Denpasar airport, where a fleet of Australian Defence Force Hercules had begun ferrying injured Australians to burns units in Darwin and Perth. Dozens of people were lined up on gurneys on the airstrip awaiting evacuation. We managed to talk our way into the airport, only to be bailed up by Indonesian soldiers who stopped us filming and escorted us off the tarmac, ignoring my furious protests.

It was 3 or 4am by the time we finished filming and returned to our hotel to grab a couple of hours' sleep before heading off the next day to Solo in Central Java, to track down the JI leader Abu Bakar Ba'asyir, now suspect number one.

People often ask how journalists are affected by the scenes they witness, such as those we saw that night. It seems inadequate now, but all I remember feeling was dazed from tiredness and sensorial overload, and emotionally anaesthetised by the adrenalin that keeps you going on an assignment like this.

Our report, 'The Network', which aired on 28 October 2002, was the first of a series on the terrorists who had set their sights on Australia. We returned the following January to make 'The Bali Confessions', a forensic reconstruction based on the accounts of the bombers. Other programs followed: 'The Australian Connections' in June 2003 and 'Still at Large', on the bombers who had evaded capture, in November 2003.

Terrorism would remain an enduring preoccupation for the world, Australia, *Four Corners* and me, for the decade that followed. But as the years passed and the abuses perpetrated in the name of the 'war on terror' became ever more apparent, the story and our approach to it changed. I became less fixated on the terrorists and more intrigued by the personal stories of those who had joined their cause, like Australians Jack Thomas and Mamdouh Habib, who were both arrested in Pakistan after 9/11 over their links to Al Qaeda. While sharing the horror felt by most Australians at the atrocities, I came to admire the profound conviction of some of the people attracted to the Islamist cause. The fact that Jack Thomas was re-tried on terrorism charges as a result of the interviews he gave to me and *Four Corners* in 2005 and 2006 caused me deep distress. I had got to know Thomas, his wife and children quite well in the year we spent filming with them on and off, and felt personally responsible, having prevailed upon him to do the interview, for the fact that it resulted in him facing trial.

Thankfully he was acquitted of the terrorism charges, which were always flimsy.

By 2008 I was reporting on the growing revulsion over the United States' use of torture against terror suspects, and the Australian government's complicity in Mamdouh Habib's incommunicado detention and torture in Egypt and so-called 'rendition' to Guantanamo Bay. It was stories like these that eventually persuaded me that the tactics used by the supposed good guys in the war on terror were as evil in their own way as those used by the terrorists. My last report for *Four Corners* was 'Good Cop Bad Cop' in October 2008, which documented the excesses of Australia's leading counterterrorism agency, the Federal Police.

Well, not quite last. You see, leaving *Four Corners* is one of the hardest things a journalist can do — apart from working for it — simply because there is no better job in journalism in Australia. I personally know nowhere else where journalists are given the time, resources and support to produce tough, consistent, incisive, investigative public affairs reporting, week after week.

After three years as a freelance print journalist, I returned to *Four Corners* in 2011 to work with producer Peter Cronau, researcher Anne Worthington and reporter Nick McKenzie from the *Age* on an exposé of human trafficking and sexual servitude in Australia. 'Sex Slavery' went to air on 6 October 2011.

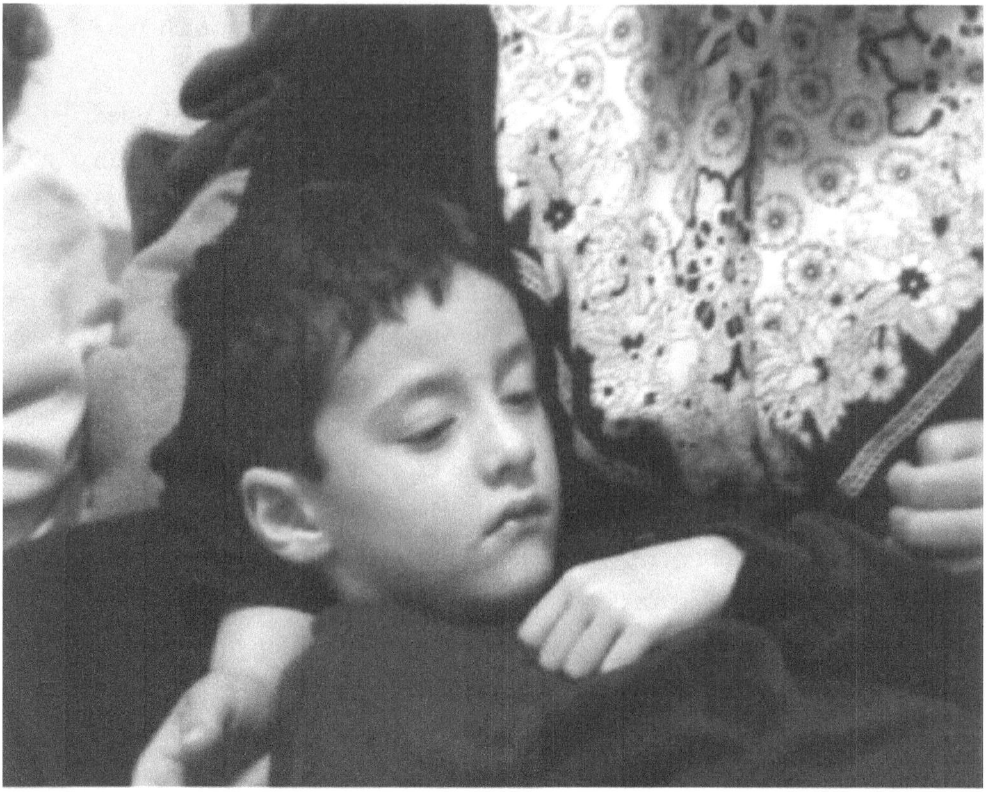

'The Inside Story' (2001). Debbie Whitmont's smuggled images of Villawood detention centre uncovered a heartbreaking tale. Shayan Badraie, a six-year-old Iranian boy held behind bars, channelled his trauma and despair into an illustration (below).

13

REPORTING FROM ANOTHER COUNTRY: STORIES ABOUT ASYLUM SEEKERS

by Debbie Whitmont

The 1961 census, held the year *Four Corners* was born, recorded that more than 90 per cent of Australians considered themselves British. In keeping with the times, *Four Corners*' first presenter, Michael Charlton, spoke with a plummy English accent. By coincidence, he and his family lived in the same block of flats as I did. The first time I heard the *Four Corners* theme music, I was in the flat downstairs playing with Michael Charlton's children. It never occurred to me that, years later, I'd be working on *Four Corners* myself.

I didn't realise, either, that my own family, who had fled wars in Europe, was part of a minority in Australia. Or that the most disturbing stories I would report for *Four Corners* would be about a new wave of immigrants and the way they were treated.

By 2001, as *Four Corners* was getting ready for its 40th birthday, Australia's cultural diversity was a trademark. That year's census found one in every five Australians had been born overseas. Back then, the World Trade Center was still standing, a Norwegian freighter called the *Tampa* hadn't yet appeared on the horizon and Australia was still basking in the glow of the successful 2000 Olympics. Few Australians knew that while preparations for the Olympics had been going on in Sydney, asylum seekers were being beaten with batons in nearby Villawood detention centre.

Divisive as the asylum-seeker debate remains, it's hard to overstate the fear and anger that gripped the nation in 2001. From a few hundred arrivals a year, the number of asylum seekers entering Australia by boat — then routinely called 'illegals' and 'queue jumpers' — had suddenly swelled to thousands. Immigration detention centres were bursting at the seams. Reports of riots and fires in the centres only hardened the popular view, supported by the media and both sides of politics, that 'boat people' weren't wanted in Australia.

At the time, I had other concerns. I was about to go back to work after taking maternity leave. *Four Corners*, with its long hours and often gruelling workload, isn't exactly a family-friendly work environment and I didn't know how I would manage with two small children. Luckily, as it turned out, my partner, Peter McEvoy, who had been the Executive Producer of the ABC's *Media Watch*, had transferred to *Four Corners* after *Media Watch* was axed under Managing Director Jonathan Shier. Peter and I arranged to work together, to help juggle child care.

Often, the hardest part of working on *Four Corners* is deciding on a story. Some stories, about big events or important people, are obvious. Others come from viewers or tip-offs. But sometimes, the idea begins with simple curiosity. In this case, I was intrigued by a piece in the *Good Weekend* magazine's 'The Two of Us' column about the friendship between Zachary Steel, a clinical psychologist, and Dr Aamer Sultan, an asylum seeker. The two had collaborated on a damning study of the mental health of asylum seekers which had been published in the respected medical journal *The Lancet*. It was a rare glimpse behind the razor wire. But what particularly interested me was that Dr Sultan was an Iraqi.

I'd been the ABC's Middle East correspondent, had lived in Jordan and travelled a number of times to what was then Saddam Hussein's Iraq. I knew Iraqi doctors were well trained and that escaping the country would have been difficult and dangerous. I wondered why Dr Sultan had been held so long in detention.

I found out later that immigration officials, who seemed to have very little information about Iraq, had simply chosen not to believe Dr Sultan and had refused him a refugee visa. But because there were sanctions against Saddam Hussein's regime, he couldn't be sent back and had been left indefinitely in detention. Locked up in Villawood, he'd found nearly all his fellow detainees were suffering severe depression and had tried to help them. After two years, he was overwhelmed and exhausted.

Both Aamer Sultan and the Refugee Action Group, who were in contact with a number of detainees, told us they were most worried about one Iranian family detained in Villawood. The Badraies, with their young son and baby daughter, had spent 11 months in Woomera detention centre during its most violent riots. Their six-year-old son, Shayan Badraie, had witnessed guards hitting his father and seen other detainees threatening or attempting to take their own lives.

As a result, Shayan had become so traumatised he'd stopped eating, drinking and even speaking. Consequently the family had been transferred to Villawood and, after two months in Westmead Hospital, Shayan had begun to recover. But as soon as he was sent back to Villawood, Shayan became ill again. By mid-2001, he was being hospitalised every four or five days, to be rehydrated and fed through a drip. On top of that, it was feared Shayan's father was about to be sent back to Iran.

At first, it seemed impossible to tell Shayan's story on *Four Corners*. The media was — and still is — totally banned from Australian detention centres. Even if we could tell viewers what was happening to Shayan Badraie, how could we prove it? And what if our questions meant his father was deported? A 45-minute *Four Corners* program needs people and pictures, and we had neither. Surprisingly, a few days later, it seemed that although we couldn't get into Villawood, part of Villawood might come to us.

In mid-July 2001, 46 detainees broke out of Villawood in two mass escapes. The first problem was how to find them, the second was that talking to them would almost certainly mean breaking the law. The government had recently increased the penalty for helping or hiding an escapee to ten years in jail or a $10,000 fine.

Our interview with two of the Villawood escapees, at the end of a very long night which began at a Sydney railway station, was probably the most surreal experience of my life. I'd secretly interviewed wanted terrorists in places like Beirut and Gaza, but I never thought I'd be sneaking around Sydney risking imprisonment to meet people who had come to my own home country seeking asylum. And until then, I wouldn't have believed that what I heard that night could have been allowed to happen here in Australia.

The two escapees we met told us that a group of detainees had spent nearly two months digging their way out of Villawood — from a hole in the floor under a carpet in a room used as a mosque, down two metres to the drains and through about a dozen sets of new gratings the Immigration Minister had recently shown off to the media as an anti-escape measure. Their escape was the stuff of a POW adventure. They'd drawn a map and rostered escapees to leave in small groups. It had taken nearly an hour to crawl along the muddy airless drainpipes to the other side of the razor wire.

The two men told us they'd emerged in suburban Villawood muddy and terrified. 'Mohssen', a 28-year-old Iranian, said he had joined the escape at the last minute: 'For me, the end of the road was deportation, so I decided to escape.' The second man, 'Stefan', from Algeria, had been the last to leave. He'd had to cut a fence to reach the mosque, which had set off an alarm.

But it was what the two told us about Villawood detention centre that was most disturbing. Until then there'd been very few reports from inside the detention centres and neither Peter McEvoy nor I had ever heard anything like the descriptions we were given that night of life in detention.

The conditions — a dormitory shared by 60 people, newcomers sleeping on the floor, boredom, constant identity checks and no exercise facilities — were one thing. But the despair was another. Mohssen said he knew two Iranians who'd tried to kill themselves. He'd seen one of them carried away on a blood-soaked stretcher.

Zachary Steel, the clinical psychologist, later told us he believed the people in Australia's detention centres were among the most traumatised on the planet: the horrors they had fled compounded by their experience in Australian detention. More than a decade later, it could still be true.

'When you are at Villawood you ask yourself, "Why am I here — why?",' said Mohssen. 'Maybe it's a crime because I came to this country? Because I applied for a protection visa? ... To tell you the truth, sometimes I tell you that I am not in Australia. Maybe I am not. Maybe I am in another country.'

I always expected we'd get into trouble — once the program aired — for interviewing the escapees. But the police didn't knock on our door. Maybe it was because the program included something much more controversial.

After meeting the escapees, we became convinced that somehow we had to see the inside of Villawood and show what was happening. Using a mobile phone the detainees had hidden in the grounds, Peter spoke to Aamer Sultan and asked him if he'd consider filming if we could get him a camera. Aamer had never used a video camera before but he courageously agreed. Just as courageously, Jacquie Everett, a lawyer who'd been visiting the Badraie family in Villawood, said she'd try to smuggle the camera inside.

Jacquie explained her rationale in an interview for the program: 'If somebody came to me carrying an ill child — no, there would be no dilemma. I would want to do whatever I could to help them.'

Mobile phones did not routinely contain video cameras in 2001, and since the *Four Corners* budget didn't stretch to a spy camera, we had to make do with a cheap video camera from the local electronics store. It was midwinter and as Jacquie always wore a collection of jangling silver bracelets, she put on a heavy coat and hid the camera under her arm, hoping to blame any beeps from the metal detector on her jewellery. Luckily, back then, Villawood's metal detector wasn't too sensitive and the plan worked. Jacquie also took in the camera's instruction book.

While Peter organised the camera, I took a day trip to Auckland. New Zealand has never imposed mandatory detention on asylum seekers and we wanted to compare the two systems. We'd also discovered that a Villawood escapee had made it to Auckland, so I arranged to interview him. In contrast to the clandestine interviews with the escapees in Sydney, he and I strolled around a park together, talking about Villawood.

Flying back from Auckland, I thought about the various reports I had made from the Middle East about injustices in other people's countries. Now, it was Australia that stood alone, as the only developed country in the world with mandatory detention for all asylum seekers. My own country was detaining more than 500 children, abusing human rights and breaching international conventions. Yet mandatory detention was supported by both sides of politics, and according to the polls and the media, the majority of Australians. Why did the standard seem so different? Why were so few people complaining?

There had been allegations of abuse in Australian detention centres — including one of sexual assault against a child — but because the victims hadn't been identified and the claims hadn't been publicly proven, the government had been able to deny them. Peter and I knew this *Four Corners* would be different, because Aamer Sultan and Shayan Badraie and his family would be clearly identified and their claims would be detailed. We feared repercussions for them, but they wanted to go ahead and we wanted to tell their story.

I was convinced that if we could show the asylum seekers were real people and explain why they had come here, Australians would understand and accept them. I felt Shayan's story should be reported as if it had occurred in any other country. I decided to start the program with images of the opening ceremony of the Sydney Olympics. It was an uncomfortable contrast and in some places, it wouldn't make us popular.

I doubt either Peter or I will ever forget seeing the first video Aamer Sultan made inside Villawood. He'd filmed it the night before, while our own children were tucked up in their beds at home. Zahra and Mohammed Badraie were in a bare white room with six-year-old Shayan slumped in his father's arms on a mattress on the floor, barely moving. Shayan was limp and lifeless, a little boy who was clearly seriously ill lying in what looked like a cell.

'He's very fearful and anxious, and he just sits in a corner not speaking,' his father Mohammed told Aamer's camera. 'Sometimes they tell us the child can survive for five days, meaning that only when he is about to totally collapse will they take him to hospital.'

I found it almost impossible to believe that the little boy I was looking at, who was so obviously in need of help, was only about 40 minutes' drive from where we were sitting.

When I first started at *Four Corners* as a researcher in the 1980s, the journalist who encouraged me to become a reporter was the late Andrew Olle. Then Andrew was *Four Corners*' presenter, doing interviews and sometimes studio-based programs. We researchers took turns to work with him, which could be very demanding and sometimes quite scary. Andrew Olle never accepted second best or took no for an answer, and often drove everyone crazy with last-minute changes. Being a perfectionist helped make Andrew Olle one of the country's finest journalists. I had never fully realised how much the same applied to Peter McEvoy.

When Peter saw Aamer Sultan's first video, he decided, shocking though it was, that Aamer could tell us more, especially about his own thoughts on detention. Aamer agreed and the next day Peter visited Villawood to smuggle more tapes in for him.

The video statement Aamer Sultan ended up making was devastating; he understood the reasons behind the detention regime better than almost anyone. He said, speaking straight to the camera: 'After a time I realised these fences around us are not to prevent us from escaping — never. No, these fences have been set to prevent you, the Australians from approaching us. It's pretty clear.'

When Dr Sultan explained why he was risking serious repercussions by recording the video, I was surprised to hear him say he remained optimistic. 'Still feeling that Australians, if they knew — and that's what I am trying to let them know — they wouldn't accept it.' At the time, I believed the same. But I was wrong.

When 'The Inside Story' aired on 13 August 2001 and Australians saw Shayan Badraie in Villawood detention centre, the ABC's internet forum went into meltdown. It was the biggest online response *Four Corners* had ever had. Thousands of people emailed expressing outrage and offering assistance to asylum seekers. Among several thousand supportive messages, less than a handful were negative. But the tide soon began to change.

In Canberra, the press gallery was strangely silent. So was the Labor opposition. Not one journalist, other than the ABC's *7.30 Report*, contacted us to follow up the story. And before long, some in the media began to attack *Four Corners*.

'Exploiting a troubled six-year-old boy for political purposes is a despicable act,' wrote the *Daily Telegraph*'s Piers Akerman. 'A parody of investigative journalism,' shrieked the *Sydney Morning Herald*'s Paul Sheahan. 'Detention centres are not meant to be holiday camps,' weighed in the paper's leading columnist, Alan Ramsay. Not one of those who criticised the program ever contacted *Four Corners* to ask about it, and Alan Ramsay, judging from the basic errors of fact he made, hadn't even bothered to watch it. When *Four Corners* wrote to the paper pointing out Ramsay's errors, the *Sydney Morning Herald* refused to publish our letter.

About a week later, talk-back radio joined the fray. Suddenly, a new flood of phone calls hit the *Four Corners* office. Unlike the earlier, positive messages from people who had watched the program, these ones were negative and sometimes abusive and came from radio listeners who openly admitted they hadn't even seen it.

In 2002, journalist Mungo MacCallum wrote in his Quarterly Essay, 'Girt by Sea' [March 2002] about the reaction to *Four Corners*' 'The Inside Story':

> By any measure it was an appalling story of neglect, cover-up and sheer brutality; a clear case of child abuse by all the authorities involved. It was the kind of case which would normally have the tabloids and the radio shock jocks screaming for blood. And yet almost nothing happened. The popular media were simply not interested; perhaps they were already reading the public mood of sullen resentment that they had helped create.

MacCallum suspected the response to 'The Inside Story' inspired the Howard government: '... if the decision to use the boat people as election fodder had not already been taken by the time of Shayan's case, it was certainly taken then.'

It took the Minister for Immigration, Philip Ruddock, several days to put out a media kit criticising *Four Corners*. The delay, wrote Piers Akerman, was only due to the fact that the program was 'so riddled with errors'. The Minister's response didn't even mention the mandatory detention of children, instead listing 15 pages of Villawood's amenities, such as computers (though they were still on order), and boasted that dozens of people at the centre played tennis every day (though there wasn't a tennis court).

After *Four Corners* went to air, one of the few journalists to take up its substantive concerns was the *7.30 Report*'s Kerry O'Brien, who interviewed Philip Ruddock the night after the program. Asked about Shayan Badraie, the Minister did all he could not to humanise him, referring to Shayan on four separate occasions as 'it'. ('I understand it receives foods and liquids ... We are working at getting the child into an environment in which its condition can be managed.') Finally, in an echo of future claims that asylum seekers threw their children overboard, the Minister laid the blame for Shayan's trauma on his family, telling O'Brien, 'Well, I'll simply say that the child is not a natural child of the mother — it's a stepchild.'

The Minister had argued that journalists had to be kept out of detention centres to protect detainees' privacy and when we had asked him about Shayan Badraie, he had told us that he couldn't comment on individual cases. Now, when it suited, he didn't hesitate to breach the family's privacy on national television. Shayan, who'd been very young when his parents had divorced, hadn't even been told the truth himself. For Shayan, the Minister's revelation was yet another trauma.

Soon, the *Telegraph* was carrying on the Minister's story, with Piers Akerman publishing numerous false claims, including that Shayan had been stolen from his mother. Peter McEvoy obtained Mohammed Badraie's Iranian divorce papers, showing he'd been awarded custody of Shayan and proving Akerman's allegation (and others he made) were untrue but the *Telegraph* wasn't interested.

The *Four Corners* program had included a black-and-white line picture drawn by Shayan Badraie inside Villawood. It showed Shayan and his sister with big tears falling from their eyes. Another stick figure held a raised club and in one corner, there was a man with what looked like blood dripping from his wrist. The picture was covered by a grid of black lines, with a curl of razor wire running across the top.

Lawyer Jacquie Everett told *Four Corners* that while in Woomera, Shayan had seen riots and fires and a man who had threatened to kill himself by jumping from a tree. 'He saw guards with batons, using the batons to quell the riot, and that's when he started to withdraw. And that's when the family became quite worried. So they came to Villawood and then, not long after they arrived in Villawood, he walked into a room where one of the detainees had cut his wrists, and there was blood and he saw all this happening. And he ran out and he spoke to his mother and he said, "There's a man dead." And he hasn't spoken since.'

In a follow-up program on 20 August 2001, the *7.30 Report* interviewed a former Woomera counsellor and registered nurse, Wayne Lynch, one of the first detention centre staff to speak out publicly. Lynch said he'd seen Shayan looking on when the man had threatened to commit suicide by jumping from a tree. In the same program the Minister for Immigration argued the suicide attempt couldn't have been serious because the tree wasn't high enough. 'I know Woomera,' said Philip Ruddock:

> I know the nature of the trees. And quite frankly, I don't think we are talking about serious suicide attempts when people are sitting in the trees that you have at Woomera, largely. I mean, they are not trees which lend themselves to people being at the sort of height that's going to occasion very significant damage.

By then, the Minister had known about Shayan Badraie's case for well over two months. *Four Corners* had copies of letters written to him by a senior doctor at Westmead Hospital. The doctor had made it clear that Shayan's illness was caused by his traumatic experiences at Woomera and Villawood and recommended to Ruddock that Shayan be allowed to live outside detention with his family. But the Minister preferred to argue about the height of a tree.

Unlike the politicians and most media, many Australians were outraged by what they'd seen on *Four Corners*. Diane Hiles, a young mother working in IT, organised a group of concerned parents and citizens to meet in response to the program. They went on to form ChilOut, and led the public campaign to release children from detention.

Solicitor Michaela Byers also took action after seeing the program, offering to act for the Badraies pro bono. Later that year, Byers helped take the family's case to the Federal Court, which decided there had been an error of law and sent it back to the Refugee Review Tribunal. In 2002, helped by Byers and others, the Badraies were found to be refugees and were granted temporary visas.

Peter McEvoy and I were thrilled to meet up with the whole family in a park one day and watch Shayan and our son kicking a soccer ball. It was almost normality.

But Shayan's trauma had long-lasting consequences. In 2002, the Human Rights Commission made a finding that Shayan had become ill due to the traumatic events he witnessed and the Australian government's failure to protect him. The Commission recommended compensation and an apology, but the Department of Immigration dismissed the finding.

* * *

Exactly two weeks after 'The Inside Story' was broadcast, the Norwegian freighter MV *Tampa*, rescued more than 400 asylum seekers from a sinking asylum boat. The Prime Minister, John Howard, refused to allow the *Tampa*'s captain to land them on Australian territory. A few weeks later, Al Qaeda attacked the World Trade Center and killed nearly 3000 people, and within another month Australia had joined the United States in its attack on the Taliban, which was harbouring Al Qaeda in Afghanistan. But even though most Afghan asylum seekers were in Australia because they were fleeing the Taliban, the war in Afghanistan only made life in the detention centres worse for them. Once the war started, the Department of Immigration stopped processing nearly all Afghan visa cases. In Woomera, hundreds of Afghans tried to find out what was happening but couldn't get any answers. Frustrated, and terrified they'd be sent back, they began a series of hunger strikes.

I wanted to see Woomera for myself and I visited it on a baking hot day in early 2002. It was soon evident that *Four Corners* would never be able to smuggle in a video camera — the metal detectors were high-tech, and the search at the gate was extremely thorough.

Visitors were kept away from the detainees' compounds. But on the way to the visiting huts, I was able to see across the centre to a red dirt area. It was the middle of the day, and the hunger strikers were outside under the burning sun, sitting or lying on mattresses they'd dragged out of their boiling metal dongas. Some had covered themselves with sheets. It would be more than a year until I would see their faces and realise that many of them, including some children, had stitched their lips together.

In September 2001, within a week of the *Tampa* stand-off, Prime Minister Howard had announced the so-called 'Pacific Solution'. All asylum seekers were to be detained outside Australia, and the Defence Forces would step up the surveillance of waters between Indonesia and Australia. The new mission was called Operation Relex. By the time an election was called a few weeks later, the navy had already taken nearly 800 asylum seekers to Nauru.

Throughout the election campaign, apart from the 'children overboard' scandal, there was a complete news blackout on Operation Relex. Journalists weren't allowed near navy ships, there were no press briefings, no maps and no detail about the operations. Sailors on the ships weren't allowed to talk to the media and detainees were locked away, either on the ships or in detention.

In early 2002 *Four Corners* began trying to piece together what Operation Relex was all about. We knew that asylum boats had been turned back and I heard that some of the asylum seekers on board might now be on the Indonesian island of Lombok. I phoned local Lombok guesthouses asking a classic journalist's question: 'Is there anyone there who was on a boat to Australia and speaks English?'

I found Mohammed Ali, an Iraqi. Ali told me the boat he'd been on had been turned around by the navy and had then run aground and sunk. Three men had disappeared. In early March, I travelled to Lombok. *Four Corners*' 'To Deter and Deny' was broadcast in April 2002.

Mohammed Ali was living with a number of other Iraqi men in a run-down local hotel paid for by the Australian government. The Australian warship HMAS *Arunta* had intercepted their boat carrying 230 asylum seekers in October 2001, just as the election campaign was beginning in Australia.

The first to talk to the Australians, Mohammed Ali had asked for the UNHCR (the UN Refugee Agency) or the International Red Cross. But instead, the asylum seekers — including children, many suffering from sunstroke, dehydration and conjunctivitis — were held on their boat for six days, with no food or drinking water. A source in the navy (who risked court martial by speaking to *Four Corners*) said the *Arunta* crew believed the boat was held up so as not to interfere with the Liberal Party campaign launch.

Four Corners later obtained an unedited video filmed by the navy on Mohammed Ali's boat after it had been boarded by the Transit

Security Element. The TSE was a unit made up of infantry, military police and intelligence officers, put together for Operation Relex. In the video, the Australians are driving the boat. During the night before, Ali and others had noticed it had changed direction to head away from Australia.

The video shows the asylum seekers just after they are told they are being sent away and are now only three hours from Indonesia. A man shouts, 'You can kill me now, kill me now. Saddam will kill me.' The Australians clearly feel threatened. One man jumps overboard and another holds up a child, in a scene that is still often used in TV reports about asylum seekers. What the man says is reported less often: in Farsi, he asks the Australians, 'What law allows Australia to deport this child in a broken wooden boat?'

'You couldn't control all those people at that time,' Mohammed Ali told *Four Corners*. 'They were all hysterical and they were ready to commit suicide. They lost everything; this is as if you are killing them, shooting them. This is a decision of execution for them, so they don't care.'

The Australians tried to control the asylum seekers with batons and double-strength capsicum spray. When the roof of the boat's wheelhouse started to collapse, the Australians chocked it up with milk crates. Then they left.

'They took their boats and they left us there to face our destiny of 230 people: women and children, sick people,' Mohammed Ali said. 'People passed out, you know. I cannot describe that moment because they were very horrible. I cannot describe it at all. All the people were down, crying, you know, shouting, hitting themselves, slapping, you know. It was a very horrible situation.'

Twelve hours later the boat went aground a few hundred metres from the Indonesian island of Rote. The asylum seekers swam and waded ashore. Some who had conjunctivitis told us the capsicum spray had blinded them. Three of the asylum seekers were never seen again.

Four Corners interviewed dozens of Iraqi, Afghan and Iranian asylum seekers who had been turned back. One boat carrying more than 200 Afghans had spent two days adrift. A baby onboard had died and another baby was born. The new baby's mother, Fatama, named her Ashmorey after Ashmore Island. She didn't know the island had recently been excised from Australia for immigration purposes.

The navy frigate HMAS *Warramunga* held the Afghan boat for nearly a week, bringing food and water. But Fatama was bleeding severely and vomiting blood. A worried navy doctor wanted to take her to hospital and her husband, Saeed, agreed. But Saeed told *Four Corners* the doctor said the decision had to be made by a higher authority. 'He said he had asked for a security permit but hadn't got it yet but that he would try and get it soon to take her away.' Fatama was never taken to hospital. *Four Corners* was told she bled for more than a month.

Four Corners went to air just as a senate inquiry, which later revealed the details of Operation Relex, was beginning. The next morning I heard Sydney shock jock John Laws talking about the program and agreeing with a caller that the *Four Corners* reporter was 'unAustralian'. I phoned up and Laws and I had a very civil conversation on air. He admitted that he hadn't seen the program and I promised to send him a copy.

Months later, the UN confirmed Mohammed Ali was a refugee and, eventually, Norway accepted him and some other Iraqis for resettlement.

In mid-2002, Dr Aamer Sultan, who won a human rights award for his work in Villawood (though he wasn't allowed out to receive it), was granted a visa and released after nearly three years in detention. He now works as a doctor in Sydney.

Through 2002, I kept trying to make a program about Woomera. I talked to everyone I could — lawyers, former staff and some detainees. I found Alley Crace, a former welfare officer who had been an office assistant when Woomera first opened and had stayed there two years.

The first time we met, we sat up most of the night talking. Alley said that until then, she hadn't been able to talk about Woomera. Talking to Alley, I began to understand for the first time, how a place like Woomera had come to exist in Australia.

Alley Crace said that when Woomera first opened, it was intended for about 400 asylum seekers. There were only a few besser-block buildings, several demountables and a handful of toilets. But within weeks, Woomera was overwhelmed by the arrival of nearly 1000 asylum seekers. Many were brought in sick, collapsing or vomiting, dehydrated or with diseases like malaria. There were only two nurses and the unqualified Crace. They were told if they didn't process all the asylum seekers within 48 hours, the private company that ran Woomera, Australian Correctional Management (ACM), would have to pay a penalty to the Australian government.

By April 2000, Woomera had nearly 1500 detainees — as Alley Crace put it, 'living in that compound with, you know, maybe two washing machines or three washing machines and five toilets. Um … no communication being passed to them about what's going to happen to them. And not enough … no resources or facilities set up for them to actually keep busy.'

Crace said that after six months, some detainees still hadn't even been interviewed, while others were getting rejection letters they couldn't understand. The detainees started protesting, demanding to see the Department of Immigration.

But when the Immigration officials finally came, Crace said they abused the detainees, telling them, 'They should be grateful that they were in Australia, that they are being looked after in good conditions, and that we were not responsible for them coming here and that the process will take as effing long as it will.'

Alley Crace said the Immigration meeting was a turning point. A month later there was a mass escape and a few months after that, the centre was in flames.

After meeting Alley Crace, we decided that even though *Four Corners* couldn't get inside Woomera, we should still try to make a program. Producer Jo Puccini and I went to Adelaide and almost melted our mobiles, phoning what felt like everyone in South Australia. Immigration staff were too afraid to talk and most ACM staff had signed confidentiality agreements. But we found a group of nurses planning to lodge compensation claims against ACM. And then Jo Puccini found a lawyer who was about to settle a claim by the centre's former operations officer, Alan Clifton. We drove to Woomera to see Clifton. It had been his job to try and control the riots. And his story dovetailed with Alley Crace's.

Alan Clifton had arrived at Woomera in early 2000, after a long career in private prisons. He found Woomera desperately understaffed, with no firefighting equipment and only six sets of riot gear. When he complained to ACM, he was told not to be paranoid. ACM told him the same thing when he found plans for the mass breakout and tried to stop it. The problem was, ACM had no financial interest in preventing disturbances.

Despite the understaffing, Clifton said ACM consistently overstated staff numbers and claimed government funds for nonexistent workers. Senior Immigration officials knew it happened but did nothing. If extra guards were needed to control a riot, ACM flew them in from one of its private prisons and charged the government double rates. If the centre was damaged, it was the government that paid to repair it.

Alan Clifton agreed to an interview and trusted our promise not to show it until his claim against ACM was finally settled. We also interviewed a number of former Woomera nurses and psychologists and a doctor. Lack of medical staff (such as one nurse for 1300 detainees) led to shocking incidents, including chemical sedation. One nurse said the centre manager prevented her sending to hospital a boy who had been sexually assaulted, then destroyed her medical notes. Files disappeared and hourly reports for detainees on suicide watch were filled out retrospectively in bulk. 'If they're still alive at 4pm, they must have been alive at 2pm,' one officer told us off camera.

During our research, we heard there might be copies of videos filmed inside Woomera by ACM. We managed to obtain them. The source can't be revealed for legal reasons.

I first watched the Woomera videos late one night at *Four Corners*, after everyone else had gone home, wearing headphones and playing them one after another. It took several hours. The videos showed detainees throwing rocks and having panic attacks, men and children covered in blood and slash marks, a man threatening to kill himself with a shard of glass and guards threatening to take a man on suicide watch to the local jail because there weren't enough staff to look after him. The sounds were just as bad — detainees screaming, guards making off-hand comments and constant radio calls for emergencies in other parts of the centre. The filming was continuous and unedited, like a security camera. By the end, I almost felt as if I had been in Woomera myself. I couldn't imagine what it would be like to be trapped there. Or what I would do if my children were.

But shocking as the images were, we had no details to explain them. All we knew was the dates they were filmed. It took a while to work out how to really use them.

As well as the videos, we had been given three years of ACM's computer records documenting incidents of self-harm, suicide attempts and disturbances. There were several thousand reports, each listing the detainees involved only by number. In the last week before the program went to air, Jo Puccini, researcher Trish Drum and I spent a couple of long nights going through every one of them, building up histories of individual detainees from their numbers, then matching the incidents to dates on the videos and other information.

'About Woomera' went to air on 19 May 2003. It began by showing a young Afghan man climbing into the razor wire and yelling that if he couldn't see the Department of Immigration about his visa he'd kill himself. As he slashed at his arms with a razor, a group of detainees, including children, watched him.

The program also showed the Afghan hunger strikers, filmed around the same time I'd seen them. Guards offer food and water but no one takes any. One man asks for a visa. Others, including a child, have sewn their lips together. One man needs to be taken away on a stretcher. A young Afghan man sobs: 'We are crying. We are screaming. We have nothing. This is what you want? This is [what] Australia say to us?'

After 'About Woomera' went to air, the critics were silent. It was impossible to pretend not to know the truth about what Australia has done to asylum seekers.

In 2005, after months in court, the Department of Immigration offered Shayan Badraie $400,000 in compensation for the harm he had suffered in detention. The government's legal battle against Shayan cost taxpayers an estimated $5 million. As soon as his parents accepted the settlement, the family was granted permanent visas.

More than a decade after Australians first saw Shayan Badraie inside Villawood, the Australian government says it no longer holds children in detention centres. But as this is being written, more than 400 children are being held in what are called 'alternative facilities'. At one Darwin facility, a ten-year-old girl who's been detained for a year has just passed a note to a visitor: 'Our lives are very sad, depressing and hopeless … We don't know who will help us.'

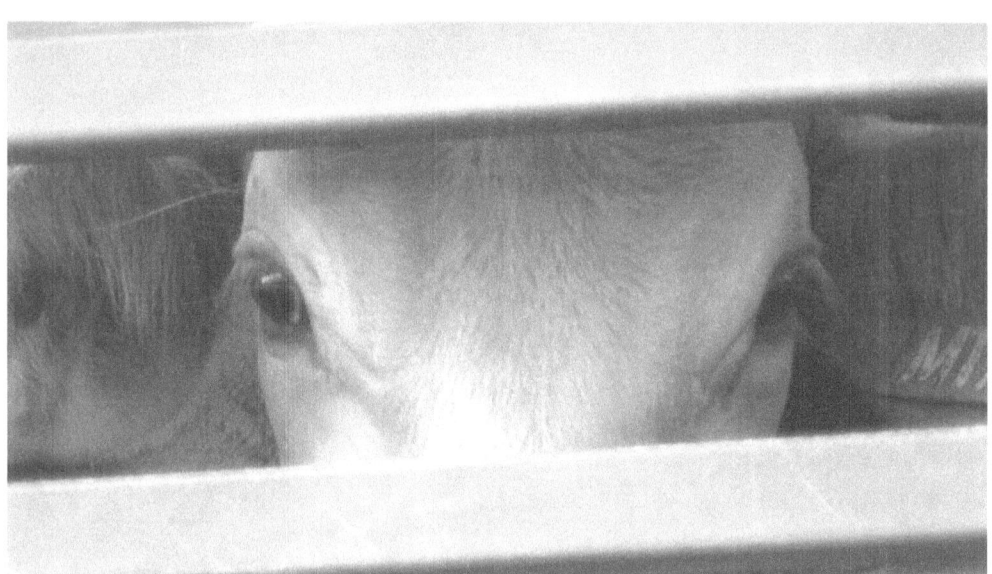

'A Bloody Business' (2011). Sarah Ferguson's report on Australian cattle exports to the slaughterhouses of Indonesia attracted the lowest ratings and had the biggest impact of any story that year, winning Ferguson a Gold Walkley Award.

14

THE WAITRESS, THE REFUGEE AND THE KILLING BOX

by Sarah Ferguson

One of the best moments for a reporter on any story is immediately after it is commissioned. It's the moment where anything is possible, before setbacks and the pitiless approach of the deadline can trim the story's ambition. For 50 years, *Four Corners* reporters have set out on stories with the same visceral determination. Styles of filmmaking change, edits are faster, the grabs are shorter but the essentials of a classic *Four Corners* investigation are unchanged. A meticulously researched, well-told *Four Corners* has the same potency to shock and provoke now as it did in John Penlington's time or at any time since.

One of the biggest media stories of 2011, 'A Bloody Business', an investigation of the live cattle trade to Indonesia, sat right on the margin of acceptability for shocking and provoking the audience. Animal welfare campaigners Animals Australia first took their footage of brutality in Indonesian abattoirs to Channel 9. *60 Minutes* looked at the material and rejected the story because they judged that the pictures would be bad for ratings. When producer Michael Doyle and I sat in our conference room a few days later, looking at the same footage, we were unable to hide our discomfort at the gruesome pictures. *Four Corners* Executive Producer, Sue Spencer, commissioned the story that afternoon, urging us to be uncompromising in our choice of images.

The significance of 'A Bloody Business' is not just that *Four Corners* would run such confronting images in prime time but as an example of how the program deals with source material. Lyn White from Animals Australia and Bidda Jones from the RSPCA came to us with more than ten hours of powerful visual material and detailed scientific analysis to support it. The footage was shot from two cameras and in key scenes the timecode was unbroken (meaning the camera was not switched off at any point) giving us an unusually high level of confidence in the integrity of the material. For most media outlets it would be enough to go straight to publication. Instead, we explained that we would conduct our own independent investigation, and that was likely to take six weeks. Jones and White were taken aback and uncomfortable with the proposed delay, but that is the way *Four Corners* works, accepting neither documents nor vision at face value, no matter how compelling a case they appear to make.

Weeks later, cameraman Erik Havnen, Michael Doyle and I arrived late at night in Jakarta, dropped our bags at the hotel and headed straight to an abattoir on the outskirts of the city. As we got closer to the building, an open doorway framed the bloody scene inside. I was suddenly unsure of myself; I hadn't admitted to the others how squeamish I was. I recalled the figure of Lyn White in the footage we'd watched in Sydney, video camera in hand, almost spectral in the dingy light, standing as close to the dying animals as she could. Once we passed through the doorway of the abattoir, my discomfort evaporated, replaced by certainty that the story we had come for was there.

In the hot fetid air, the floor awash with blood and animal parts, a large Australian steer, roped around the ankles was thrashing its head on a concrete slope in the corner, each crash of its skull echoing around the room. A metre or two in front of the flailing beast, the slaughtermen cut the head off another animal before dragging the carcass across the floor and, with a thick clanking chain, hoisting it into the air. The quick rasp of knives being sharpened mixed with the gurgling sounds from the dying animal's throat.

The Indonesian owner of the abattoir, Hendri, pointed excitedly at the metal restraining box where the animals were roped before being pulled over for the kill, *'Australi! Australi!'* he said. The words 'Meat and Livestock Australia' were stamped on the sides of the box. We knew this abattoir, Gondrong, was one the Australian cattle industry had invested in heavily and within minutes of our arrival almost every cruelty we had anticipated was on display.

No one besides Hendri seemed interested in why we were there. Buyers with wads of cash and receipt books sat impassively at the back of the room, watching the slaughter. Another large beast crashed out of the box and struggled to get to its feet, almost swimming on the slick surface of the slope as a slaughterman tossed buckets of water over its head. Outside more Australian cattle waited in the half-lit pens. The coloured plastic tags in their ears spoke of the vast distances they had travelled: Wave Hill in the Northern Territory, AACO Queensland. Only when an Australian steer with a broken leg was dragged away in front of us did the owner order Erik to stop filming.

The previous week we had driven through the neat paddocks of Newcastle Waters in the Northern Territory, the showcase property of the former Packer cattle company, Consolidated Pastoral. CEO and industry-founder Ken Warriner spoke candidly about the failings in Indonesia. The contrast between his almost pampered animals and the pitiful creatures we saw in Indonesia struck us more than anything else while making the program. Expensively reared animals would be sent hundreds of kilometres across the ocean to spend months in sometimes luxurious feedlots to end up in a broken rusty raceway waiting for a blunt knife in an untrained hand. As a number of inquisitive white Brahmin nuzzled at the window of Warriner's truck, I asked him if cruelty would be tolerated on his property,

>WARRINER: **Here? No. Oh, no. They're made very clear in their induction that any cruelty will not be tolerated and —**
>FERGUSON: **So why would you tolerate it when they're in Indonesia?**
>WARRINER: **Because I think it's going to take time to 'get there'.**

Warriner was hospitable despite the threat our upcoming program posed to the industry he had forged. Over tea taken in the shade of the back of his truck, served with freshly baked cake, he argued that the live cattle trade was so vital to the north of Australia, the industry should be allowed all the time it needed to make improvements in Indonesia.

The industry's dilemma was best expressed in a moment of silence that only broadcast media could capture when we put the question to another cattle farmer, Rohan Sullivan.

>FERGUSON: **You say we've got to have patience, but why should animals suffer while we help Indonesia get its act together …?**
>SULLIVAN: **Because I think that um … [very long pause]**
>FERGUSON: **It's a hard question, isn't it?**
>SULLIVAN: **Yes.**

In Jakarta, we returned to the abattoir for a second night to see if what we had witnessed on the first evening was an anomaly. The slaughtermen had put on uniforms for our second visit, the hangers-on had been shooed away, but everything else was the same. Within earshot of our translator, the abattoir owner told his slaughtermen to lie about their training and technique. After two days we had almost enough material to be able to go home. Instead we travelled for ten days through West Java and Sumatra, the two areas of Indonesia where live Australian animals are shipped to, testing the assumption that the conditions we had seen ourselves and in Lyn White's footage were widespread.

The further we travelled the more tension we seemed to encounter. When we reached Medan in the north of Sumatra, the location of the most brutal scene of torture in Lyn White's footage — where an animal with a broken leg was beaten, kicked and gouged in the eyes and nostrils — we were forbidden entry to the main abattoir. The security guards threatened us to stop filming in the street outside.

In Australia, all that remained was an interview with the Minister, Joe Ludwig, who was responsible for the live cattle trade and directed taxpayers' money to the abattoirs we had visited. We offered Ludwig the same deal that the live cattle industry group had accepted: to see a representative section of the footage in advance of an interview. Ludwig refused to be interviewed. His staff went further, demanding that *Four Corners* hand over all the footage shot by us and by Animals Australia *before* the broadcast. We refused.

On the Friday before broadcast, we sat in a crowded edit suite for the viewing of editor Alec Cullen's final cut. As well as the program staff, the ABC had sent two senior managers to view the material. As the story progressed, Michael Doyle and I scribbled on our scripts the cuts we both thought would be demanded. When the final scene faded to black on the monitor, Spencer turned to the room and said, 'Change nothing.'

Animal welfare campaigners Lyn White and Bidda Jones didn't like the program at first. They hadn't expected the program to include the recent efforts made by Ken Warriner and business partner Greg Pankhurst to import stunning devices to small abattoirs in Sumatra.

That is the critical difference between advocacy and journalism. Their initial reservations were forgotten once they witnessed the extraordinary response to the program.

As 'A Bloody Business' was being broadcast, a wave of revulsion swept through the viewing public. The volume of responses on Twitter and Facebook was unprecedented for the ABC, the *Four Corners* website crashed, MPs reported a deluge of calls demanding action while the program was still running. Animals Australia and the RSPCA teamed up with social activists Get Up! to harness the momentum of that impassioned response, calling for a total ban on live export. By the end of the week, the government had suspended the cattle trade to Indonesia. The ABC's Managing Director, Mark Scott, observed that truckloads of media coverage were being delivered to him every day for weeks afterwards.

In the immediate aftermath, much of the cattle producers' distress was turned on its own representatives. Cattlemen phoned in to rural radio programs weeping. The government's decision was supported by some industry heavyweights, like Peter Holmes à Court, who called for tighter regulation in Indonesia. But the response to high-impact programs comes in waves, and sooner or later someone turns on the ABC to take a shot at the messenger. During periods of intense scrutiny like these, as a reporter you are intensely grateful for the rigour the program demands. We had hours of our own footage as well as the footage from Animals Australia, the RSPCA's analysis and documents from the industry and their own veterinarians backing up our assertions. In probably the lowest moment, West Australian Senator Chris Back accused Animals Australia of paying an abattoir worker to torture the cattle. His allegation was specific; one look at the uncut footage would have shown the events he described could not have taken place. The Senator never asked to see the footage but nor did the journalists who reported his allegation under the headline, 'Animal Footage Faked'. Uncritical news reporters under pressure to produce a fresh headline, especially in online news, reported the allegation without checking whether it could be true or seeking any comment from us. Disappointingly, that included reporters at the ABC.

While slaughter practices in Indonesia have changed significantly as a result of the program, the greatest impact was on the profile of animal welfare in Australia. Bidda Jones from the RSPCA said this about 'A Bloody Business':

> **Never before had the treatment of animals received such sustained and widespread attention in the media or government. The program not only led to a fundamental shift in government and industry policy on live exports, but the *Four Corners* program shifted animal welfare in Australia from a fringe issue to the mainstream.**

The ratings for the first broadcast of 'A Bloody Business' were the lowest of 2011 for *Four Corners*. After the broadcast, ten times as many people as usual came to the *Four Corners* website and they kept coming as the story developed. Almost 50,000 more people watched the program on the ABC iview. By every calculation, Sue Spencer's decision to run the program in the uncompromising way we did, paid off.

* * *

A few stories we do are obvious, demanding to be done; many more are based on an instinct that a bigger story lies beneath an apparently minor event or series of events. It takes painstaking research to get those stories to air. The opening of the 2009 NRL football season provided an example of this phenomenon. Several sordid incidents involving rugby league players and the mistreatment of women dominated the first weeks of the competition. One Monday morning, the headlines of yet another weekend's drunken scandal splashed across the sports pages, and Sue Spencer slapped the Sydney *Daily Telegraph* on the conference table demanding to know what was going on. The resulting program was 'Code of Silence', produced with Ivan O'Mahoney.

In the weeks leading up to its screening, it seemed as though the program would never make it to air. Researchers Kate Wild and Anne Connolly searched for women who'd been involved in incidents with footballers, scouring social media for contacts, leaving messages with friends and relatives. Not only did the women not want to appear on camera but initially they didn't want to speak to the researchers at all. Their fear of the public backlash was too overwhelming. Women who'd tried to bring assault charges were so scarred by their experiences with the media they were unwilling to go public again. The researchers persevered. Kate Wild found the stories depressingly similar: 'It was always about sexual predation. In the situations we were hearing about, women were treated by players as little more than the spoils of victory.'

Ivan and I sat with a softly spoken policeman from a state Sex Crimes Squad who'd supported a woman bringing charges against a player, only to see her pull out just before trial. She also turned down our interview request. The ex-wife of a well-known player poured out a tearful recollection of a drunk, abusive ex-husband, but she was too afraid of him and of the vitriol of the club's devoted fans to go public. One woman, whom we called 'Caroline', who did take part in the program said this about her decision not to press charges for assault: 'There's no way. It's not like if he was just another guy. I would be going up against him, the football team, the NRL, their fans. I'm not going to take that on.'

Meeting this young woman was the first breakthrough. She had been the victim of a drunken rampage by Newcastle Knights players who had broken curfew after a game and wandered into her university dorm; it was her first week at university.

Seated under a pool of light in a darkened ABC studio, Caroline described how she had been woken from sleep in her dorm-room bed by a man climbing on top of her, his hands reaching round to her breasts. She struggled to find the right words to describe what happened next: 'H-he put his hands down to — I don't know — what do you say? Touched my private parts ...' He told Caroline to roll over as she struggled to push him off.

The 48 hours after the assault were almost as bad as the event itself. The policewoman who examined Caroline later that night for physical evidence was unsympathetic. The following day Caroline took refuge in a university office, hiding behind its shuttered blinds from the media pack camped outside. Two days later she dropped the charges.

After the program went to air, the father of the Newcastle footballer texted angry messages to *Four Corners*, saying we had no right to include the story, that his son had suffered because of it. He did not ask about Caroline or the affront and shame that she had lived with since.

The most dramatic story within 'Code of Silence', the group sex incident involving the Cronulla Sharks and a young New Zealand waitress, was the easiest to track down. Sports journalists had known about the story in 2002 but chose not to report it — as they admitted — out of loyalty to the players.

Anne Connolly located the young woman at the centre of the story, whom we called 'Clare'. Clare had been offered money immediately after the incident to tell her story to Australian networks and magazines; she had refused. Once Anne explained the breadth and purpose of the program, Clare readily agreed to take part on the condition her identity was disguised. Seven years after the incident, she had only just reached a point in her life where she was able to talk about it. The intervening years had seen her personality disintegrate in shame and self-loathing; binge drinking and depression took over her life to the extent where she was barely able to leave her house, having abandoned work and study.

The bare bones of Clare's story had made news headlines at the time. Members of the Cronulla Sharks tour of New Zealand in 2002 were accused of sexually assaulting a young woman during an incident at the Racecourse Motel in Christchurch. The CEO of the Cronulla Sharks told the media that, as far as he was concerned, nothing had happened. After the team's return to Australia, New Zealand police flew to Sydney to interview 40 players and staff. According to police, they admitted that 12 men had been in the room during the course of the evening; six had sex with Clare while others had watched, but Clare had consented to all of it. The police decided there were no assault charges to answer; the case was closed. One of the investigators remarked afterwards, 'The young woman was manipulated to the point where she couldn't give meaningful consent.'

For *Four Corners* though, this story wasn't about consent but, like the other examples, the demeaning abuse of a young woman by high-profile sportsmen, including the practice of 'gangbangs' or 'buns', to use the players' jargon. In the program, veteran sports journalist Roy Masters described how the practice had been viewed by some in the game as a form of bonding:

> **It has been a vehicle of team bonding ... there could be little doubt that a girl that might've accommodated three or four players was all part of players becoming a closer knit unit, for want of a better word. I do think it in the past may well have been a focus of team players relating to each other.**

Gangbangs were not a new topic for *Four Corners*. (See pages 21–22 for John Penlington's recollections of his 1968 story about outer suburban Sydney youths discussing the practice.)

During their 2002 investigation, police noted Clare's naivety and her confused attempts to mitigate the shame and embarrassment about what had occurred, admitting her distress only to her closest friends. Investigating officer Neville Jenkins said: 'She was a nice girl. She was young, naive, not worldly, just a growing up teenager. But even for 19 she was quite young I felt.'

In the weeks that followed, Clare's sense of self-worth unravelled, until one night the Christchurch police took a call from her, alone in her car sobbing and threatening to commit suicide. Clare was brought to police headquarters and kept on suicide watch. The New Zealand Accident and Compensation Commission funded her ongoing psychiatric care, noting she remained suicidal, had cut her wrists and brought a rope to hang herself with. The New Zealand police's commitment to supporting Clare continues today.

I met Clare in the lobby of a hotel overseas. She was polite and neatly dressed and worried about how she would get me a receipt for her taxi journey home. We sat in the coffee lounge drinking tea from delicate china cups, surrounded by groups of men holding business meetings. Almost whispering, we talked about the sordid events in the motel in New Zealand. I introduced baldly one of the more grotesque elements of the sex that the players had volunteered to the police. Her self-possession evaporated; through tears she said, 'I don't even remember that.'

In 2002 Clare was a young 19-year-old, newly out in the world. Listening to the still naive young woman struggle through the retelling, she seemed to be looking for a way of making some sense of the destruction that had followed. Her distress was hard to witness; there were moments when I thought about stopping the interview.

The individual Clare best remembered from the night at the motel was also the most famous person in the room: then 30-year-old rugby league star Matthew Johns. It was the morning after the Logies when I first called him and he was in a buoyant mood, *The Footy Show* had just won a Logie. Johns wasn't hostile, he was polite. He said he had been expecting a call like this for years, that he knew the incident would catch up with him one day. He was most worried about his family and the details we planned to broadcast. I carefully told Johns how distressed Clare was in the interview and the catastrophic effect the incident had had on her life. She had singled him out and I wanted him to do an interview so that his role that night would be clearly understood. He didn't agree to the interview but subsequently said that he had left the room before the other men joined in.

The researchers, Ivan and I tracked down as many of the Cronulla team and staff as we could. Some players and player-managers were abusive and threatening; one prominent player said it didn't matter about the other players; only he and Johns mattered because they had 'profiles'. Although some of the touring party provided details off the record, none of the other players and staff was willing to go on camera, ensuring the attention remained almost solely on the celebrity Matthew Johns.

As the broadcast approached, an increasingly nervous Johns rang again to check which details we were running; he also agreed the worst outcome would be for the media to go after the girl. We had warned Clare and all the program's participants to expect a vitriolic response from some sections of the audience and the media. I don't think any of us quite expected the force of it. Much of the coverage was positive and sincere, especially from the NRL as an organisation, but the negative responses were vicious in a way I had never seen. We urged Clare unsuccessfully to stay off Facebook and the internet; the anonymous attacks there were the worst. The Executive Producer and I worked around the clock for weeks, trying to protect Clare from some of these excesses, including media stories featuring people she didn't remember ever meeting claiming to know her intimately in order to attack her credibility. Clare made a single statement:

> They have got people speaking of me that are not my friends or people I have ever met. It feels like I am living in

a nightmare. All I wanted to do was to make people aware of the culture and stop it happening to other girls.

Newspapers and TV programs hunted her down to the point where we became afraid for her safety and sanity. One of the networks had a graphic ready to reveal not only her identity but also that of her new husband. At the last minute, at our urging, they decided not to run it.

Three years later, Clare is proud of playing a part in improving the way women are treated in sport. After the broadcast, Phil Gould described 'Code of Silence' as 'the sledgehammer to the back of the head' that the game needed:

> For so long we've been having incidents like this, whether it was drugs or alcohol or abuse of women, and we all say, 'Well, that was a wake-up call', but no one wakes up. What comes out of this report now should be a message to all players, and all young people and all young girls, that there are no winners in any of this. The behaviour has to be addressed.

The idea was perhaps best expressed by Caroline, one of the other women in the program:

> I have the vague hope that maybe something will change. That every season there isn't going to be another girl hiding with the curtains shut and the blinds down, hoping like hell that her name and her face isn't going to get out in the media. That it's not going to happen over and over and that the football players involved and named aren't just going to go straight back on the paddock the next weekend, the next Saturday or the next Friday night.

* * *

In early 2010 producer Michael Doyle and I were sitting in a café in Jakarta, watching my mobile phone on the table, waiting for it to ring. It beeped, delivering a text: 'I got problem the got pen'. It took me a minute to work out what it meant: our Iraqi colleague Hussain Nasir, who had sent the text, was letting us know security officers at the Indonesian Department of Immigration had caught him using a camera concealed in a pen. Hussain had been looking for evidence of a corruption racket in which senior officials were soliciting large bribes from asylum seekers in return for releasing them from detention centres into the hands of people smugglers.

There was nothing Michael and I could do. To reply to the text message would have endangered him further. Hussain had worked with the US Special Forces in Iraq, if anyone could escape, he could, but at that moment we were unsure if we would see him again.

At Immigration, the guards unscrewed the data key from the pen, plugged it into a computer and watched the vision of their own office play on the screen. They demanded Hussein call someone to pay a large bribe or they would make him disappear into prison beyond anyone's reach. While we endured an agonising wait, Hussain pretended to make phone calls, then asked the officers to take him to the foyer where he said the cash would be delivered. As he looked around the busy foyer for a means of escape, the Muslim call to prayer sounded through the building. Some of the guards in the foyer drifted off to pray. Hussain asked to use the bathroom and slipped through a side door in the cafeteria. He ran across the car park, jumped into a taxi and drove a short distance. Then he switched to a motorbike taxi, pulled the helmet visor down over his face and urged the driver to speed up, away from Immigration, through the busy traffic on Rasuna Said.

In the café my phone beeped again: 'ok I run away already'. When Hussain walked into our hotel room hours later, moustache shaved off, dressed improbably in perfectly ironed new clothes, you might assume the story we had come to film was over. It was just beginning.

It took a further six months and a second trip to Indonesia to gather together the material for 'Smugglers' Paradise'. Over a single week in Jakarta, meetings were set up in a small hotel in the seedy area of Jalan Jaksa between Hussain and a number of Indonesia's most successful people smugglers as well as a couple of new operators trying to break into the lucrative market. With Hussain posing as a would-be passenger, they discussed the details of their operations in front of our hidden cameras. Hussain even persuaded one smuggler, Abbas Al Kurdi, to go away and video the boat he planned to use. In the footage he brought back, Al Kurdi's girlfriend provided running commentary like a travel agent showing off a cruise ship. 'See, inside it's like a café,' she boasted as the camera panned across the hull of a splintered wooden fishing boat.

Not all the people Hussain filmed would come to Jalan Jaksa. An army colonel who provided cover for one of the smuggling syndicates insisted the meeting take place in the army-owned Hotel Borobodur. This time Hussain had to slip the camera past the hotel metal detector and security. In the back seat of the car driving away from the meeting, Hussain played the video material on his laptop; there in full colour was Colonel Hotman, leaning back in his chair in his hotel slippers, discussing the large sums of money he needed to make worthwhile the risk of providing cover to the boats.

The last scene was filmed in a private room of a restaurant called the Ali Basha: a group of smugglers stretched comfortably on cushions, discussing business. The head of the syndicate, Abu Ali Al Kuwaiti, spoke urgently into one of his three phones, demanding money from passengers. Next to him, Haider Hani sat idly puffing on a hubbly bubbly. Haider Hani now faces charges in Australia of sending the boat that smashed on the rocks of Christmas Island, killing 50 people in December 2010.

The key to 'Smugglers' Paradise' (like 'A Bloody Business') was the abundant footage: people smugglers, corrupt officials, agents, military officers caught on screen conducting their business. No one had seen this sort of material before in such detail and abundance. It revealed the extent of the task facing the Australian authorities and showed clearly how cynical the smugglers' operations were. *Four Corners*, with its ability to sustain difficult, sometimes dangerous and lengthy investigations, is one of the few means that exist in Australia of bringing such comprehensive revelations to the audience.

Following the screening of the program, many of the smugglers in the story were detained by the Indonesian authorities. What we didn't anticipate was the response of the United High Commission for Refugees.

'Smugglers' Paradise' had revealed that a number of major people smugglers were living in Indonesia under the protection of the UNHCR, their food and accommodation paid for by an Australian government program to assist refugees. The UNHCR's chief representative in Indonesia, Manuel Jordao, said on camera that getting their assessments of refugee status wrong was 'not a main worry'.

Hussain Nasir, his wife and four young children were also UNHCR-registered refugees awaiting settlement in Australia. We had checked Hussain's bona fides with the US Special Forces unit he worked for in Iraq. The work he did in Najaf after the US invasion was so dangerous he was eventually forced to flee the country. An officer from the Special Forces unit he worked with said it was much too dangerous for Hussain to go back to Iraq now as a number of the people he had helped them arrest were being released. In Indonesia, Hussain had also helped the Australian Federal Police with their anti-smuggling operations following an introduction by a senior UN official in Jakarta. When we asked the UNHCR for help protecting Hussain, they instead reviewed his case and cancelled his refugee status.

The decision stranded Hussain in Indonesia with his wife and children at a time when people smugglers were threatening to harm him. I was with friends in Sydney when Hussain called from Jakarta to tell me about the letter from the UNHCR. I told him he must have misunderstood the contents and asked him to scan the letter urgently and email it to my host's computer. I tilted my head as the pages of the letter loaded slowly, sideways onto the screen and was unable to believe the words I was reading. In a few sentences, the UNHCR stated that it had no evidence against him to support the decision to cancel his refugee status. They said they had made the decision on the basis of an assumption that as a young conscript in the Iraq army, he may have been party to war crimes.

The UNHCR, it appeared, had made no attempt to check their facts before cancelling Hussain's refugee status. They asserted that he might have been connected to crimes that didn't exist. *Four Corners* started checking the facts in Iraq and consulted more than 15 of the world's leading experts on the situation in Iraq at that time — academics, NGOs, leading Iraqi jurists and military experts — who all said the assumptions made by the UNHCR in their decision were dangerous and unjust.

For Hussain, the injustice was almost unbearable. He had tried to help Australia in its fight against people smugglers and he was being punished. Soon afterwards, Hussain survived a stabbing attack in a market on the outskirts of Jakarta. His wife became increasingly distressed with their predicament. In a decisive response, the Australian government brought his wife and children to safety in Australia, where they were settled as refugees. In Indonesia, Hussain moved frequently to stay ahead of the smugglers, while Michael Doyle and I searched for information to challenge the UNHCR's decision.

In November 2011, a year after Hussain said goodbye to his wife and children, the UNHCR's determination was over-ridden by the

Australian government. When Hussain arrived in Australia, Michael and I picked him up from the airport and drove him to his new home. He sat nervously in the front seat of the car, clutching a bunch of deep red roses. Having lived with their story every day for many months, Michael and I stood back shyly while Hussain and his wife held each other in a long embrace. No moment in journalism has meant as much to me as that one.

Author Biographies

**Jenny Brockie** reported for *Four Corners* in 1983–85, returning briefly in 1986 and 1990. Her media awards include the Gold Walkley for Excellence in Journalism, two AFI Awards, a Logie, a Human Rights Award and two United Nations Association Media Peace Awards. She has produced and directed groundbreaking ABC TV documentaries such as 'Cop It Sweet', about Sydney's Redfern police, and 'So Help Me God', about Campbelltown local court. She also presented *The Morning Show* on 702 ABC Radio in Sydney and her own interview series, *Speaking Personally*, on ABC TV. Jenny currently hosts *Insight* on SBS TV, where she drives a lively debate each week involving more than 50 people.

**Mary Delahunty** is the CEO and National Director of Writing Australia Ltd, a Gold Walkley Award-winning journalist, with a prominent career in television news, current affairs and the arts. She is a published author (*Public Life, Private Grief*, 2010). Mary was a senior Victorian government minister in the portfolios of Education, Planning and the Arts and is the longest serving Victorian Arts Minister. She is the Chair of Orchestra Victoria and director of the not-for-profit boards Harold Mitchell Foundation, Melbourne Recital Centre, and Centre for Advanced Journalism at Melbourne University. She also established a residential writers' retreat at Rosebank in the Macedon Ranges.

**Sarah Ferguson** began her journalistic career in newspapers in the UK and worked in France and Washington DC before moving to Australia. For four years at SBS she was a producer and reporter for *Dateline* and *Insight*, then she spent four years at Channel 9, working on the *Sunday* program. Since joining the ABC's *Four Corners* in February 2008, Sarah has won three Walkleys, including the Gold Walkley in 2011 for 'A Bloody Business'. Her reports 'Code of Silence', 'Smugglers' Paradise' and 'A Bloody Business' won the Logie for Most Outstanding Public Affairs Report 2010–2012. 'Code of Silence' also won a Queensland Premier's Literary Award and the George Munster Award for Independent Journalism in 2009.

Allan Hogan joined the ABC in 1967 and was a reporter on *AM* and *This Day Tonight* before going to London as a staff correspondent in 1971. He was a reporter for *Four Corners* (1974–78). He left the ABC to join *60 Minutes* and started the *Sunday* program in 1981. He rejoined the ABC in 1987 as staff correspondent in Washington and in 1990 he was presenter of the Queensland edition of the *7.30 Report*. In 2005 Allan became the Executive Producer of SBS TV's *Insight* program. He joined *Enough Rope with Andrew Denton* as script editor in 2007. Allan is currently writing a screenplay and playing the guitar.

Jonathan Holmes was born and educated in Britain. He spent 12 years with the BBC, working behind the camera on programs like *24 Hours*, *Nationwide* and *Panorama*, before moving to Australia as executive producer of *Four Corners* (1983–85). Jonathan has served as Head of ABC TV Documentaries, executive producer of *Foreign Correspondent*, *The 7.30 Report* and of Channel Ten's short-lived current affairs program *Public Eye*, and worked as an on-air reporter. Since 2008 he has presented ABC TV's *Media Watch* program. A four-times nominee for a Walkley Award — though never a winner — with Jill Jolliffe, Jonathan won the 1998 Logie Award for Best Documentary for a Foreign Correspondent Special — on the Balibo Five.

Liz Jackson graduated with first-class honours in Philosophy and Literature before studying Law. In 1986 she joined the ABC as a reporter on Radio National, then joined *Four Corners* in 1993. She has covered the fall of the Soeharto regime in Indonesia, corruption in international cricket, the war in Iraq and sexual abuse in Aboriginal communities. During her time at *Four Corners* she has won three Logie Awards for Outstanding Coverage of Public Affairs and eight Walkley Awards for her coverage of Indigenous issues, international affairs, sport and social equity. In 2005 Liz presented the ABC's *Media Watch* program, returning to *Four Corners* in 2006. In 2006 she won the Gold Walkley for Excellence in Journalism.

Caroline Jones was the first woman reporter on *This Day Tonight*, and the first woman reporter and anchor of *Four Corners* (1972–81), concurrently with broadcasting on Sydney morning radio (1977–81). For eight years, on ABC Radio National, Caroline presented *The Search for Meaning* programs (1987–94), in which hundreds of Australians told of their lives. Caroline is the author of six books, most recently *Through a Glass Darkly: A Journey of Love and Grief with My Father*. Caroline has contributed to and presented *Australian Story* since its inception in 1996. Among many honours, she has been voted one of Australia's National Living Treasures, is an Officer of the Order of Australia and an Ambassador for Reconciliation.

Peter Manning counts himself privileged to have worked on *Four Corners* for seven and a half years: as field producer (1982, 1983), Associate Producer (1984–1985) and Executive Producer (1985–1989). This period saw the program's uncompromising investigative style win many Walkley and Logie awards and prompt several Royal Commissions and some spectacular jailings and demotions from high office. Later, while the Controller of ABC TV News and Current Affairs, Peter initiated *Lateline*, *Foreign Correspondent* and the ABC's first website. He also served as Head of the Seven Network's current affairs output. He has lectured at UTS and Monash University, and is the author of *Us and Them: Media, Muslims and the Middle East* (2006).

Chris Masters is *Four Corners*' longest serving reporter. His first program, 'The Big League' (1983) — an investigation of judicial corruption — precipitated the Street Royal Commission. 'The Moonlight State' (1987), on Queensland corruption, helped trigger the Fitzgerald inquiry, the first of a series of national inquiries into policing. Chris is now an author and documentary-maker. Among many accolades, Chris has received a Logie Award and four Walkey Awards, including the prestigious Gold Walkley — for his report on the sinking of the *Rainbow Warrior*. A three-time author, one of his Walkley Awards was for *Jonestown*, his unauthorised biography of broadcaster Alan Jones. Chris was awarded a Public Service Medal in 1999 and a Centenary Medal in 2002.

David Marr is one of Australia's most influential commentators. Over the past 25 years he has worked at various outlets: for ABC TV's *Four Corners*, as a presenter for Radio National and for the *Sydney Morning Herald*, where he works today. In 2002–04 he hosted the ABC's *Media Watch* program. In addition to journalism and commentary, David has written a number of highly acclaimed books, including biographies of Sir Garfield Barwick (1980) and Patrick White (1991), and *The Ivanov Trail* (1984), the story of a spy scandal that rocked the Hawke government. *Dark Victory* (2004), co-written with respected journalist Marian Wilkinson, analysed the 2001 *Tampa* incident and the subsequent election campaign.

Sally Neighbour was a reporter with *Four Corners* in 1996–2008, during which time she won three Walkley Awards — for her stories 'The Crown Deals' (1996), 'Catch Me If You Can' (2001) and 'The Kilwa Incident' (2006). Sally is the author of two books on terrorism and Islamic extremism: *In the Shadow of Swords* (HarperCollins 2004) and *The Mother of Mohammed* (MUP 2008). After leaving *Four Corners*, she spent three years as a freelance journalist writing for the *Australian*, principally on terrorism and security-related issues, and the *Monthly* magazine. In February 2012, Sally was appointed as Executive Producer of ABC TV's nightly flagship current affairs program, *7.30*.

 **Kerry O'Brien**, one of the most prominent names in Australian journalism, has six Walkley Awards, including the Gold Walkley. Kerry was the host and editor of *The 7.30 Report* for 15 years. Since early 2011, he has presented *Four Corners*; he reported for the program in 1975–77 and 1985–86. Born in Queensland, Kerry started as a news cadet in 1966. He has worked in newspapers, wire service and television news and current affairs, as a general reporter, feature writer, political and foreign correspondent, interviewer and compere. In recognition of his distinguished service and contribution to the community, Kerry was made Doctor of the University for both Queensland University of Technology (2009) and the University of Queensland (2011).

 **John Penlington** was born in 1938, educated at Ascot State School and Brisbane Grammar School and completed part of a Diploma in Journalism at Queensland University as an external student. He began a cadetship at the *Queensland Times* in Ipswich and moved to the *Courier-Mail* in Brisbane. In 1961 he switched to broadcast journalism with *ABC Talks* in Sydney. He was a *Four Corners* reporter for eight years, then an overseas correspondent in Hong Kong and Chief Correspondent in London before becoming Executive Producer of *Nationwide* for three years. He then moved to the Nine Network's *60 Minutes* program as a senior producer for 16 years.

Peter Reid's journalism career spans over 45 years. He was a reporter on Melbourne newspapers, then worked overseas as a sub-editor with Reuters and the *Daily Express*. Switching to television, he served as scripter–sub with Visnews and ITN. In 1965 he returned to Australia, joining *Four Corners* as a reporter–producer; he was Executive Producer through the 1970s. Peter headed ABC TV current affairs programs then worked for ABC's TV Features as senior producer of major documentaries, including 'First Among Equals', in which five former prime ministers and their wives recounted life at the top. Since retirement, his articles on media issues have appeared in the *Australian*, the *Sydney Morning Herald* and *Walkley Magazine*.

Debbie Whitmont trained and practised as a legal aid lawyer before entering journalism. A former ABC Middle East correspondent (1993–96), she has reported for news, *Foreign Correspondent* and the *7.30 Report*. She is also the author of *An Extreme Event*, about the fatal 1998 Sydney to Hobart yacht race. Debbie has worked at *Four Corners* for more than 20 years — as a researcher, producer, Associate Producer and now as a reporter. As a producer, her programs have been nominated for an Emmy and won a Logie. As a reporter, she has won two Walkley Awards and is a three-time winner of the Australian Human Rights Award for TV.

www.ingramcontent.com/pod-product-compliance
Lightning Source LLC
Chambersburg PA
CBHW022042290426
44109CB00014B/946